Hypno
Advanced Techniques of Hypnotherapy and Hypnoanalysis

A handbook of advanced techniques to use within or without the state of hypnosis

Terence Watts

©Terence Watts 2005

Other books by Terence Watts:

Warriors, Settlers & Nomads
Rapid Cognitive Therapy
(with Georges Philips)

Hypnosis: Advanced Techniques of
Hypnotherapy and Hypnoanalysis

Watts, Terence, 1941 -

BIBLIOGRAPHY
1. Hypnotherapy
2. Hypnosis
3. Self Hypnosis
4. Psychotherapy

ISBN 0-9709321-3-8

CIP DATA
497-W   615.851   2-dc21
by Terence Watts
Copyright 2005
All Rights Reserved

Published by
Network 3000 Publishing
3432 Denmark Ave. #108
Eagan, MN 55123

Order: (612) 616-0732
Fax: (651) 365-0524

Table of Contents

Bibliography 368

None of the material in this book may be reproduced in any format without the written permission of the author.

PART ONE

This book is in three sections; the first is about advanced methods of working with hypnoanalysis and analytical psychotherapy. The second is about a more abstract way of working, via **Archetypal Parts Imagery,** a powerful and modern version of PARTS therapy. The third is an integrated collection of miscellaneous ideas, concepts and scripts, all relative to the rest of the book, which will complete a powerful therapeutic tool for both the working professional therapist and the neophyte.

All the work here is based on the author's practical therapist's office experience and much of it is suitable for teachers and coaches to deliver in workshop form. For this reason, much of the book contains **Practical Work** hints to use in a workshop format.

CHAPTER ONE
Getting to grips with the idea…

Analytical Hypno-psychotherapy gains its strength from the fact that it is more flexible and more interactive than straightforward hypnoanalysis. We can work with a wider variety of psychological conditions and can even achieve positive results when working with the logical and analytical client.

It is more interactive than hypnoanalysis, more flexible than 'direct regression' and allows the skilled worker enormous access to the individual workings of the client's psyche. We can work with people in their sixties and seventies, logical and analytical clients, individuals who are 'hypnophobic' or 'hypno-incapable', even those who strenuously seek to avoid confrontation with whatever trauma has caused their presenting problem.

We can even work with those who have not experienced *any* trauma but are, in the words of the late C.G. Jung, "Suffering only from the problems of living."

Conventional hypnoanalysis often appears to fail – usually because the therapist has not the training to recognise that he or she is using it for the 'wrong' type of symptom or the 'wrong' sort of client, more of which later. Hypnoanalysis is a relatively brief therapy, when taking into account the type of problem for which it is normally employed as a work methodology. The problem is that the oft-quoted 'eight to ten sessions' format is really only applicable when working within certain parameters – and there are many clients and their presenting problems who fall outside these guidelines.

The advantage of the work methodology that we are looking at here is that it is far more versatile; its disadvantage is that we are not looking at a truly brief therapy here – we are looking at getting the client better and the timescale is going to vary enormously according to the client personality type and presenting difficulty. In any case, a conscientious therapist should completely ignore the *"I can fix that in two sessions, what on earth are you doing?"* brigade – therapy should never be a race. It is the emotional health and well-being of the client that is important, not the ego of the therapist.

We will examine the difference between the 'text-book' hypnoanalytical encounter and the extreme of what can actually happen.

The Text Book Analytic Encounter

The 'text book' format of the hypnoanalytical encounter is pretty much as follows:

- **Session 1:** Take Case History. The client is open and communicative.
- **Session 2:** Perform a 'primer session', evoking some emotion.
- **Sessions 3 – 6:** The client moves closer to the repression, continually relating thoughts as they occur, with minimal input from the therapist.

- **Session 7:** The client accesses and releases the repression, the therapist simply checking to make sure that 'it's all out'.
- **Session 8:** Tidy up and send the now-happy client on his/her way

It is important to remember that when the client can work effectively in this manner it is in many ways the best way to work.

When it becomes apparent that the above scenario is either inappropriate or ineffective, it is the therapist who can deal easily and smoothly with the unexpected who is going to provide the best help for his clients. Most clients will exhibit some form of resistance and you will encounter some of the following scenarios, though hopefully not all in one client (though this has been known!).

The Real Life Analytic Encounter
- **Session 1:** Take Case History. Client is clearly keeping quiet about something and/or is evasive.
- **Session 2:** Perform a 'primer session'. The client lies like a stone in the chair and shows no reaction to the emotive section of the session.
- **Sessions 3 – 6:** The client 'forgets' an appointment; turns up too late to do anything; insists 'it' is not working at all; asks the therapist why he doesn't learn proper hypnosis; says that it IS possible to have a blank mind; develops a 'no go' area and insists that it has nothing to do with the presenting issue. There are protracted silences with an apparent refusal to communicate.

- **Session 7:** The client comes in sullenly, claiming to have just experienced "the worst week of my life"; refuses to talk whilst in hypnosis; starts talking when *out* of hypnosis and has you running considerably over time
- **Session 8 – 10:** The client goes over the same ground repeatedly, insisting that "something just doesn't feel right"; decides to finish therapy then becomes irritated when you agree; complains about how much therapy has cost so far; decides to go on holiday for two weeks
- **Session 11:** The client spends the entire session in hypnosis giving a chronological account of the two week holiday and complaining about the other guests in the hotel.
- **Session 12:** The client bounces in and tells you that a friend said something that suddenly put the whole problem into perspective and now he/she feels absolutely wonderful.
- **Session 13:** The client doesn't turn up; the message left on the answering machine says that the friend fixed the entire problem; the therapist wonders uncomfortably what went wrong and may even decide not to do analysis any more…

Of course, there is some exaggeration there – but only a little. And it is more than likely that therapy can go on a good while longer than those 13 sessions, too. We'll see how best to address some of those issues later on.

Higher Numbers of Sessions

There is a school of thought that says you should quit if you haven't got a good result in 12 sessions; in general this is reasonable rule because if you haven't got there by then, then it may well be the case that this particular therapeutic combination (you and the client) is not going to be effective. But there are several exceptions:

- The client is extremely reserved and takes the first 6 sessions just learning how to feel comfortable and accept that you are seeking to help.
- The client is 50 years of age or older; sometimes, it is more difficult to begin to get the memories of childhood 'flowing'.
- The client is afraid to 'look back' because of repeated childhood trauma. Some desensitisation and reassurance is needed before we can work properly.
- The client is extremely resistant and has a tendency to be non-communicative. Memories have to be coaxed or dragged out of the psyche.

There are other reasons why the therapy might go on a bit longer than we would like but these are the main ones. Some teachers suggest that these clients would not be ideal candidates for analytical therapy, and this may be so. Not ideal, maybe... *but with the right tools and the confidence to use them well, you will still be able to achieve a good result for many of these individuals.*

Therapist Confidence

Therapist confidence is paramount; if you have even the slightest doubt that you can help the client, then that's the time to refer on. But truly understand one vital fact about the way that the mind and brain works and you will never again feel such a lack of confidence. It's a simple fact and doesn't sound so special, but it becomes steadily more profound as you examine it:

In the psyche, everything is connected to everything else

It doesn't sound particularly important until you recognise that the way we understand anything that happens to us is by referencing everything that has already happened to us. When you see a pair of spectacles, you know instantly that it's a pair of spectacles. Not a pen. Not a hairbrush. Not a ship, or a mountain, or a car, or a person, or an animal... It's a pair of spectacles. But your mind has had to scan everything that you know in order to work out what it is that you are looking at. Everything that you have experienced... everything that has happened to you.

And what happens when it is something you have never seen before? It takes longer to recognise that you *do not* know what something is than it does to identify something that *you do* know. Your mind takes longer because you are trying to match the item to the templates that you already have stored in your mind. You are still searching everything that has ever happened to you to discover that this is something new. Then, something interesting happens – that new experience itself becomes a template by which you will recognise all future occurrences of the same event.

The Childhood Learning Process

Now, this is very important: when we are a child, this process is happening all the time as we begin to discover the world that we live in. But there is a problem. Some of the things we discover, we interpret wrongly – but we don't know this, so our template develops errors of judgement, errors of understanding. So, if or until we somehow manage to learn what those errors are there, we interpret every bit of life that we encounter with that slight 'skew' that is created by our own personal templates, because they are being continually accessed to make sense of our world. We actually have two templates; the instinctive one with which we are born, and the one that is learnt that is subject to constant modification. The Chapter on 'inherited instincts' explains more about these templates, how they are formed, and how they affect our psyche.

So, truly, everything in the psyche is connected to everything else in the psyche, even if only by the slightest basis of understanding or misunderstanding. This is immensely useful to us, especially if we are working without hypnosis – and later on we will examine some of the circumstances in which we might do that. We can use a kind of 'guided free association' to help our client find the real reasons for their emotional responses and behaviour patterns.

Consider the following scenarios:

1. **Somebody decides to learn to drive because he or she wants to.**
2. **Somebody is forced to learn to drive by a dominant individual.**

16

3. **Somebody is ridiculed for wanting to learn to drive but does so anyway.**
4. **Somebody is forbidden to learn to drive by a dominant individual but does so covertly and keeps quiet about passing the test.**

It is easy to understand that each individual will react differently to driving because of their early experiences. Unfortunately, we cannot employ any sort of formula here, since the basic personality of each will have an effect, too; nonetheless, it is inevitable that the attitude towards driving will be coloured by those early experiences. It goes further, though; *the reaction of an individual to each of those 4 different stimuli will be governed by what they experienced during their formative years.*

A Gateway to Core Thought Processes
And now we can complicate things even further... thanks to the fact that the subconscious cannot have a 'nothing' experience – there must always be a response – the experiences of learning to drive will either reinforce that 'personal way of being' or fall into conflict with it, just as everything else in life does. As unlikely as it may seem, the way we react to, say, giving a speech in public is governed by the same psychical processes that come into play if we decide to learn a new skill, buy new clothes, form a new relationship, decide where to go on holiday, or any other pursuit we might follow.

So by examining <u>any</u> emotional response pattern that an individual might experience, we can find a gateway to his or her core thought processes; obviously, the more profound the

17

emotion, then the wider the gateway for us to work with. This is very good news indeed for the analytical worker, for it means that the reasons for the existence of the client's symptom pattern are *definitely* available for us to work with; no matter that they might be hidden from conscious thought when the client presents. It is 'guided free association' that will make it accessible and later we will explore fully how that can work.

Core thought processes are those which are fundamental to our 'way of being'; the more situations that a thought process or belief might affect, the more fundamental they are and the more we can achieve for our client by helping him/her to make whatever adjustments are necessary. Here are a few core beliefs – there are many more:

- *I'm different from other people*
- *Other people think I'm weird*
- *Things don't work properly for me*
- *I'm less confident than other people*
- *I'm naturally <clumsy, awkward, stupid, slow-witted, timid> etc.*
- *I'm not loveable*
- *I'm basically a bad person*

The Jigsaw of the Mind

Because these core processes govern everything that we do, our mind is like a huge jigsaw puzzle, and asking questions about exactly why an individual carries out a particular behaviour can provide an enlightening illustration of subconscious links. Here is an example of a train of processes linked to fast driving:

18

*"Driving quickly gets me to places faster and **I don't like waiting for anything.** I'm the same with everything, come to think of it – **I always want things straight away.** Driving slowly is boring because it holds me up and **I like to be getting things done.** Anyway, I like the feeling of driving quickly because I like to show off a bit, I suppose – **I do tend to be a bit of show-off...** Also, driving quickly is exciting. **I like a bit of excitement** in my life…"*

You can easily see how many inter-connected links there are here, all coming from core thought processes. Sometimes, you will find the original process quickly gives way to something quite different and questioning reveals something like:

- Driving quickly to get to work early in order to please the boss.
- The need to please others.
- Guilt complex.
- Fear of being caught out in some way.
- Outrage at people 'getting away with things'.

Practical Work

You might want to practice some of what you have read so far; the outline below shows how we work in a workshop situation and this can easily be adapted to other formats.

➢ Working in groups of 3, in the format of 2 Therapists, 1 Client
➢ The 'client' will choose two simple behavioural processes that have a psychological value and attempt to discover the links between them, with the aid of the

'therapists'. You will notice that other processes often become involved.

➤ Be sure to work with a behavioural process, rather than a task. For instance, *"Driving my car"* is a task but *"I like to drive my car quickly"* has a psychological value; *"Watching Television"* is a task, while *"I hate watching the news on television"* has a psychological value. In this example, we are talking about conflicting reactions ('like' and 'hate') so we would be likely to find some conflicting responses in the connections between them. As an example, here are three different ways in which these two processes could be linked:

1) *Watching television news is boring and 'old', whilst driving quickly is exciting and connected with youthfulness.*

2) *Watching television news is about other people; driving quickly is about self.*

3) *Driving quickly is irresponsible; watching the news can be a reminder of irresponsible people.*

➤ The connections are easily found by examining the mental imagery that they create, the psychological reactions ('like' and 'hate' in the examples here), and by examining exactly why the individual carries out each process. In this context the 'why?' question is better than 'because?' since it potentially creates a wider response.

➤ It is important that the 'client' chooses his/her own behavioural processes to work with, since they will be chosen via the connection that exists between them. It can actually be extremely educational to choose two processes that initially seem impossible to link up.

➤ When you have confirmed that you can find links between the two behavioural processes, search out other psychological processes to which they are linked.

➤ <u>Remember that we are not looking for core thought processes at this stage.</u> We are simply exploring the connectedness of the behavioural processes.

The Total Learning Machine

There is another factor which is also important to us as analysts and that is that the brain is a total learning machine. When we learn or understand something, everything around us is taken into account, not just the subject matter; this is why, if you forget the reason that you've gone into a room, going back to where you were when you first thought of going into that room will usually trigger the memory. Again, it's rather like a Jigsaw puzzle, but with one or two pieces missing – moving back to your original location and your mind is now given *almost* everything that was in the 'picture... all that's missing is the thing that we've temporarily forgotten. And that connectedness of everything instantly fills in the gap, reminding us of the missing element.

Practical Work

Again, here is a format used in workshops for practicing working with the 'Total Learning Machine' concept.

- ➢ Working in groups of 3, in the format of 2 Therapists, 1 Client.
- ➢ The 'client' thinks of an event from last year and describes just the event itself.
- ➢ The 'therapists' ask relevant questions, keeping the 'client' focussed on the event, even if there is a temporary 'drift' to another time/event. Statements along the lines of: *"That reminds me of when I was..."* or *"My* (relative/friend or other acquaintance) *always behaved like that..."* or anything that is 'looking outwards' of the event should be met with a question concerning something that is directly associated with it. <u>In a true therapy setting, though, we would move dynamically with the client, exploring, via 'guided free association', the other thoughts that came to the surface as they did so.</u>
- ➢ The 'therapists' will make notes of any of the 'looking outwards' thoughts/events for use in a later exercise.
- ➢ It soon becomes clear that the more the actual event is explored and kept in mind, the more vivid becomes the recall, often with more details suddenly being available to awareness. This exercise is designed to clearly show that the more we explore any psychological event, the more the core thought processes are made accessible.

Working Interactively

To work in an interactive therapeutic manner with the client's psyche we need to ask questions but we must always be absolutely certain to adhere to the following 'rules':

1. The questions are designed to guide our client in the right direction.
2. Each question is asked for a specific purpose and **never just to ask a question.**
3. The questions are completely 'clean'.

We will briefly examine each of these rules.

Rule 1: It escapes the recognition of many therapists that ALL questions are leading, in that they actually guide your client to think about the future, the present, or the past. (In this context, 'future, present and past' is relative to the time of life the client is currently talking about.)

Consider this client statement: *"I remember walking in the park"*. We can respond with:

a) *"How did you get there?"* or maybe: *"Have you been there before?"*

b) *"Is there anybody else there?"* or perhaps: *"What time is it?"*

c) *"And when you've walked in the park long enough, what happens then?"* or possibly: *"And where did you go after that?"*

It is easy to recognise that we will be guiding our client into completely different circumstances with each of those questions. For instance, if we ask those questions at *(a)*, our client will have to access everything that had happened before that time, in order to recognise the answer. Although the subconscious does not seem to work chronologically, there does appear to be some sort of mental filing system that places things in connection with other things that happened at around the same time. So asking a 'backward-looking' question focuses the entire psyche behind the current event.

Rule 2: This is related to rule number 1 – we must always know exactly why we are asking a question. Far too many therapists just ask what comes to mind and the result of that can so easily be that the client's thought processes are not kept 'in focus'. We need to be aware of where we want out client to 'look'. For instance, if we feel that a situation needs to be explored further, then our questions will be designed to keep the client in that place in their mind. On the other hand, if we want out client to look in a different place and/or a different time, then we need to ask questions that will carry them there. We cannot plan in advance which way we need our client to 'move' – but when we understand what our questions will do, then we are in greater control of the session overall.

As a very rough guide:

- *If the client is talking about an event we explore it until we find a 'pointer' to another time/place which we then follow.*
- *If the client is referring to a psychological process which has clearly been acquired or learnt at an earlier time, then we ask 'backward-facing' questions.*
- *If the client is complaining of feeling uncomfortable in some way, we ask 'forward-facing' questions. Sometimes, the discomfort then diminishes*

Rule 3: Clean questioning is essential of we are to keep contamination of the client recall to a minimum – and rest assured that you cannot interact with a client *without* contaminating their thoughts in some way. After all, you are there and they cannot but react to you, and since everything is connected to everything else, you will be subtly affecting their thought processes.

Consider our possible responses at *(a)*, *(b)* and *(c)*, above. If a therapist said instead: *"Who took you there?"* or: *"Who were you with?"* our client is being encouraged to believe that there was somebody else with them, which may or may not have been the case. Other possibilities are: *"Were you all on your own?"*; *"Were you frightened?"*; *"Did anything happen in the park?"*; *"When you left the park, what happened then?"* (subtly different from the question at *(c)*, above). All those responses are putting thoughts into the mind of the client, rather than encouraging the client to explore what actually <u>did</u> happen.

Remember the absolute rule: It doesn't matter what <u>we</u> believe, think, or feel about the symptom(s) or the situation the client is talking about, we can have no idea of the event that caused it, *because we were not there when it happened.* Keep it clean!

ISE and SSE

The ultimate aim of this style of therapy is the discovery and release of an initial sensitising event (ISE) which may have occurred many years before a secondary sensitising event (SSE) triggers the resultant symptom pattern. The SSE is then often thought of by the client as the originating cause of the presenting problem – and SSEs should always be fully explored, for they are directly linked to the ISE, due to that 'connectedness of everything', even if the connecting processes are 'invisible' at the time the client presents for therapy. It is useful to think of the SSE as shield of neurotic response that is protecting the ISE; working through it will help to detach that neurotic process making the ISE more accessible.

Just occasionally, after working though an SSE, the client experiences enough improvement in his/her 'way of being' to believe that therapy is complete and successful. Usually – though not always – such improvement is only temporary and the client will re-present, often with the claim that something has 'worn off'; this is one of the few circumstances in which it is worth working a second time with the same client. Generally, though, there is little or no improvement obtained by working at the SSE (one of the indicators that we have *not* found the originating cause is that the client experiences no improvement); it simply helps to clear the path to the ISE.

Theoretically at least, we *must* release the ISE if we are to help our client to good emotional health. The problem is that it sometimes lurks behind an SSE which is creating a 'false' symptom pattern. Most therapists would tell you that you can only do this by using hypnosis and that we cannot easily work with the logical and analytically orientated client. Both of those concepts are incorrect, as the next chapter will show...

CHAPTER TWO
Effective conscious working techniques

Working Without Hypnosis
We will start this chapter with a look at a case that was worked through over several sessions without any formal hypnosis. The client suffered a form of epilepsy, which often precludes the ability to get into hypnosis, yet there was clearly a need for an analytical style of working.

The client presented with Agoraphobia. Guided free association revealed that there was a strong fear of dogs, and the client eventually recognised that this was possibly contributing to the Agoraphobia. The client became anxious and resistant for fear that the Agoraphobia being 'cured' would bring her into contact with dogs. After some considerable time, she said: "But if I get bitten..." and more resistance ensued during which time the Agoraphobic response improved not one bit. A SSE of being chased by a large dog and being absolutely certain that she would get bitten came to the surface but this made scarcely any improvement to her anxiety. More questions eventually got to the real fear: if she got bitten she would have to go to hospital – and it was this that was the result of an ISE and which needed resolution. She could think of nothing that terrified her more than the idea of going to hospital – in fact, she would prefer to take a dog for a walk!

27

This understanding led eventually to the recognition of cause: The client's mother had disappeared for some days when the client was young and she was told that 'Mummy's in hospital' and given no further explanation. When mother returned home, she brought a baby with her; for many years, the client detested this sibling and the attention it got and blamed it all on the hospital.

With hindsight, you should be able to see the connection between the ISE and SSE (the potential hospital visit), though it would otherwise be difficult to understand the relationship between the birth of a sibling and Agoraphobia.

This is exactly why this style of therapy can be so successful, of course. Along the route to discovery of the originating cause of the problem, many other ideas and anxieties were thoroughly explored, so that when the client arrived at that final understanding there was little resistance left to defeat the therapy.

Analysis Without Hypnosis

The ability to carry out an analytical style of therapy without the need for a deep state of hypnosis is an enormous asset to the therapist, for there are other reasons why we may wish to do so. Here are a few:

- The client is hyper-vigilant and cannot enter hypnosis. Hyper-vigilance means that the client is permanently 'on guard' and is completely unable to relinquish constant checking of his/her surroundings.

- The client is of a logical and/or analytical nature, hypnosis is difficult to achieve and free association is poor.
- The client is 'hypno-phobic' or 'hypno-resistant'.
- The client's religious beliefs are opposed to the use of hypnosis.
- The client is insistent on the fact that his/her eyes must be kept open.

During the initial consultation, we should be assessing the suitability of our client and his/her presenting symptom for our style of work; whether we should use hypnoanalysis or analytical psychotherapy may only become clear during our first working session. The major difference between the two is that analytical psychotherapy does not use a formal trance induction and there will be far more interaction between therapist and client than with hypnoanalysis.

As far as suitability of client and symptom is concerned, we should always bear in mind that the free association model of working was devised and used by *Sigmund Freud* for the treatment of hysterical illness. Most symptoms which have a physiological content that is likely to be of psychological origin can be considered to be the result of a hysterical illness. In general, a hysterical illness will have been caused by an emotional process rather than a conditioned response – there is clarification on this point later on.

Hysteria

This connection to what Freud termed 'hysteria' has been largely forgotten, or perhaps misunderstood, and as a result there are many therapists who attempt to use it in inappropriate circumstances and then claim that it is ineffective. It is definitely not suited to every ailment. But with the 'right' client and a relevant symptom, there is still no finer way of achieving a resolution of the presenting difficulty. It is when there is a departure from this situation that we might need to modify the procedure somewhat in the ways shown in this book.

Conscious Questioning

Later on, we will consider the importance of personality type and specific symptoms; now, though, we are going to have a look at a conscious questioning technique that can produce remarkable results, often in a relatively short time. Sometimes, we will simply access an aspect of the client's core thought processes, sometimes gain an understanding about a conditioned response pattern, while at other times we will access an SSE or ISE.

Again, it is important that the questions we ask are completely 'clean' and devoid of any expectation on our part – it is the client's truth that we seek, not our own. Here are some examples which can be applied to almost any situation:

- *"When did you first think that?"*
- *"How did you recognise it?"*
- *"Who taught you that that was what it was?"*
- *"What did that feel like?"*
- *"When did you first feel like that?"*
- *"What other times did you feel like that?"*
- *"Where were you?"*
- *"Why did she/he teach you that?"*

- *"What does that feel like as you remember it?"*

You will notice that many of those questions could be asked in response to the answers to others. The important thing is that you don't ask a question just for the sake of it but <u>always</u> to guide the client to access those core thought processes that were created as a result of events that occurred during his/her formative years. We should never accept *"I don't know"* as a valid answer, instead asking the client to state the first answer they can think of, even if they feel they are making it up. Remember, everything is connected to everything else, so no matter how outrageous the response a client invents, it will still be connected in some way and the response, even if imaginary, will keep the process active.

You may well find the need to ask other questions during this technique that are relevant to the client's responses, but the same 'rules' hold; keep it clean, know why you are asking the question, and constantly seek to guide in the relevant direction. Here's an example:

Therapist: *"How old were you then?"*

Client: *"I don't know. I think it was after my sister was born."*

We should always follow up potentially important statements, so:

Therapist: *"Do you remember your sister being born?"*

Client: *"No... It felt like she was just suddenly there."*

Again, there is a need to follow up:

Therapist: *"How did you find out that she was just suddenly there?"*

Client: *"I don't know... can't remember."*

Therapist: *"Just pretend – the first thing that comes to mind. It'll be connected so it doesn't matter if it seems odd."*

    Client: *"She was just in the front room."*

Now we can begin to get back on track:

Therapist: *"What did that feel like?"*

    Client: *"I can't remember..."*

Therapist: *"Pretend again."*

    Client: *"I was pissed off."*

Therapist: *"When did you learn to be pissed off?"*

    OR: *"What other times did you feel like that?"*

    OR: *"How did you know that was a pissed off feeling?"*

Clearly, to get the best out of it, this technique needs experience and clarity of thought on the part of the therapist; learn the skill thoroughly, though, and you will be able to guide many clients to an ISE which they may not otherwise have been able to access.

Practical Work - Questioning technique

Another workshop format is shown here, which you can easily adapt.

> ➤ Working in groups of 3 in 'standard' Therapist, Client, Observer format this time.

> ➤ Working with the same conversational subject as previously, if possible, the 'therapist' now pursues any of the 'looking outwards' responses that were noted previously.

> ➤ If there were none, the 'client' will choose a different event with which to work. The task of the 'therapist' is to access core thought processes.

This is a good place to remind you of an important fact: <u>If the client can work in hypnosis and continually free associate without lengthy pauses, then that is a better way to work for most suitable problems.</u>

Pushing the Client

Sometimes, it is necessary to give the client a little 'push' to get the therapeutic ball rolling. This is particularly so when a client is exhibiting a secondary gain or hidden agenda being exhibited as a destructive rationalisation or resistive process. Here are some examples:

- *"Well, I think the real problem is that I was adopted..."*
- *"I believe it all stems from the day my father walked out on us..."*
- *"It may be because I was so severely bullied as a child..."*
- *"Well, you see, my mother was rotten to me when I was a child..."*
- *"My partner cheated on me and I've never been the same since..."*

The work shown now is somewhat provocative in nature – some might even consider it to be a little judgemental in places. It certainly needs a fine assessment of how the client is *genuinely* functioning at an emotional level and how the client will react to this intervention. The fact is, though, that under the right circumstances it will produce an almost instantaneous and highly beneficial change in thought process.

Sometimes, the client will simply be giving us what he or she believes to be useful information. Quite often, though – and this is where fine assessment is needed – such statements will be made with a sad shake of the head or other body-language indicator that what is being sought from the therapist is a response along the lines of: *"Oh, no! You poor thing!"* which is what he or she would normally get when telling their 'sad story'. This is, of course, the reason for the existence of the hidden agenda – sympathetic attention. But sympathy never made anybody better. In fact, it will tend to focus the client *inwards* to his or her woes, rather than *outwards* to psychological health. Sympathy is something to help the giver – and we should not be seeking anything for ourselves when we are working with a client.

Occasionally, the search will instead be for evidence that the therapist is in some way impressed with the awfulness of the circumstances that are being discussed; again, this is most likely to be a defence mechanism to avoid change.

Cognitive Dissonance

So let us bring a bit of *cognitive dissonance* into the therapeutic equation. Let's do something that the sympathy-seeking client probably will not expect at all and ask a quite reasonable question, without making any comment on what we have just been told. *"So what do you want me to do?"* (In the case history shown later, you will see that just *"So what?"* can be used under the right circumstances) It works best when a totally normal conversational tone is used, as if, to you, it is a normal response.

Even on the occasion that the client believes the information is helpful, this is still a valid question, and one which is essential anyway, if we are to be successful. The response we get will tell us much; when it is something along the lines of: *"I'd like you to help me get past it,"* we can proceed with whatever intervention we decide will be the most effective. It is when the original statement is repeated or when there is an attempt to get us focussed upon it, that we can safely assume that the client is seeking to avoid change – you, the therapist, are being required to confirm that there is nothing that can be done.

We have to get our client past this resistive state as soon as possible if we are to be of any real help. The best way – maybe the only speedy way – is to point out that the event that the client believes caused the problem simply cannot be changed. The only change that *can* happen is change within the client. While this 'new' viewpoint is being considered, you can and should reassure the client that you are an expert at helping people get the best out of themselves. It is also good to say something like: *"I wonder how it would actually feel to shake yourself free from that stuff?"*

Sometimes, a client will simply refuse to consider this, or perhaps may try once again to focus on the original statement in some way; when this happens then it is up to you to decide how best to proceed, for this particular technique has not produced the desired result and something different is needed. If you have handled the session well enough, though, most clients will now be eager to start work.

A case History

'Alan' presented himself for therapy with the information that he was virtually unemployable and had never kept a job for more than three months. He then regaled

35

me with stories of the unpleasant bosses who had sacked him without giving him a chance; he stated that somehow or another, they always seemed to find out about his origins; and that 'it's obvious' that he would always be at a disadvantage. Then, with a small sad shake of his head and a helpless shoulder shrug, he said: *"I shouldn't be surprised really. I was born as a result of a rape."*

Here is the conversation that followed:

Therapist: *"So what?"* [A 'shock tactic' to break a destructive thought chain]
    Client: *"Pardon?"*
Therapist: *"I wondered why being born as a result of a rape would cause you to be unemployable..."*
    Client: (looking acutely uncomfortable) *"Well, it means I'm sub-standard, I suppose... I mean, some bastard raped my mother and I'm the result!"*
Therapist: *"Ok, I see... so what do you want therapy to do?"*
    Client: (puzzled) *"Erm... I'm not sure what you mean, really..."*
Therapist: *"Well, I can see that you believe that the rape caused you to be sub-standard, although I wouldn't actually agree with that. The problem is, the rape happened and can't be UNhappened, so there's nothing we can do about that part of it, is there?"*
    Client: *"Er, well, I suppose not..."*

Pause

Therapist: *"Mind you, if you want to create a change in what you believe about yourself, I'm a bit of an expert at helping that to happen."*

Client: *"But you can't change the past."*

Therapist: *"That's right. We can change only the future."*

Client: *"OK - let's say I go along with that. How will you do it?"*

The effect of such work is to 'normalise' the situation as far as it possibly can be; such normalisation empowers the client to let go of the belief that the presented situation is responsible for all his/her ills which makes the search for a resolution of symptoms a whole lot easier.

The ensuing therapy, mostly conducted in an Ericksonian style was frequently verbally colourful. It started with the premise that Alan wasn't there when the rape happened and therefore he had nothing to do with it. Along the way, there was some Archetypal Parts Imagery, some logical work concerning DNA and also much exploration of the concept that had his parents been married, *he* would still have been the same person, though with a possibly quite different view of himself. It transpired, too, that he actually *enjoyed* being a victim and lost no time in telling workmates of his origins. He had also 'acted up' to the extent that his various employers had no option but to dispense with his services.

Therapy was highly successful in that Alan's eventual view of self was that he was a worthwhile being and would study to gain new skills and a worthwhile job.

The last thing he said as therapy finished - and he said it with a grin - was: *"I'm just a happy sod, but you're a clever bastard!"*

Remember, fine judgement is essential when using this technique. If you do not receive the indicators that the client is searching for a specific reaction, then don't use it!

CHAPTER THREE
Brainwork and Personality

The Invisible Therapist

It is a distinctly useful skill to work invisibly! There are several ways in which this can be achieved and we will experiment with one or two of them here. We are going to concentrate on accessing whichever part of the brain is relevant to the work we are doing. If we want our client to use a logical thought process, then we need to access the left hemisphere; if we are looking for an emotional response, then we need to access the right hemisphere. We need to do this as invisibly as we can:

Looking into the relevant eye

Although you may not have realised it, you always tend to look at the same eye when you are talking to somebody. Intellectually orientated people tend to look at the right eye, therefore accessing the left hemisphere, whilst emotionally orientated people will tend to look at the right eye, to access the right hemisphere. It's interesting to change this and see what it feels like. You will notice that you access different responses from those that you talk to, as well, even though they may not consciously notice you looking at the 'other' eye from time to time. It's interesting to note that when you know about shifting the gaze like this, you can become aware that the person you are talking to has changed eyes – often more by what you can feel than what you can see.

Leaning/looking to the relevant side

Again, if we shift our body position, or just turn our head slightly, we can access the part of the brain with which we wish to work. This should be done as invisibly as possible, body shifts being disguised as simple adjustments of position, for example, and made casually enough that the client simply doesn't notice it.

Both these techniques are immensely useful when working consciously. For example, we can:

1. Address the left side of the brain to access time-orientated matters, including memories of events.
2. Address the right side of the brain to more readily gain access to the emotional and instinctive work associated with those events.

As an example, the question: *"What's the earliest school memory that you have?"* you would seek to address the client's RIGHT side of body (facing your left side) in order to access the chronologically-orientated left brain. You might follow with: *"And how did that feel, to you?"* whilst transferring your attention to the client's LEFT side (facing your left side) to access the emotionally-orientated right brain. Some people do this automatically, other have to learn it. But it becomes so instinctive that you scarcely notice what you're doing it – it just becomes apparent that your communication skills seem to have improved!

Practical work - Accessing the hemispheres
Here is the way that this can be practiced in a workshop setting:

> - Working in groups of 3 – 'standard' Therapist, Client, Observer format.
> - Choose a subject to discuss – your journey to this class and the class itself so far is suitable. It does not matter where the conversation moves to, since we are experimenting with technique here, rather than content.
> - Experiment with looking at the 'wrong' eye when you talk and also with looking at the 'wrong' eye when listening. ('Wrong' = the eye that you <u>do not</u> normally look at)
> - Experiment with shifting body/head position.
> - Choose a situation to work with and apply both the above, thoroughly exploring the psychological experiences within the situation.

Personality and Therapy
Now we come to the importance of personality type in relation to therapy. Of course, there are many people who dislike any classification of personality intensely, claiming that everybody is so different that you cannot possibly classify them… and if you come into this category, then that itself classifies you in some way. It is a fact that we automatically classify everybody that we meet. We classify them as male/female, young/old, attractive/unattractive; we classify them by colour, apparent social status, the work they

do; we even classify them by that most subjective of methods, whether we like the look of them or not.

So let us reappraise slightly what we are going to do. We are going to quickly access the way that our client *truly* thinks and behaves, rather than the way that they might like to show us. This will allow us to understand several things about them and will most certainly allow us to provide a more effective therapy than we might otherwise have done. We will be working with three different types:

1. **Resolute Organisational (RO):** Control focussed, practical and 'thinking-orientated' individuals who tend to question things.
2. **Intuitive Adaptable (IA):** Emotionally focussed, communicative and 'feelings-orientated' people who tend to be compliant.
3. **Charismatic Evidential (CE):** Self focussed enthusiastic and 'sensation-orientated' people who must have excitement or drama in their life.

Although everybody will possess something of each group, there will usually be an evidently predominating 'driver'; sometimes, this is not the case, and then we are looking at a **Combination Personality**. There will, nonetheless, still be a 'leaning' to one of the three types – it will just be a little more difficult to observe it.

Full personality profiles of each type are given at the end of this chapter.

Later in this book, in the section on 'Archetypal Parts Imagery', you will see how our personality may be related to the behaviour of or ancient ancestors, via the process of inherited instincts.

The **RO** type is the one least likely to be successful with 'ordinary' hypnoanalysis, thanks to the tendency to apply logical thought to everything, as well as the instinctive need to be in control of self, emotions, and the environment. There is also an instinctive urge to safeguard against any threat to integrity and, therefore, a tendency to not report recalls which they believe will bring this into doubt. Depth of hypnosis is *sometimes* difficult to achieve (though can sometimes be profound) and there is usually difficulty with free association – this individual is compelled to bring logic, conscious understanding and rationalisation to bear upon each recall, thus interfering with the free associative process. Analytical psychotherapy, because of the interaction and its intellectual orientation can be very successful for this individual.

The **IA** type can generally work very successfully with hypnoanalysis; the rather trusting and communicative nature will usually comply with the request to 'tell all' and there is less of an egocentric need to preserve integrity. Depth of hypnosis is usually adequate and free association is good. Being predominantly emotionally-centred, this individual can benefit greatly from this style of working.

The **CE** type enters hypnosis particularly easily and usually makes a 'flying start' at hypnoanalysis; problems arise out of the low boredom threshold and the tendency to exaggerate emotional responses – it can be difficult to observe a true abreaction and one which is acted out for the sake of the therapist. There is occasionally so much interest in impressing the therapist that free association becomes scanty. If you can keep them focussed, then straightforward hypnoanalysis is probably the best methodology; if not, then analytical psychotherapy may produce a good result. Failing this, one of the forms of PARTS therapy, shown later in this book, can be startlingly effective with this type.

It is important to be aware that Hypnoanalysis is primarily for use with Hysterical illness (which any one of the three groups may acquire) and can be less effective for other problems.

Note that it is possible for some of the following conditions may have physical cause.

Probable hysteric illness

Hysterical illness originates from an emotional response and includes:

Anything dramatic; panic attacks, spontaneous vomiting, blackouts, fainting fits, hysterical paralysis, hysterical blindness, failure to conceive, promiscuity, 'phantom' illnesses of all kinds from blackouts to crippling or catastrophic conditions.

Physical problems with an evident psychological process; Irritable Bowel Syndrome, anorgasmia, vaginismus, withheld ejaculation, premature ejaculation, erectile dysfunction, and 'nervous' conditions like rashes, coughing, nausea and some asthmatic conditions.

Most of these should respond well to analytical therapy, especially with the IA or CE personality types, though you will probably do better using analytical psychotherapy with the RO individual.

Possible

Some commonly presenting problems which <u>may</u> be of hysterical origin but which might alternatively be the result of a conditioned response include: *Most phobias/fears, excessive regard for authority, guilt complex, psycho-sexual difficulties, sleeping difficulties (esp. insomnia), migraine headaches, neurotic paranoia, timidity, general anxiety, stress, unexplained physical pain, memory/concentration problems.*

Unlikely

Some commonly presenting problems which are usually <u>not</u> of hysterical origin and therefore maybe unsuitable for hypnoanalysis include: *All obsessive disorders including sexual jealousy and obsessive emetophobia, most depressions, inferiority complex, low self-esteem, fear of what others think, sexual fetish, addictions, gambling, anorexia, bulimia, binge-drinking.*

The lists given here are not exhaustive, though they do contain the most commonly presented difficulties. At any rate, they should allow you to identify where something 'fits' with a reasonable degree of confidence.

Personality Testing

It is entirely possible to work without going anywhere near a personality test, of course. It is also entirely possible to make such a mistake about the person that you're working with (because even skilled therapists can make mistakes in assessment!) that communication is less effective than it might otherwise be.

It is worth remembering that even if you don't like personality tests, many people love them and they can certainly give a little more insight into how any one person 'ticks', provided that: (a) There is no evidently correct or 'best' answer, and (b) The therapist avoids influencing the answer according to his/her pre-existing beliefs.

The problem at (a) is easily resolved. We can either ask questions that are difficult to assess what they are directed at, or we ensure that, in a multiple choice question, there appears to be no particular benefit to any one answer. Each response 'resonates', though, with a different personality type. This is the approach that has been taken on the questions we are using in the test here.

An Easy Personality Test:
On each question, note down the order in which each statement applies and write your answers on a single line. For instance, if you think on question (1) that your most likely course of action would be to research thoroughly, your second most likely would be to make a spontaneous decision, and your third to ask other people, then that line will read 'a, c, b'.

When you have completed the test, you'll get something like:

a, c, b
c, a, b
a, b, c
b, a, c

Question 1

When buying a medium-priced new item, you are most inclined to:
a) Research what you want and seek it out
b) Get a clearer opinions by asking other people what they think
c) Make an spontaneously instinctive decision

Question 2

In a minor disagreement, you are likely to:
a) State your case very firmly
b) Try to find middle ground with a fair compromise
c) Use personality and wit to make your point

Question 3

You have to go a party where you don't know anybody. You are likely to:
a) Not give too much away about yourself
b) Be a bit nervous but go out of your way to make friends
c) Enjoy playing to a new audience

Question 4

How do you think other people are most likely to describe you?
a) You are positively orientated and determined
b) Usually in a good mood, an agreeable person to be with
c) Different from the crowd – an individual

When you have answered all the questions, the dominant parts of your personality will be shown in the first two vertical lines. So, on the example shown above, there are 4 (a) answers on the first two lines and 2 each of (b) and (c). Since (a) answers = RO; (b) = IA; (c) = CE, that 'reading' shows a predominantly RO personality. Somebody with this profile would possibly find difficulty with free association and if you look at the statement to which the answers refer, you can see why. The equal amounts of IA and CE which influence the profile make analytical psychotherapy a good work methodology here.

Practical Work - Assessment Techniques

Again, here is a practice method suitable for a workshop setting.

> ➢ Working in groups of 3 – 'standard' Therapist, Client, Observer format.
> ➢ Assess the client; first just by talking, second by the questionnaire.
> ➢ Compare the results.

Phobia and Obsession

A brief look now at an interesting aspect of one of the most commonly presented conditions, the phobic response. There are occasions when an apparent phobia is actually an obsessive illness; the most common one of these is **Emetophobia** – the fear of vomiting or vomit. In its phobic form, it will often respond to hypno-analytical techniques; in its obsessive form, it will not. It's actually quite easy to tell the difference between the two forms. When it is a true phobia, the sufferer only suffers the associated anxiety/panic when he/she feels nauseous or is confronted with somebody who feels nauseous. There is also a reaction to discovering that somebody has vomited on the pavement, for instance.

In the obsessive form, the sufferer has all the above symptoms but additionally self-tests frequently – often every few minutes – to see if he or she has started to feel sick. If there is the tiniest awareness that something 'feels different' the panic will start, subsiding only if and when the physical sensations stabilise.

This self checking will start upon waking and continue throughout the day. There is also a great deal of anxiety about what foods may or may not be eaten, often embracing colour and texture. Usually, only food cooked at home can be consumed and even then, there are certain foods that the sufferer will consider to be 'high risk', often including shellfish and chicken.

Almost any phobia can hide an obsessive illness. The giveaway is as shown above:

- If it is truly a phobic response, there will be little or no anxiety unless the phobic object is either present or imminent. There will be a slight increase in tension if talking about it but any anxiety is usually at manageable levels.
- If it is an obsessive process then there will be a constant watchfulness. Simply talking about the trigger can frequently trigger a severe panic reaction.

Hypnoanalysis is not suitable for working with obsessive illness; Cognitive Behavioural Therapy is the best methodology in these circumstances, although change can also be brought about with the conscious analytical psychotherapy techniques shown in this book. There is a section later on concerned specifically with this illness.

The Importance of Preparation

With any style of analytical therapy, good preparation is essential. Obviously, some of that work will be done during the initial consultation when you explain to your client how you are going to work and why. It is the first working session, though, that will set the tone for the whole therapy; 'get through' to your client then and a successful therapy is assured. What we need is a primer session, something which gets the mind thinking about those formative years with some intensity, whether we are using hypnosis or not.

A suitable primer for use in hypnosis is included in another part of this book but it is not really suitable for those occasions where you have already decided to work consciously. Then, you need 'bullet points' of issues and concepts that you will bring into the conversation, in order to be able to apply the questioning technique that we used earlier. The trick is to always focus on events and situations that have happened in the client's formative years – you will have some idea of this from your case study, which should always be as detailed as possible. Some examples shown here, though you will be able to think of others and it is likely that you would not use *all* of them at any one time:

- Starting School
- Birth of Sibling(s)
- Hospitalisations

- Parental Arguments
- Arguments with Friends
- Changing to the Big School
- Starting Work
- First Sexual Discovery
- Guilty Secrets
- Injustices
- School Exams
- Superiorities
- Inferiorities

The main difference between this first 'primer' session and all subsequent sessions is that you will be more in control of the subject matter on this one. The client will introduce new concepts but for the moment, you will simply make notes of them and keep to the primer session material. On second and subsequent sessions, you will pick up on one or two of the concepts that the client introduced and explore them, allowing as much free association as possible.

A point worth remembering is that you should always adopt a 'normal' conversational style when working consciously, remembering to use the 'invisible' techniques of accessing the relevant brain hemispheres.

Personality Outlines

Now here is an outline of the three personality types shown earlier, along with a 'quick recognition guide'

Resolute Organisational

Personality Profile:

Forceful: Can always make their presence felt.

Resolute: High levels of tenacity and determination.

Organisational: Able to plan well and bring those plans to fruition.

Achilles heel: The need to always be in control.

Areas of conflict: Concerned with issues of loss of respect/dignity/integrity or any sort of 'attack' – being frightened, picked on, humiliated, punished, bullied, etc.

Symptoms: Usually based around phobic response patterns or control issues – body <u>or</u> mind. There are often physical manifestations of the digestive tract, including ulcers, IBS, constipation, etc.

Abreaction type: Sometimes almost invisible – any tears are likely to be sparse, though s/he will feel as if they have been laid totally bare. The approach of abreaction will often be indicated by fear or anger.

Personality: The RO personality tends to have a reputation for firmness and a no-nonsense attitude to life. Psychologically stronger than either the IA or CE personality types, they find no difficulty in taking charge of things and easily attain the respect of others. They are cautious yet rapid thinkers who are unsurpassed at finding and exploiting the flaw in any argument. On the negative side, there can sometimes be a problem with cynicism and jealousy and there is not the immediately friendly response generally found in the IA. Indeed, there will sometimes be a significant pause before answering any question that is put to them and even then, the answer will often be carefully phrased in such a way to leave as many options open as possible.

Physical traits: This type is the least physically animated of the three groups. There are few changes of face expression during conversation, and few changes of body position. The angle of the head, in particular, may remain unchanged for longish periods making them reminiscent of an excellent card player, giving away absolutely nothing about inner thought processes. They appear to be – and indeed are – watchful and perceptive, with a steady gaze which may be away from their conversation partner if they are nervous. Any tension or anxiety will show in a taut body shape and a set facial expression leaning towards irritability or hostility.

Positive attributes: Determined and tenacious; methodical and organisational; perceptive and easily able to spot the pitfalls in a plan/situation; sound but not <u>necessarily</u> fast decision making abilities; natural team leader and co-ordinator; quick thinker in discussion or argument, able to easily see and exploit loopholes or advantages; practical and logical; good at recalling/using facts and figures.

Negative attributes: *As with the other two groups, these traits are only possible tendencies and are not necessarily evident in any one individual - indeed, it is unlikely that any one individual will show <u>all</u> these traits. The positive traits in this group are very decisive and specific, and this forthright attitude tends to also be reflected in the negative traits.*

The RO character is inclined to force rather than subtlety and in negative mode is usually pedantic, domineering and impatient, and can appear rude and sarcastic. They have a driving need to be in control and can sometimes be quite ruthless in their determination to be so, being very good at manipulating people and events to their advantage – this, of course, may be viewed as positive trait under some circumstances. The two things they hate most are: not getting their own way, and having to admit that they are wrong. Underneath all these attempts to maintain power and control, there are often secret feelings of self-doubt, leading to cynicism and jealousy. They are prone to phobias, hypochondria and/or obsessive thought or behaviour patterns and sometimes actually take a considerable amount of actual pleasure in being bad-tempered or unreasonable.

Intuitive Adaptable

Personality Profile:

Sociable: Gets on well with almost anybody

Intuitive: A high level of instinct and general awareness.

Adaptable: Able to make the best of any situation.

Achilles heel: The need to be liked.

Areas of conflict: Concerned with emotional states, predominantly guilt, shame, and injustice issues.

Symptoms: Usually concerned with feelings – inadequacy, depression, inferiority, low self-esteem, fear of what others think, excessive regard for authority, guilt, shame, etc.

Abreaction type: Usually tearful and childlike. The approach of abreactive states will often be indicated by sudden quietness and an increase in hypnotic flush. A hand may be raised to the mouth, which may tremble or straighten. Within the abreaction, tears and weeping can be copious.

Personality: The IA personality, being able to fit in with almost any situation, is necessarily a kind of psychological chameleon. The most obvious traits are a pleasant and responsive attitude to others but sometimes with a tendency towards mood swings from happy to miserable – or the other way round – at the slightest provocation, the smallest event. There is also often an 'all or nothing' tendency, in which if they cannot have *absolutely* what they want, they will simply refuse to have any part of it at all and will 'cut off their nose to spite their face'. Excellent talkers and communicators, they are unrivalled when it comes to having an instinctive grasp of all that is going on around them. They are usually reliable and come over as 'nice' people, which they usually are.

Physical traits: Easy to recognise from their physiology, they are responsive during conversation, with active but not excessive body/head movements, nodding when they should, smiling when they should, any disagreement being expressed politely and tactfully. Their face expressions are reactive to the conversation and there is a tendency to smile often unless they are depressed. Any tension/anxiety present tends to speed up body movements and speech, and increases the visibility of any lines on the face, and there will then be a leaning towards a worried/anxious expression.

Positive attributes: Instinctive understanding of others; caring and compassionate; excellent communication skills; generally optimistic, cheerful and polite; tolerant and easy-going; powerful instinctive responses (it can seem as though they possess a genuine sixth-sense of the unadmitted attitudes or mood-shifts of others); flexible approach to the plans of others.

Negative attributes: *There are many IA individuals who appear to show none – or very few – of the following traits. They are only tendencies and not necessarily present.*

The complexity of this character can be exasperating to others if they once get into a negative mode of operation. They can be just on the brink of success when they will suddenly give up, claiming that they simply have not got what it takes, even if other people think they have; feelings of inferiority and inadequacy can lead to problems with decision making and displays of under-confidence or unassertiveness; and they can seem to take far too much notice of the opinions of others, an excessive need to be liked sometimes leading to difficulty in saying "No" when necessary. There are often feelings of failure or of being in some way fraudulent. They are prone to shyness, depression and/or bouts of debilitating melancholia/depression.

Charismatic Evidential

Personality Profile:

Restless: Must always have something 'going on'.

Charismatic: Naturally outgoing.

Evidential: What-you-see-is-what-you-get.

Achilles Heel: The need for constant stimulation.

Areas of conflict: Concerned with image issues and loss of freedom or things that they really did not want to do/face. These can seem to be quite minor events.

Symptoms: Anything dramatic. Hysterical blindness, paralysis, 'massive' panic attacks, spontaneous vomiting, 'phantom' illnesses of all kinds from 'blackouts' to crippling or catastrophic conditions.

Abreaction type: Noisy and often may include screaming and shouting, as well as thrashing arms and legs. Anything that *dramatically* illustrates how bad they are feeling. The approach of abreaction is usually rapid and almost indeterminable from the abreaction itself.

Personality: The CE personality in its purest form tends towards extremes in many things. They enjoy life to the full and can give much pleasure to a great many people along the way – except for the occasions when they get carried away with frivolity and excitement, loving to shock others with loud and embarrassing behaviour and being amazed when someone complains about their excesses. This exuberance tends to show itself quite often and can be quite exhausting for their companions. Most of the time, though, this personality is tempered by more sensible traits from the other two groups, not unusually producing an individual who can quite often uplift others with their irrepressible sense of fun and enthusiasm.

Physical traits: Animated behaviour is the most obvious trait here but, as with most things in this group, it tends to be exaggerated. There are excessive movements of the head and face, the body, and especially the hands, and they can liven up any gathering with sparkling wit - as long as not too much serious stuff is expected from them. Often quite generous and outgoing, and almost exclusively extroverts, they are always on the search for something new and exciting to do. They adore telling jokes and stories with lots of noise and action and always do it well. Under any sort of pressure, they tend to become louder and more expansive in their gestures and movements.

Positive attributes: Enthusiasm for new projects; lively approach to life and work; inspirational in outlook and communication; exceptionally confident and outgoing; uninhibited in all areas of life; quick eye for creating an image; uncomplicated personality – what you see is what you get; good presentation skills; ready wit, especially in response to others.

Negative attributes: *As with the IA and RO personalities, these negative traits will not necessarily be apparent.*

The biggest problem for the CE personality is in maintaining application of effort and as a result they can appear unreliable or fickle. They themselves are unconcerned about this, however, relying on sheer force of personality/charisma to see them through and usually getting away with it; they may even boast about it. There is a childish need for instant gratification – they cannot abide waiting about for things to happen – and a distinct tendency to flamboyantly exaggerate their successes. Their relationships are usually distinctly one-sided and they are masters of tactlessness and bad taste. Under pressure, they are prone to dramatic illnesses like paralysis, apparent blindness, 'black-outs', memory-loss, etc., which may or may not be genuine.

Quick Recognition Guide

Now, here is a quick recognition guide for each group which, while it is not as accurate as the questionnaire, will give you a good idea of where anybody 'fits', just by watching them for a moment or two.

Intuitive adaptable

Physiology: Responsive body and head movements. Frequent smiles.

Positive: Caring, cheerful, pleasant, talkative and tolerant. 'People' people.

Negative: Depressive, indecisive, underconfident. Prone to mood swings.

Dress: Conservative, 'sensible', with a tendency to co-ordinating colours.

Resolute organisational

Physiology: Fairly straight-faced, few body response patterns, steady gaze.

Positive: Practical, tenacious and self-sufficient. Quick thinkers. Often personable.

Negative: Suspicious, dictatorial, manipulative. Cannot easily admit mistakes.

Dress: Plain, sometimes austere, sometimes tends towards dark-ish colours.

Charismatic evidential

Physiology: Often expansive in gestures. Can be animated or noisy and often laughs easily.

Positive: Fun-loving, enthusiastic, outgoing. Inspiring and optimistic.

Negative: Unreliable, childish, and boastful. Prone to exaggerate mild success.
Dress: Individualistic, either 'designer' or deliberately downbeat. Can often be 'showy' with accessories.

CHAPTER FOUR
Useful techniques for the professional therapist

Dissociation

Every therapist should have in their 'toolbox' several dissociative techniques for use when a client simply cannot bring him/herself to think/talk about a past event; it was just too traumatic. The first technique shown here is very powerful and can help a client to access memories which are otherwise 'just too painful' to contemplate.

The Book of Life

This method can sometimes have one or two advantages over the very similar 'movie of life' routine that has been published elsewhere. In particular, whichever part of the book we are working on can be devoid of pictures if the client is more comfortable that way.

To begin, you need to introduce your client to the idea of imaginarily writing a book of his or her life. It is essential that you carefully make the point that you will not attempt to force any conversation about the feared event. What is *not* a good idea is to promise that the event will not have to be accessed or discussed in any way at all. What *is* a good idea is to reassure the client that he or she will be in full control of the conversation at all times.

Next, ask how many chapters the book will have, then which chapter your client is currently in. The answer here will tell you a great deal about the mental processes with you will be working; where you are told that the book has, say, 20 chapters and the current one is 10, then it's a fair bet that there is a recognition that change is entirely possible – there is a natural optimism and optimism works very much in our favour. When a number close to the total of chapters is given, then there may some benefit in discussing why the client feels this way and doing what we can to create greater optimism. It is not necessary to spend too much time at this; if there is no evident interest in exploring the situation, simply carry on as shown here.

The Work Proper

Now we are ready to start the therapeutic work proper: The first of the following stages can be skipped if necessary:

1. Ask about a list of characters, with brief biographies, who will appear in the book – this can speed things up no end but does not work well with particularly nervous clients. In any event, if the client displays any unease at all you should move on.
2. Ask which chapter the client wants to write first – if option 1 has been skipped, you will find yourself having to take time to get the background of each character as they appear.

Now the work proceeds easily, though it is important that you make notes throughout. Ask your client what happens in this chapter, the timescale and chronology and so on. Flashbacks are allowed, as are references to chapters not yet written, though it is useful to discover what chapter anything of that sort will fit into; just get the number, write it down, then continue.

It is essential that you *never* lead the client; if this therapy is to be successful it must be kept totally 'clean'. To this end, you simply make notes about what your client tells you, without judgement or criticism, though it is completely in order to point out any contradictions, which can then be analysed where necessary – and again, totally without judgement or criticism. This will gain the client's confidence and trust, which will eventually allow **'The Biggie'** chapter to be written – the one with the trauma.

There may be several 'blind alleys' and diversions before the client is ready to approach this point; the work cannot and should not be rushed. Therapy is not and never should be a race and the reason that this routine can be so successful is that the client is given enough time to gain the confidence necessary to talk about a hitherto 'no go' area and discharge the associated and quality-of-life-damaging emotion.

Practical Work – The Book of Life

Here is a suitable format for practicing this technique in a workshop setting:

  ➢ Working in groups of 3 – 'standard' Therapist, Client, Observer format.
  ➢ Be sure to create a short biography of each of the main characters.
  ➢ Keep to 'lightweight' issues as far as possible for this exercise.

Not Today

Another dissociation routine, indicated when the client feels that history might repeat itself in some way. Often, we can use a simple collapsing anchor technique from NLP but there are times when this is ineffective or otherwise not a suitable technique.

'Not Today' works with a different form of dissociation from the previous method shown; rather than dissociate the client from an event while she or he tells us about it, it seeks instead to dissociate a current or future situation from the trauma of something past.

To achieve this end, it allows and encourages open exploration of a past upsetting event which is being echoed in some way in the client's current life. The following examples are not at all uncommon, though there are many other circumstances in which this method may be employed.

- The client needs to make a flight but has a previous experience where there was a problem which he or she believed at the time was potentially disastrous. Where this is the only time a flight has been made, this routine is invaluable.
- The client suffers 'commitment neurosis' after a relationship in which he or she suffered some sort of abuse.
- The client wants to start/restart a business but is held back by the memory of a venture which went wrong as a result of a third party's involvement.

The client will often feel that he/she was out of control at the time the sensitising event occurred and where we can demonstrate that this was not so, we are 'home and dry'. In this situation, we can work on the basis that our client will have learnt from the experience and now has more resources available - even if this happy fact has not been recognised before our intervention.

Situations like the 'bad flight' scenario are obviously different; here, the event would always *genuinely* have been out the client's control. As a result, this type of neurotic response can be rather more difficult to resolve and we will need to rely on natural desensitisation and logic - and this should cause us no problem at all, since most individuals suffering this 'can't let go' type of problem are of logical orientation.

Method

The client may well have talked through the event with friends and family a good few times, yet achieved no relief from the problem. Of course, friends and family can so easily have compounded the difficulty by offering 'helpful' advice that has proved ineffective. So one of the first things we have to do is to convince the client that talking to a qualified and highly skilled therapist is a whole different situation.

"Did <name> *know how to help you to dissociate your fears?"* is a good question. Usually, the answer will be a 'no,' or 'I'm not sure,' or something similar and we have made a step forward. The client now knows that there is something that **can** be done that has not been done **yet.** Even when the answer is a 'yes,' we can turn it to our advantage with: *"Good – that means I can get straight to work*

immediately." Inevitably, belief and expectation will now be on the way up.

Getting the Client Talking

We now need to get our client talking and we will at first do the exact *opposite* of what we have indicated; we will seek to get *association* with the past event before we start to work our therapeutic 'magic'. This, of course, is extraordinarily easy to do, via <u>determinedly non-leading</u> questioning. (For a full description of the importance of this sort of work, read **Rapid Cognitive Therapy Volume One**)

The following are useful, introduced at salient points in the client's narrative. They do not by any means comprise an exhaustive list and are only here to illustrate the type of question you should ask. In general, avoid asking too much about the event - it's the client's reactions we are after.

The first question is by far the most important:

"How did that feel?" Ensure that the client *does* tell you how 'it' felt, rather than just the way things were. You want the 'psychological experience' - in other words, a full account of what was going on in the client's mind. You could instead ask: "How did that seem to you?" which is a little more permissive and will sometimes be useful. Here are some more:

- *"What did you do then?"*
- *"Was there anybody else there?"*
- *"What were other people doing?"*
- *"What happened then?"*
- *"What were you thinking when that happened?"*
- *"Had you felt like that before?"*

Advanced Hypnotherapy and Hypnoanalysis

Any of these questions, along with others that you might decide to use to explore a past event in detail, can occasionally produce an abreactive state, the resultant catharsis ensuring that the client's symptom pattern will soon start to fade. Most of the time, though, this will not happen. Instead, your client will stat to show signs of unease and that's where we start the dissociative work.

How we do this seems so ridiculously easy and obvious that you could be forgiven for thinking that it cannot possibly work! This is actually a useful circumstance, for our client will not actually realise that we are doing anything therapeutic and will therefore be most unlikely to resist.

At the very first sign of discomfort, we simply say: *"That's ok - it's not going to happen today. In fact, it's a guaranteed fact that that particular event will never happen again, is it not?"*

You must get a 'yes' from the client here, however long it takes and however many times you have to point out that once something has happened, two irrevocable rules come into play:

1. When something has happened it can never be *un*happened.
2. Once something has happened, that particular event **can never happen again.**

You can also use, where relevant: *"Well, you haven't got to do it today. Does that make sense?"* This is especially useful when dealing with fears related to a specific event, like flying in an aeroplane.

67

And this is especially useful *and* important: *"I wonder if you've ever thought that you are in total control of whether or not you even have the chance of encountering a similar situation ever again? You can just choose not to do <thing> We can all choose that option – it's just a question of the price! Can you see that?"*

You might need to explain the concept of the 'price' of making a choice to some clients, of course, and the example the author likes to use is: *"If Tom wants to play on the computer but his wife wants him to do some decorating, he's the one with total choice and control. He can choose to play on the computer, and the price will probably be domestic strife!"* This is said in a light-hearted manner and will usually introduce a little levity into the proceedings – never a bad thing, in moderation.

When the client gives us a 'yes' response to these concepts, we seek more of the same; be sure to use a totally conversational tone when you ask the following questions and also be sure to weave them into an apparently innocuous conversation. Invisible therapy is always the best!

- *"Does it make sense to you that because the moment of 'now' is always brand new, every event is a totally new event?"*
- *"Can a football team ever beat a team that has beaten them in the past?"*
- *"If you threw three 2's on a dice, is there a chance that the next number will be different?"*
- *"If you toss a coin and it comes down 'heads' is there a chance that it'll be 'tails' next time?"*

It should be possible for you to come up with a few more examples of your own but even if not, those given here will help you provide a good therapy – it will now be possible for your client to talk easily and in depth about the sensitising event. In effect, a full 'debriefing' can now take place, so that we can help our client to relegate the connected emotional work to where it belongs - in the past.

Two 'Ace' Cards

Where it is relevant, we have two 'ace' cards to play, both related. The first is: *"I don't know about you, but when something goes wrong, I want to discover what my part of it was. That way, I don't have to wonder if it might happen again, because I can do something different the next time."* Discussion about this concept with the client will usually bring some enlightenment.

The second 'ace' is: *"How easily would you recognise a similar situation in the future?"* This is an empowering question and far more positive than asking: *"What have you learnt from that experience?"* which can create feelings of inadequacy if the client forms the view that he or she was foolish not to have recognised it in the first place.

Either or both of those 'focussing' questions can be followed with: *"How would you handle that situation differently now?"* Where the circumstances of the original sensitising event were such that our client *did* have a share of the responsibility, exploration of this concept can be enormously empowering.

By now, your client is likely to be feeling much more at ease with himself and all that is needed is to wind the session up.

If you decide to utilise a hypnotic intervention at this point, then relevant ego-strengthening is indicated. You should also make plenty of reference to the newly discovered resources and/or the notion that, contrary to popular belief, history *cannot* repeat itself.

Regressive Progression

This simple routine can be very useful for those clients who present with the 'I used to be different' type of statement. It works particularly well when an individual needs to recapture some of the vitality of youth.

It is used in a specific manner; unlike 'standard' regression, where we would focus on the presenting problem – on what *is* – here, we will focus on what it is that our client needs that is missing – in other words, on what *is not*. Also, we work *forwards* to when the problem event arose, rather than backwards. The therapist can help here by working chronologically, using the body/eye mind accessing techniques. Occasionally, when the quality and type of recalls changes abruptly, it becomes evident that the client has 'skipped' the traumatic area; all we have to do here, of course, is to work at the period of life that seems to be missing and here you could use the Book of Life routine to help if necessary.

Let us assume, for a moment, that our client has presented with a general shyness or other social phobia, perhaps, but remembers distinctly that he/she used to be confident and outgoing. The first thing we have to do is to help our client build a strong image of a time when he/she *was* confident and outgoing. The use of the 'Total Learning Machine' technique you practiced earlier will help here.

70

From there we conduct the session exactly as in standard regression techniques, exploring each concept in full, but moving forwards through time instead of back.

You will often discover abreactive states occurring here, though this will often happen with less ferocity, for some reason, than in other regression techniques. This <u>may</u> be because, in the normal way, we are asking our client to go further back through time and they are approaching the trauma from a position *after* repression has occurred and created resistance. With regressive progression work, though, they are thinking back to *before* repression and therefore approaching it with less resistance.

The effect is the same as for any regression style of therapy, in that once the ISE has been discovered and worked through, there is catharsis and a steadily lessening emotional attachment to the event as a result.

Practical Work – Looking for revitalisation

Here is a guide for practicing the technique in a workshop setting. We are using 'revitalisation' as a search object since it is evident when we find it!

> ➤ Working in groups of 3 – 'standard' Therapist, Client, Observer format
> ➤ Search back until a truly energetic part of self is found; this might be many years in some cases.
> ➤ Experiment how this can 'rejuvenate' by accessing the feelings that existed then, using the 'Total Learning Machine' technique.

The Miracle Box

This routine is so delightfully simple that you could be forgiven for thinking that it couldn't possibly do anything useful!

We simply ask our client to imagine they are holding a small box, and ask for a description. Allow total freedom of choice here, for it really doesn't matter how he or she actually sees the box; we are simply increasing concentration. Once you are sure that you client can visualise the box, ask the client to imaging shaking it until it starts to rattle, then just hold it steady.

Then we say, building expectation: *"Now, in that box is something that will remind you of everything you need to remember right at this moment. It might be one thing, or it might be a lot of different things – a whole world of things, perhaps, in just that tiny box – which you will only be able to see one at a time. So when I ask you to take the lid off, I want you to tell me the very first thing you see...or even the first thing you think, because it might be that some of the things in there are just thoughts."*

Pause for a few seconds before asking the client to take the lid off the box. The language we use is very important here; asking the client to simply 'open the box' would not have the same effect at all – asking him/her to 'take the lid off' has a much stronger subconscious meaning.

Whatever the client reports, we follow up, exploring as fully as we can. Then we ask the client to put the lid back on the box and continue with: *"And this is why it's called the 'Miracle Box', because next time you take the lid off it, you will see something quite different, though that something will be connected to the first one..."*

We continue with this until the client reports that 'there's nothing there', when we can safely assume that the particular thought train with which we have been working is exhausted. If we need to, we can curtail the work with the suggestion: *"At some point, you'll see that the box is empty and that means that your mind has exhausted that train of thought for the time being..."* but this should only be used if it is essential to end the session.

Practical Work – The Miracle Box
> Working in groups of 3 – 'standard' Therapist, Client, Observer format
> Be sure to create the right 'aura' of mystery, which can easily be done with voice patterns.

Tell Me a Story
This one can be great fun! It is based around the fact that we cannot actually ever invent anything at all; everything we imagine must be based upon our own previous experience, even if that experience is 'second-hand' in the form of a tale that we ourselves have been told. Because of the 'connectedness of everything', the subconscious will seek to match everything that happens to us with something that has happened previously, in order to understand it. So when the client starts this story-telling technique, he or she is already tapping into the memory banks and will pretty soon recount a real tale from the past.

Here is the best way to use the technique:

Ask your 'stuck' client to choose a childhood age – it often turns out to be seven. Then follow with something like: *"Good, ok, you're (age). Now I want you to make up a story*

*about something that a (age)-year-old (boy/girl) might do...
not something outrageous like taking a team of elephants
across the Alps and skiing down the other side in record
breaking time, but something absolutely normal that a (age)-
year-old child might do. When it turns into a real memory,
just keep on talking. It doesn't matter how boring it is or how
anything else it is – what matters is that you start talking...
now!"*

You might need to 'prod' your client a bit, but *do not*
give any help or suggestions about what the story should be
about. When they do finally start, you can rest assured that
what they are telling you is in some way close to a real
childhood experience. And it soon will be the experience
itself, because there are very few people indeed who can
'survive' for long without realising that they have 'fallen'
into a real memory of some sort. Of course, since the
memory is from his/her own subconscious, it is perfectly
valid for therapy purposes, and there are times when it will
lead directly to an abreaction.

Here is a snippet from a 'live' session – it is obvious at
which point it all became a real memory, actually before my
client realised it was so:

*"When I was eight, I went to the park with my friend
Darren. We were going to play football but Darren's mum
had told him not to get dirty... she was always moaning
about him not keeping his clothes clean, just like my mum..."*
And now the thoughts are flowing again, of course.

Practical Work – Tell Me a Story
Here is how to practice the routine in a workshop
setting:

74

➢ Working in groups of 3 – 'standard' Therapist, Client, Observer format
➢ The therapist gets the 'client' started while the observer watches for evidence that a real memory is being accessed
➢ The 'client' must play fair and own up when challenged!

The Single Frame of Film
This is probably one of the shortest routines that anybody has ever taught... when your client is avoiding detail in his/her recall, just say: *"If I was to take a photograph of your thoughts, just a single frame of film, what would I be looking at?"*

Here is an example:

Client: *"I'm remembering a day trip to the zoo with the school."*

Now, everybody reading this will form an entirely different image from that statement; but it's the client's image/thought that we want, not our own, so we ask the question as above, and we might get:

Client: *"Well, actually, I'm looking at somebody being ill on the coach."*

That the second statement is vastly different from the first; the first statement was *a translation* of the original idea or concept and it is that original idea or concept that our client finds that we need to explore.

Practical Work – The Single Frame of Film
Again, a method for practicing the technique in a workshop setting:

75

➢ Working in groups of 2 or 3
➢ The 'client' chooses as vague a description as possible
➢ The 'therapist' extracts the actual image

Recall Types

Throughout the analytical encounter, you will hear your client relating at least 5 different types of recall: **event, scenic, rote, chronological, composite.** Of the five, it is event recall in which we are most interested and we need to guide our client in the direction whenever he or she drifts.

Event recall, of course, is about something that has happened one time. This is what we want our client to access.

Scenic recall is generalised recall of a geographical area, something along the lines of: *"I'm just looking at the outside of the house where I used to live...there was a park just round the corner, and the main road wasn't far away..."* The 'antidote' is to ask about a specific event that must have been associated; we take the first part of the recall and work with that: *"Tell me the earliest thing you can remember about that house,"* is a good example. *"Who else lived in that house?"* is also good.

Rote recall is something that is told *by rote;* that is, without actually accessing any real thought processes – an example here would be something like: *"I always used to go the same way to school every day...and when I got home, I used to watch television or play in the garden."* A good response here would be: *"Tell me about something that happened one day on the way to school."*

Chronological recall is a sequential narrative: *"I remember once we were going on holiday and dad yelled at* *my mum to hurry up or we'd be late and mum yelled back that she'd been ready for ages... they kept on arguing all the way to the airport and when we got there we'd missed the 'plane so they had to put us on another one..."* We can be very direct with this one: *"Tell me about another time when you felt just the same way as that."*

Composite recall is sometimes difficult to spot but is very important; it tends to serve the same purpose as a screen memory, hiding something relevant to our client's problem by confusion. It will always be a mixture of 2 or 3 fragments of memory, seldom, if ever, of an event. Sometimes, you will be very aware of it and sometimes the client will confess that something 'doesn't seem right'. The answer is simple: *"If I took a photograph of your thoughts..."* etc.

The important thing with all of these is speed; we have to get our client back on track as quickly as possible because he/she is steadily moving further away from the original concept or idea that started the recall. Yet we must also be unobtrusive and our intervention must be ease our client back to event recalls as invisibly as possible. You would follow each of the interventions with more interaction designed to keep the client focussed.

Practical Work – guiding the client to events

➢ Working in groups of 3 – 2 Therapists, one Client format.

➢ On this exercise, the 'client' should be as determinedly awkward as possible; think of an event that has happened within the last year, and then talk about anything connected with it but not the event itself. The 'therapists' will find as many ways as possible to guide to a description of an actual event.

The Mini 'PARTS' Session

A wonderful way to finish analysis is with a mini 'PARTS' session. 'Archetypal Parts Imagery' is easier to use than the system originally taught by Charles Tebbets, as well as being light-hearted and fun. It will 'tidy up' effectively and ensure that we leave our client with an effective set of tools with which to tackle the rigours of life when they no longer have us as their support system. It is shown in full detail later in this book, but here is a 'taster' session to introduce you to the idea.

We are going to use **Terence Watts'** 'Warrior, Settler and Nomad' concept, since it embodies the three main behaviour patterns of the human psyche; *Survival, Security* and *Pleasure.* You have already seen the three types, in Chapter Three, though listed by their 'professional' names of:

- **Resolute Organisational** – the **'Warrior'**
- **Intuitive Adaptable** – the **'Settler'**
- **Charismatic Evidential** – the **'Nomad'**

If we were doing a complete therapy based around the concept, then we might spend some time explaining something about inherited instincts (as shown later on and where the origins of the names is given) and the instinctive behaviour patterns inherited from our ancient ancestors... but for our purposes here, we want something elegant and quick, something which will introduce our client to the idea speedily and clearly.

So here is the 'quick way in'.

Just as there are three primary colours, so there are three primary behaviour patterns in the human mind. Just as we can find any colour by mixing those three primary colours in the right proportions, so we can find just the right mix of personality in the same way, to deal effectively with any situation in life, no matter what it is.

The first primary behaviour pattern is based around Survival – we call that part the **'Warrior'** because it will fight for what is right and will use tenacity and practical abilities to achieve an objective. It is the part that helps us to stay in control of our life. Warriors can include: *Celtic Kings and Chieftains, Warrior Queens, Normans, Vikings, Crusaders, Knights, Native Indians, Samurai, Zulus, Shoguns, Trojans, Nubian Kings and Queens, Roman Gladiators and Centurions, Chinese and Japanese Emperors, Ancient Huns, Saxons.*

Next, we have the **'Settler'**; the Settler settles things and is the part of personality that needs security and love, and the part that will give those things to others, too. It is the nurturing 'looking after' part that likes to be settled and secure in any given situation. Settlers include: *Homesteaders, Ancient Farmers, Livestock Workers, Ancient Builders, Carers of all descriptions, Healers, Craftsmen of all types, Teachers, Monks, Nuns, Prophets and Seers, Clothiers and Dressmakers, Barbers, Shopkeepers, Researchers, Philosophers, Artists, Musicians, Composers and 'Searchers for Truth'.*

And finally the **'Nomad'**, the part that doesn't want to remain stuck in one place all the time. The Nomad is all about pleasure and light-heartedness, and likes to entertain and be entertained... we need the Nomad part so that we can lift other people's spirits as well have fun ourselves from time to time. *Nomads include: Gypsies, Wandering minstrels, Tinkers, Ancient Arabs, Actors, Tricksters, Travellers, Sorcerers, Witches, Warlocks, Wizards, Itinerant musicians, Soothsayers, fake Prophets and Seers, minor Thieves and Pick-pockets, Pirates, Highwaymen, Outlaws, Court Jesters, Story-tellers, Dancers, Magicians and Conjurors, Illusionists.*

You'll notice that all those listed here are 'ancient' but their modern counterparts are perfectly acceptable for our purposes here.

The next thing we do is create a mind-picture of each of those parts and develop it into a vivid mental image – a ''VMI' – which can be used as an anchor to the associated resources. Work with the idea that:

- **The Warrior** is a determined, resourceful and practical individual who is good at being in control, but can be pessimistic.
- **The Settler** is a kind and helpful person who has an intuitive understanding of others, is versatile, adaptable and likeable, but can have problems with asserting self.
- **The Nomad** is the fun-lover and fun-giver, enthusiastic, lively and very persuasive, always optimistic but can sometimes be self-centred.

Practical Work – Creating the VMI
- ➤ Work in pairs and create an image of each archetype
- ➤ The images can be whatever seems to fit the style of behaviour and can be modern or old. For instance, a Warrior might be an ancient Norseman, a Roman Centurion or a modern Jet Fighter Pilot.
- ➤ The images need to be as detailed and complete as possible – how the person looks, sounds, moves, even smells. What she or he is wearing and what he or she seems to be doing, etc.
- ➤ 'Cross sex' archetypes are acceptable. A female can have a Farmer as her Settler and a Male can have a Sorceress as his Nomad.

As a 'tidy up' at the end of our therapy with a client, the best way of using this concept is to revisit some of the life difficulties that have beset our client before therapy so that she/he can compare how they will be able to deal with the same sort of thing in the future, now that there are 'new' resources available. This is great confidence booster and instils a high belief of lasting success.

This can be done in or out of hypnosis and will show our client the effectiveness of the technique; what we teach him/her to do for the future is to simply hold the relevant VMI in their mind for a few moments if they ever find a need to change a behaviour process – in this way we can actually begin to overcome the problems that have arisen as a result of a conditioned response pattern or a damaging core belief.

Practical Work – Using the VMI
- ➤ Work in pairs.

- ➤ The 'client' thinks of a recent situation that was difficult in some way.
- ➤ Decide which archetype would deal with that problem most effectively.
- ➤ The 'therapist' induces a light state of hypnosis (optional) and helps the 'client' to explore the situation with the new resources.

When the above work is completed, take a few moments to test the effectiveness of the VMIs that have been created:

- Access your Warrior, and see how he or she feels about the new resources you've acquired during this session.
- Access your Settler and see how he or she feels about having something extra to offer clients or others who need your help.
- Access your Nomad and test how much YOU are enjoying the workshop session so far.

CHAPTER FIVE
More Techniques for the Professional Therapist

Different Futures

This routine, best used in a moderately deep state of hypnosis, can easily help those individuals who are in some way 'stuck' where they are in life and are determinedly resisting any sort of change; it can be particularly effective when there is fear of some future circumstance – a new job, a relationship break up, a medical operation, moving house, etc.

It is not unusual, when working with this method, that the client suddenly comes to the recognition that there is another 'way to go', that he does not *have* to pursue the feared objective. Sometimes, he will come to the recognition that staying where he is will be far more uncomfortable than even the worst case scenario in his other possibilities. On other occasions, he will simply arrive at the conclusion that his fear is irrational and that the objective carries nothing more sinister than temporary discomfort. On rare occasions there will be the sudden and determined recognition that where he is, is where he actually *wants* to be, for some reason or another, even if he did not realise it before.

There is nothing complex about the way we proceed here, though it can be lengthy, sometimes, due to the fact that we help our client to 'work through' every possible

83

eventuality that he can come up with – and even a few of our own, if necessary. The object of all this is to help the client accept that his course of action is the best possible of all that are available; in other words, we have created that empowering circumstance, **choice.**

The Method

To begin with, we need to point out to the client that he has many different futures and the one that he moves into is actually very much under his control. This notion itself is empowering, though it will not work until we have shown the client the truth of that statement.

To aid description, we will take the hypothetical case of a middle-aged male in a poor-quality relationship in which he has no wish to remain, yet is frightened of moving on. The first thing we have to do is to *forward pace* from where he is now to a point at some time in the future, with the assumption to begin with that he makes no change. Once this has been completed, create a 'VMI' of the situation or circumstance in which he has found himself.

Negative Hallucination

Next, we ask him to start creating a future where he *does* leave; allow your client's imagination to create the scenario that is instinctive to him and if it is a positive one, then your work will be easy. Usually, though, there will be obstructive thoughts in the form of 'negative hallucinations' – an assertion that such-and-such is likely to happen for some reason or another. Your job then is <u>not to tell him that such an event may not come to pass, or that it is rare,</u> but instead to ask him to work out how he would overcome that particular obstacle. We continue in this vein until our client either clears the final hurdle to a positive outcome, or moves back to one of the obstructive thoughts and deals with it in a different manner in his mind.

Once we have that positive outcome we create a VMI of it and compare how it feels in comparison with the VMI of the outcome where no movement took place. It goes without saying that there is almost always going to be a favourable reaction and we can then begin to reinforce the motivation towards the goal to finish the session.

Where there have been many negative hallucinations that have been worked through, it can be empowering to remind the client of his resourcefulness and point out to him that whatever befalls him, he has the tools to deal with it and deal with it effectively.

Example:
Using the above case scenario:

Therapist: *"So you decide to leave. And what happens then?"*

 Client: *"Well, I'd have to find myself somewhere to live."*

Therapist: *"And you find yourself somewhere to live…"*

 Client: *"It might be awful. Crappy."*

Therapist: *"And you find yourself somewhere to live and it's awful, crappy. So what do you do about that?"*

 Client: *"Look for somewhere better?"*

Therapist: *"And you look for somewhere better. And then what?"*

 Client: *"I can't cook."*

Therapist: *"And what do you do about that?"*

Client: *"I could eat out. Or cook ready meals."*

After a while comes the recognition that eating out and cooking ready meals is not particularly healthy, besides which, it is inclined to be expensive. This might quickly lead to an impasse and is where the therapist (who should have been making notes!) will need to intervene:

Therapist: *"Let's rewind a little. To where you say you can't cook. So, you can't cook, and what can you do about that?"*

Client: *"OK. Well, I could buy a book and learn how to. I mean, I can follow instructions. How difficult can it be?"*

Therapist: *"And so you learn to cook. Now what else is there?"*

It is essential that the therapist makes notes throughout this type of session, in order to avoid resistance becoming entrenched when any sort of irresolvable block is encountered. It will be necessary to observe the likelihood of such an event – as shown in the example above – and 'rewind' to the most recent salient point. In this way, the client will discover that he can easily overcome whatever obstacles are presented to him.

It is important that the therapist does little more than ask questions, if the client it to become truly self-empowered.

But Reversal

'But' is one of those commonly-used words that slips easily off the tongue and allows – indeed, encourages – all sorts of procrastination, evasion, apathy, and various other forms of avoidance mechanisms. It has been described as 'the mind's natural eraser' and this is a well-earned title, for when we say something like: *"I'd like to learn to drive* (for example) *but I'm frightened of the traffic,"* all we are left with is the reason for not doing whatever the subject of the sentence was before we replaced it with the new subject   in this case, fear. Therefore, we cease to give any thought as to how we might achieve our goal. Words can be powerfully destructive if we use them in a poor fashion, wonderfully empowering if we use them wisely. The therapist who can rapidly convert a client's negative phrasing into a positive concept has a valuable tool at his or her disposal.

Many readers will be familiar with the NLP method of dealing with the problem by replacing 'but' with 'and'. Unfortunately, though this can be useful on occasions, there are times when not only does it not help much, it can actually make things worse.

"I need to get my teeth sorted out <u>and</u> I'm frightened of the dentist," is not exactly encouraging, any more than is: *"I have to go abroad <u>and</u> I'm frightened of flying."*

The author has been using the 'but reversal' work shown here to good effect for several years. Quite apart from being effective it has the wonderful side effect of surprising the client with its simplicity, often inspiring a radical change in thought processes.

The Method

'But reversal' is simple in the extreme; we merely reverse the statements that surround the 'but' word and make any grammatical changes that are necessary to create a positively phrased statement. So: *"I'd love to learn to drive <u>but</u> I'm frightened of the traffic,"* becomes: *"I'm frightened of the traffic <u>but</u> I'm going to learn to drive."* In the same way, using the other phrases given here as examples: *"I need to get my teeth sorted out but I'm frightened of the dentist,"* becomes the far more empowering: *"I'm frightened of the dentist but I'm going to get my teeth sorted out."* And the flying fear statement becomes: *"I'm frightened of flying but I'm going to go abroad."*

Essentially, then, we fit everything into a: *"I might well be frightened but I'm going to do it,"* format. Once we have the client's agreement on the new phrase, therapy becomes a far more simple matter than it might otherwise have been; the client is looking at achieving his or her objective rather than seeking to avoid it. Obviously, this makes for a more successful outcome of whatever intervention we decide to use, if one is still necessary (which it sometimes is not).

It is not totally necessary for the client to have used a negative 'but' statement for us to employ this methodology – it is only necessary for us to discover the *implied* 'but' that is often present. For example, the individual who presents with a fear of needles is really saying: *"I have to have this injection but I'm frightened of needles,"* – which we can point out to the client.

Now, until this moment, the client has been seeking to avoid the injection; once we have worked our 'magic' on it, the whole situation changes dramatically – the client now will be looking for us to help him or her to actually *have* it. To put it another way, up until now, the therapist may well have been viewed as somebody who will seek to 'make' the client do something that is feared; now, however, we are the magician who will help them!

Don't Can't

There is absolutely nothing remarkable about this little intervention – it is only here because the author became aware of how many therapists miss out on a simple piece of rapid change work

It hinges around our client's use of the word "can't" and is similar in many ways to the work shown in the 'But Reversal' technique. Many times, a client will tell us that he or she "can't" do something or other. *"I can't go into a supermarket,"; "I can't talk to the opposite sex,"; "I can't go out on my own,"; "I can't stop eating too much."*

There are a *few* times when the "can't" word is valid; when it refers to an autonomic dysfunction, as in: *"I can't stop blushing,"* or when it refers to a specific skill, as in: *"I can't drive."* Almost all of the rest of the time we can say to our client: "Don't can't – it won't help."

Puzzlement will almost always be the response here, and puzzlement can open the psyche for a few seconds while the client searches for a meaning or interpretation. We have to catch it while it is open and put something useful in there before it closes again. *"Tell you what,"* you continue, *"We'll try something interesting. I want you to tell me the first thing you can think of at the end of this sentence: 'I **won't** go out on my own (for example) because...?' "* Be sure that your client understands from your tonality and body language that this is the point at which she/he must tell you the thought that comes to mind.

Now, here we are at an important juncture in therapy, for we are about to introduce our client to the notion that **can't** is a 'no choice' word, while **won't** is empowering because it allows choice – the client will no longer be 'stuck'.

A Blank Stare

Sometimes, your client will instantly give a reason; in the above example you might find something like: *"Because I have a panic attack."* At other times, we will get a blank stare or the assurance that absolutely nothing has come to mind. When this happens we can explain the notion of no choice/choice and keep on working until we have an answer to the 'because' question. On occasion, the answer can provide such enlightenment for the client that the ensuing therapy will proceed at an amazing rate.

Where increasing resistance is exhibited, with statements akin to: *"Well, I still can't think of anything,"* we need to apply some gentle pressure.

"How do you know that you can't go out on your own?" would be a good question, with the example we are working with here, as would: *"Tell me about the first time you discovered that you couldn't go out on your own?"*

Provocative Therapy

If we still draw a blank at this point some fairly provocative therapy can work wonders. We can get the client to imagine the feared event and investigate the reaction, or we could even suggest that he or she goes away, tries it, and then returns so that we know exactly what sort of work is needed. This might sound somewhat heartless, but many a therapist has struggled for far too many sessions trying to fix something without knowing exactly what it is that needs to be fixed.

Almost every therapists training course teaches the need to ask the all-important *"What do you want me to do?"* question. Well, if you try to work without knowing anything more than *"I can't go out on my own,"* You could be in for a very long and ultimately unsuccessful haul.

Anyway, assuming that our client has now answered our 'because?' question, we can point out that he or she actually *can* do the feared thing - it's just a matter of the price. The price of going out on his or her own, in this example is a panic attack. But: *"Knowing that you can go out on your own is better than knowing you can't, is it not?"* will almost always produce a 'yes' response – and now, as in the 'but reversal' method, the client is on our side. He or she is waiting for us to make life easier, rather than viewing us as the person who will try to 'make' him or her face up to a feared event. Something else that is often useful here is to point out that the price would seem to be an absolute bargain under some circumstances; if a building were on fire but nobody else was around, then going out on one's own to have a panic attack would be a highly desirable option...

Of course, once we know what the 'price of can' is, we can start therapy proper with most of the resistance nicely dealt with.

The Central Core

This is a simple empowering technique which can be use with or without hypnosis and can make an instant change to the way that your client views her position amongst her peers and family. It is based around a 'Central Core' induction/deepener that the author has used for many years. This particular version is phrased for conscious use, though with eyes closed.

Explain to your client that you are going to work at a technique that will allow her to position herself more comfortably around the other people in her life, which will allow her to function more comfortably around them. Tell her that she can just allow her subconscious to do the work; she does not have to try to *make* it work. Then suggest that she closes her eyes, and continue:

"I wonder if you can imagine, right in the very middle of you, a kind of central cores that runs from the top of your head all the way down through your body. It might be made of a precious metal, like gold or platinum; it might be diamond or some other precious stone, or it could be a gentle mist or a flowing liquid, perhaps golden or a misty blue or silver or some other colour that feels just right to you. Tell me what you find there."

Wait for your client's response, prompting gently if you need to. It is best to ensure that she is not simply complying (some do) by getting a description.

"Excellent! Now that central core is where the real you lives, the <u>real</u> you, that part of you that you call 'I' or 'Me', the part that some might call their essence, or maybe spirit or soul. Does that make sense?"

Be sure to get an affirmative before continuing:

"Splendid. Now, you might have been told a long time ago that the world doesn't revolve around <u>you</u>... and that is one of the biggest lies you have ever been told! Because you are the one who is always with you, in fact, the <u>only</u> one who is <u>always</u> with you, you can see that you cannot be anywhere

other than in the centre of your world. You <u>must</u> be the centre of your world, because you are the only one who is always there. Does that make sense?"

Again, wait for an affirmative.

"Wonderful! Now I want you to think of those people who are also in your world, one at a time, and position them wherever you feel is the right place. Your subconscious will know best, so if you want to place somebody far away, do just that, and if you want somebody so close into that central core that he or she is <u>almost</u> sharing it, then that's fine too. Now, tell me who you find there first."

When the client tells you, ask where she is going to position that person – in front, above, below, far away on the edge of her world, close into her central core, to her right, her left, and so on. Be sure to get the detail.

Repeat the process until she has located everybody she wants to think of and has allocated them all a position in her mind. It is almost inevitable that there will be a few surprises; it is not uncommon for evident satisfaction as somebody is placed as far away as possible, and for softness as a loved one is moved close. There can be tears and sudden understandings, and recognition of the interaction between others that causes stress or other difficulty for your client. The routine, simple though it is, can achieve much change and recognition in a short time.

Used carefully, it can even be used to resolve relationship or doubt issues by testing to see how it feels as somebody is moved further away or closer in. Always be sure, though, to let the client discover for herself where she wants to place those who come into her mind; any judgemental work from the therapist will cause the whole thing to 'fall over', since it will affect the positioning in her own hierarchy of everybody else she has thought of.

Practical guides have not been shown in this chapter, since it is immediately obvious how each technique might be practiced in a workshop setting.

PART TWO

Archetypal Parts Imagery – an introduction

Archetypal Parts Imagery combines standard 'Parts' work, inherited instincts, Creative Visualisation and Interactive Guided Imagery in a powerful combinative format. It has several unique features that allow the therapist to solve a huge number of problems, and does not rely on formal hypnosis.

The idea behind the concept of the therapy is a relatively simple one, though two-fold:

1. *Any conflict exists because one Part of the psyche wants to do something that another Part does not. The more balanced the 'disagreement' the more difficult it is to resolve or accommodate and the more stress it causes.*

2. *The interpretation of each experience we encounter is always based upon that which we already know – if we encounter something that is completely unknown to us, it cannot be interpreted and instead becomes part of our database against which all future*

experiences are measured. We cannot actually invent anything that is totally unknown to our thought processes, so all thought, all reaction, is based upon the experiences of our life to date.

There are many ways in which we can use this and this book will teach you several. There is plenty of room for innovation, though, for developing your own techniques and your own 'party tricks' to get the client to where they need to go as quickly as you can. This is a brief therapy.

We will most frequently start the process by introducing our client to the four major parts of his/her personality, the Warrior, the Settler, the Nomad and the Inner Advisor. Using conversational techniques, you and the client will be able to discover which of the three parts 'owns' the presenting problem and/or where conflict exists between two or more of them.

Agreement or Compromise

More often than not, we will continue to work with these parts, sometimes performing a type of timelining with one or the other so that we work with present and past; when any issues are resolved, we can then move forward in time to the future. In this way we can isolate issues and see what happens when we change them, whilst observing the effect upon the other parts, all the time with the Inner Advisor present to guide and reassure, working until we can find agreement or compromise between the parts.

Sometimes, the client may arrive at an impasse where it is just not possible to find this agreement. That is when we can use a different facet of this type of therapy – Abstract

Imagery – to find a solution, for there always is one, even if it is only the true and deep acceptance of the problem or conflict and the validity of its existence. When working with Abstract Imagery, it is important to recognise that, just as every thought and reaction is based upon that which we already know, so if we imagine something, then it, too, must based upon that which we already know, however bizarre the imaginary work.

If we 'seed' the subconscious with an idea, then ask our client to create an imaginary image that represents it in some way, that imaginary construct will contain all the elements of the idea, both negative and positive, albeit in some symbolic form; all we have to do, then, is help the client translate the imagery in order to find truths and fundamental beliefs about self and function of self.

The first thing...

This process shares something with the Freudian therapy model of Free Association, in that the client works with the first thing that comes to mind much of the time; but unlike Free Association it does not have to be a memory or real event that the client brings to mind, simply the first thing he or she can think of, however apparently disconnected, however unlikely or bizarre, however abstract. Also unlike Free Association as it used in most therapist's offices today, we do not necessarily work with childhood issues and the concept of repression. It is not unusual for these to be encountered, but we have no need to go looking for them.

In practice, the therapist does not have to worry about getting interpretations wrong, for it is our clients who will do most of the work – their minds create the construct and their minds know *why* the construct was created and how. We act as guides only and it is when we help them to interpret their own imaginary work that they will find enlightenment. Working with the imaginative/creative part of the psyche in this way can allow resistance to be more easily by-passed; where it is encountered, we can actually use the process itself to overcome it, by exploring the reason for its existence.

The Nature of the Problem

To begin with, we need to ascertain the exact nature of the problem from our client and it will usually be necessary to explore it with 'normal logic' for a while to establish a suitable point from which we can begin to work. We can easily discover which part it is that is creating the negative aspect of the presenting difficulty, even if we do not always convey this to our client – it is always better if we allow our client to discover which of the three 'selfish' parts is causing the problem and why.

This process not only gets therapy under way, but also successfully establishes the 'seed' that will propagate within our client's imaginative processes to eventually be expressed within the therapy.

Contra-indicators

There is really only one major contra-indicator for this type of work and that is where any form of psychosis is involved; the psychotically ill individual has great difficulty in distinguishing between fantasy and reality and this sort of work might very well make him worse.

Others of a less serious nature (as far as the therapy is concerned) are mentally impairing diseases like Alzheimers and so on, drunkenness, or the influence of hard drugs. If treating alcohol/drug related problems, it would be as well to insist on a 'dry' period of at least 24 hours before each session.

It is fair to say that the extremely logically orientated client might be a little resistant to the therapy – although these are the ones who would benefit most – thanks to their scientific nature convincing them that what we are seeking to do has no basis in reality. Also, the elderly, whose imaginative powers may be waning even though they are suffering nothing more than ageing, could well prove to be a challenge for the therapist. But these are not contra-indicators for the therapy, merely pointers that the therapist may be taking on a little more of a problem than he might have at first thought... come to think of it, that often happens anyway!

CHAPTER SIX
Our ancestral memories – the origins of conflict?

*There is no claim that what is written here is an academic study of the human race. It is simply a workable hypothesis that may well be accurate in much of its construct and assumptions. It is based on and around the known origins and development of the current species of Human animal. This first section has much valuable resource that will allow is to grab our client's attention and to set the scene for a successful therapy, though you would, perhaps, not use a great deal of it **directly** with most clients.*

Some of this chapter makes reference to more 'standard' forms of therapy than the Parts work shown here; there are times, though, when you will need to take just such a traditional approach.

Preparation

Note that while you can usefully learn the content of much of the first part of this chapter to use with your clients, there are many times when the brief introduction to Archetypal Work, as shown towards the end of Chapter Four, will be of more use. It is dependent upon personality type; the intellectually orientated individual will prefer a lengthy 'historical' explanation (in fact, will probably go into hypnosis listening to it) while the more emotionally centred client will fare better with the brief version. It is useful to

become thoroughly conversant with a working version of
each.

In the Beginning

One hundred thousand years or more ago, the human
race lived in groups of twenty-five to fifty individuals,
hunting and gathering their food from the land; they were
already a developed race, having probably been around for
some four hundred thousand years at least. But these were
the first of the race that looked like us, and – in a primitive
way – behaved like us. The first was a woman, the so-called
'African Eve' whose DNA was different from her ancestors.
From this beginning sprang the whole of our Human race as
it exists today.

Whilst they still carried the aggression of the earlier
species that were their forebears – who may have been semi-
robotic in their functioning – this new race seemed to be the
first to possess the ability to be self aware, and awareness of
their effect upon others around them. Hence, many hundreds
of millennia later, as this ability gained strength, some of
them would find the need to express their thoughts and
feelings via early art forms – cave and rock paintings,
sculpture, and primitive engraving.

For thousands of years, their way of life scarcely
changed, instincts and response patterns being handed on
from generation to generation, all within their own group in
what amounted to a genetically pure chain. They would have
had no qualms about incest or in-breeding – those concepts
simply would not have entered their realms of thought. Any
members of the tribe who did not 'fit' would have had far
less chance of survival: individuals in the aggressive tribes

who were less warlike than the other tribe members would perish more easily, for they could not avoid battle; and aggressive individuals in the less warlike tribes, individuals who chose to fight rather than run or hide, would have died at the hands of the attackers. Thus the process of natural selection ensured that each tribe maintained and strengthened its own particular attributes and behaviour patterns, each individual passing on the genes for success according to his tribal culture.

Tens of thousand of years passed… something like *fifty times* the passage of time we have experienced as a 'modern' race since the days of Jesus Christ and the Roman Empire. Then, something of extreme importance happened, something that was to affect the whole of the human race for ever more.

The first settlements were formed.

Settlements And Tribes

It does not sound like much, but would have had a polarising effect upon many individuals. For some, those that had always chosen to stay out of trouble, it would have been an ideal situation; no need any more to wander the land in search of food – simply farm your own crops and livestock and share the work within the community. Instead of fighting the land, adapt to it and tame it, and use its resources for survival and comfort. They became the **Settlers** and discovered their evolutionary destiny.

For others, those who had always simply taken whatever they wanted, this presented a golden opportunity of a different sort. They could wait until that settlement was established and everything was nicely under control, then simply move in and take over. These were the **Warriors** and any protesters would have had a choice – adapt to the situation or die. Those that were afraid to die and so acceded to the Warriors' control became slaves and so a new hierarchical system came into being, one that still exists today, where the stronger both dominate and exploit the weaker.

But there were some for whom all this would be too much. They never had had the stomach for fighting, nor any wish to work for somebody else's benefit. And now they had no desire whatsoever to stand around getting caught up in the crossfire between the Settlers and the marauding Warriors. So they adopted the instinctive Nomadic urges of their earliest forefathers – keep on the move, don't get involved, and constantly look for someplace new. They became the modern **Nomads.**

Developing Civilisation

These three tribal types still exist today, but because of the huge increase in interbreeding that would have started with the advent of civilisation, the purity of each type was soon lost.

Each of us has inherited characteristics of all three types, though there will usually be a predominant behaviour pattern in evidence. In this way, we can still identify individuals as **Warrior, Settler or Nomad** *an important fact that allows us to help create rapid and profound change.*

The problem is, of course, that we are all born with conflict, or the potential for conflict, already in the psyche; in addition to this, because genetic selection is apparently random, we can inherit a particular gene, or set of genes, from our parents which are actually not evident within them at all. So we can inherit an entirely different set of instincts for survival than either parent has – and yet they are going to teach us how to live. For example, we could be a Settler born to a Warrior father and Nomadic mother; then we are brought up by someone who teaches us to behave in a way that we come to believe is correct, but which conflicts with what our natural, inherited, instincts are attempting to insist we do. It does not stop there, either, because it also means that we do NOT have the instincts that go with what we believe is the way to behave.

So there is always likely to be a great deal of incongruence in the thought processing – tribal instincts demanding one set of behaviour attributes, family conditioning demanding something quite different. It is a fair statement to say that in order for us to feel happy and confident, we absolutely must be discharging our natural instincts, otherwise we will be trapping libidic energy within the psyche, and that libidic energy *will* find a way out somewhere or another. Unfulfilled urges and drives may well become sublimated, and instincts for self-protection which remain undischarged may well manifest as anxiety as a result. It is not inconceivable that this is the origin of 'random' panic attacks, for example.

Reactions, Not Events

Ancestral memories would not be of actual events – we are not talking about past life regressions or reincarnation – but of instinctive behaviour patterns brought about by the environment of those early tribes. The subject of genetics is highly complex and it is fortunate that we do not have to

104

have a full understanding of it to appreciate how it affects us. One or two facts are certainly fascinating, though, and definitely worth mentioning...

If it seems to you that there has to be an awful lot of 'instinctual information' passed on to each generation, then you are right. And the truth is that investigation as to how this actually happens is still in its infancy. But consider this amazing fact: There are millions of fragments of protein present within one DNA strand which are so minute that they can only just be seen with the most powerful of electron microscopes.... And the gene-carrying DNA strand itself is so minuscule that there are scores of them grouped together in clusters known as a chromosome... and the Human animal has 23 *pairs* of such chromosomes buried away in just the nucleus of each cell... and the entire human cell is around only around one hundredth of one millimetre in diameter.

Not Only Humans

The idea of inherited instincts doesn't apply to just the human race but is very evident in other species as well. Experiments to determine the validity of genetic memory have been carried out with various creatures and some experiments on rats, particularly, revealed interesting results. There were two groups of rats used, one group of which was trained to find their way through a maze, and the others just left to their own devices.

The experiments appeared to show that the offspring of the control group learned to find their own way through the same maze far more easily than the offspring of the other group, those who had not been taught. *Their* offspring found it easier still. And after a few generations, the offspring needed no teaching – they seemed already to know their way through the maze, after traversing it once. So perhaps it is not so difficult, when you take all this on board, to understand how animals instinctively know their migration routes.

The Birth Predisposition

Inherited instincts are possibly/probably responsible for our predisposition at birth towards certain responses and reactions. These are probably a physical part of the **right brain,** and are therefore 'hardwired' and unchangeable without surgery, clinical intervention, or other physical damage such as illness or accident; it is possible, too, that massive trauma might produce some modifying effect, even if not a total change.

Templates

It is useful to think of these birth predispositions as our 'basic-ideal' template, a series of stacks, if you like, of our *requirements* and *reactions* – all our natural behavioural instincts are here. Our Ancestral Memories govern how these stacks are when we are first born and therefore have a tremendous effect upon our subsequent behaviour patterns throughout life.

At birth, the logical left brain is almost empty – and like a sponge, starts soaking up information, every new stimulus, avidly and immediately. And since the logical brain *is* pretty much empty, everything perceived, though not necessarily understood, is accepted without question. From the moment of birth, but slowly, that 'basic ideal' template, the built in requirement and reaction set, begins to create the belief and expectation system. Events that are repeated and reinforced a few times soon become part of our fundamental beliefs, since we have no prior experiences for comparison and we have not yet discovered doubt to make us wary.

The Yardstick

Our first experiences are our yardstick of the world however good or bad they are; cuddles, comfort, pain, violence, and the situations which cause them are all equally accepted as being normal and what we must expect from the process of living. Later, we will investigate what happens when an individual with a predisposition that belongs to one tribal group or behaviour pattern is reared by parents that are in a different group – a situation which can actually be extraordinarily problematic.

If pain and violence can be accepted as a normal situation – and they really do have to be if they exist from the outset – and if we accept the existence of the subconscious ID as being essentially concerned with survival and pleasure, then it becomes obvious that we have a serious potential for emotional conflict. The conflict arises from the fact that for the whole of our life we are subject to a subconscious drive to seek security in order to ensure survival so that the species may continue; but our perception of security comes from being in a situation which mirrors or matches what is already stored in our subconscious as 'normal'. When that normality encompasses pain and violence, maybe abuse in one or more of its forms, then we are subject to a search for what can be thought of as **Destructive security.**

If we are brought up with pain, for instance, we will continue to subconsciously seek situations which can cause us pain, even though at the same time we are seeking pleasure… and perhaps you can now more easily understand the roots of sado-masochism, which probably arises where part of that early violence contained sexual overtones. Quite often, where there is little or no sexual content to the violence, there will be a different effect, which we can observe in the individual who determinedly seeks out partners who will beat them, for example.

First Ten Years

Even where there is no violence as such, there is still much potential for harm. By the time we are ten years old, we have a firm idea of how we fit into the world and how the world thinks of us. If we are confident at that age, we have a good chance of remaining so. But if we feel we do not fit in some way, that we are different from the crowd, then we are likely to feel like that for the rest of our lives or at least until something makes a radical change to our underlying thought processes.

A competent therapist, maybe.

So if parents or others teach us that adults are going to belittle us or hurt us in some other way, we are likely to experience problems as we grow older and begin to mix predominantly with other adults. If, on the other hand, we are taught that other children will hurt us – and many parents do just that, albeit sometimes unwittingly – then we may very well grow up hating children. Hate and aggression, of course, are based upon fear.

Now, there is something very important in all of this. If we have a subconscious process that was brought about by the creation of doubt or uncertainty – about ourselves or our environment – it becomes a neurosis and can be dealt with via a relatively straightforward therapy. *But if that same process was brought about as a result of our early conditioning, it is a part of our fundamental belief system in the way things are and may therefore be more difficult to deal with.*

Adult understanding and concepts might help, but there will always be that deep subconscious belief pattern which is likely to make itself felt if circumstances arise which seem to confirm that belief. An example might help to clarify this. If a child is brought up in a reasonably balanced environment and at some relatively late stage (after 5 years old or so) is subject to repeated harangues that s/he is stupid, then there is an affront to the fundamental belief system creating doubt and anxiety which will later lead to a symptom pattern of some sort. In all likelihood, such a symptom would be resolvable by an understanding and exploration of its origins, allowing the doubt and anxiety to be resolved and the integrity of the fundamental belief system to be restored.

But if the harangue of stupidity had existed since birth, then there will be a belief that is devoid of doubt. There will be a feeling of being stupid, that *will become part of* the fundamental belief system. There is nothing to be restored. As a result, although the adult might very well learn that s/he is not actually stupid at all, and be able to function accordingly, their symptom pattern is never going to be very far away. It is here that Archetypal Parts Imagery techniques can provide one of the few methods of providing viable and lasting help.

Fundamental Beliefs

It is probable that we continue to create our fundamental beliefs at least throughout the first stage of development, about the first 3 years or so of life, because throughout that time we are busily adapting to our environment. We make associations with everything around us to everything that happens to us and use those associations to evaluate every experience. These early evaluations, reinforced a few times, start to act upon that 'basic-ideal' template, and are *imprinted* into our psyche where they will remain for the whole of our lives and will act upon, and be acted upon, by our Ancestral Memories, to become part of our instinctive behaviour pattern.

In this way, we constantly adapt to the environment in which we find ourselves, developing patterns of behaviour that are appropriate to that environment and are therefore conducive to survival. They allow us to function instinctively and safely, responding well to any new dangers that might have developed since those ancestral instincts were formed.

The 'As-Is' Template

Gradually, the basis of the system we will use for the rest of our lives to assess threats to security begins to develop, in the form of another template; the *'as-is'* template, a reflection upon how life actually seems to be. At first, it is very similar to the *'basic ideal'*, and indeed, some of it will always remain so. But great changes will be made to much of it soon enough. Uncomfortable changes that force us to accommodate the fact that life often does not go the way we want it to. This 'as-is' template will form the basis of our beliefs about ourselves, the world, and how we fit into it.

110

Our life changes irrevocably at the very moment that we discover *doubt* – but it is doubt of a specific nature. It is the realisation that what we expected would happen actually did *not* happen – and we are thrown into a quandary. It is not necessarily a new experience that does it, just something that did not pan out as we believed it would, so that our 'basic-ideal' template of how life is, the embryonic expectation and belief system, is suddenly shown to be fallible.

We have no idea how or why it could have happened. We are completely mystified by it our sense of security is suddenly at risk. So we now have to introduce a new system into the psyche, because the survival instinct demands that we understand what is happening, and why, in order to react in such a way as to protect ourselves from danger, because danger equals possible extinction. The way we handle this situation and our success or otherwise becomes an imprint in itself.

That very moment greatly influences our future reactions to conflict. If we adapt, then we will always try to adapt; if we fight and win, then we will always try to fight; if we fight and lose, we will probably always tend to be defeatist, and if we turn our back on it and pretend it did not happen, then we will seldom follow things through and will always tend to turn away from problems. Whatever reaction we give is obviously governed by our major genetic inheritance and the influence that has been exerted upon it by our parents or parent figures.

And now the 'as-is' template starts, just slightly, to begin the process of change to indicate how life actually is, an indication of what we have survived. From that very second when we discover doubt for the first time, we behave differently towards each experience and event that befalls us. Within this new experience, we might start to seek separate elements that we already know about, that we have already experienced, that we already understand, so that we can perhaps make sense of what we do *not* understand – or ignore it if everything else seems well. We do this by evaluating the qualities of the new event against those of our previous experiences so that we can assess the likely outcome; in this way, we start to form our own unique view of the world. It is why one individual's 'truth' may be quite different from another's.

Emotional Filters

At some point during our early years we begin to develop the whole complex range of emotions that go to make up the human psyche. Gradually, what might be called our tuning filters are created, filters which search every event for like elements, creating new filters where necessary, so that we soon develop the capacity to recognise, within any event, the potential for certain emotional and physiological responses. These filters will be concerned with the potential of an event to generate... *anger, fear, sadness, frustration, guilt, pleasure, hate, love, embarrassment, sexual arousal, gratification, jealousy, inadequacy, power, control, self-liking, self dislike, and a whole host of other feelings and combinations of feelings.*

These filters continually alter and monitor that new 'as-is' template that is gradually being created. It helps to understand this concept if you imagine that for every event that occurs, the emotional response generated is recorded separately. This record, of course, has a marked effect upon our expectation and belief systems – the more there is of it, the more we expect to find it. If you imagine a stack of coins which gets added to each time a certain feeling is generated, the amount of coins being added depending on the importance of the event, you get the idea easily. In addition, there appears to be a system of counters that tell us how frequently we experience that same reaction, which will also tell us of the likelihood of finding it again.

So our 'as-is' template, our fundamental belief system which is formed by this process, accurately reflects the way we fit into the world and what the world does to us and for us. The whole thing becomes a highly sensitive detection and response system, a unique biological record of how we have conducted our life so far, how we have coped, and will therefore inevitably influence even the tiniest of decisions that we might have to make.

This core of belief and expectation is both a knowledge base and an evaluation system through which every sensorial input, however minute, every micro-second of every event, must pass before we can make sense of it. Every input is evaluated and an anticipation of likely outcome made – because if we had to wait for an event to finish before we could evaluate it, we would have no way of anticipating any form of danger. So we continually evaluate, anticipate, and behave accordingly – not just complete happenings and events, but every single micro-second of that event as it unfolds.

Precisely because evaluation *must* be based on existing experience, it follows that if the counter for any one response pattern is particularly high, then we are going to keep on finding that same response more frequently than any other. It will be compounded and reinforced, whether it is good or bad. The tuning filters will become more sensitive in that particular area, especially in the case of an expectation of negativity, to allow us an earlier chance of dealing effectively with the situation.

Experience Templates

In addition to the foregoing, each experience we have is linked to its own template, its own set of reactions and responses – either one that it has created anew, or a pre-existing one that fits well enough, one that seems to have the same qualities. You can often feel that happening in your mind when you say: *"This is just like that time when..."*

That template will be compared against our 'basic-ideal' and 'as-is' templates for evaluation as to how it might affect us and if we need to interact in some way with it. When something seems to match the worst part of the 'as-is' template, then it may well produce uncomfortable surges of anxiety, even though we consciously cannot understand why. The mind stores these templates forever. Ever been to a place and realise that you've been there before, but only once and many years ago?

That 'basic-ideal' template is the benchmark against which we will compare all experiences, the standard, if you like, by which we judge the value, the 'goodness' or the 'badness' of all future events. All our other templates – we probably have thousands – are formed, developed and constantly modified by events. Everything that happens to us is compared with everything that has already happened, in an attempt to consolidate the new event with experience, thus creating security.

Negative Responses

Although many people look upon negativity as a character flaw, there is much to suggest that it is part of our survival instinct. The prehistoric individual who was stalking his prey would not have stood much chance of survival if he became so intent on this task that he was simply unaware of the sabre-toothed tiger that was stalking *him*. It was necessary to deal with his own predators first and foremost if he was going to live long enough to *need* that prey. Looked at in this light, it can be seen things that can hurt us are naturally going to be perceived far more readily and seen as more important than things that will give us pleasure because it is indigenous to our species and exists as a predisposition.

Or, if you like, it is an inherited instinct of a behaviour pattern that was necessary for the survival of the species; and it is part of our genetic inheritance.

With practice and an understanding of the workings of our belief system, we can tune ourselves – and others – to spot opportunities for pleasure without having to 'untune' the natural search for mortal danger. Archetypal Parts Imagery allows us to do this far more effectively than most other methods.

Continual Comparisons

As the 'as-is' template develops, so it is continuously compared with our 'basic-ideal' in order to assess how safe we are, how likely we are to be able to deal with the process of living. We have all met the individual who has told us: 'I shouldn't feel like this,' even though he cannot actually tell us exactly why he shouldn't; *we should listen closely, because if he feels it's wrong, then it IS wrong, to him. He*

115

has a subconscious knowledge that his two main templates are moving too far apart.

Since the 'basic ideal' is an indicator of life should be if it were ideal, that continual comparison with the 'as-is' template allows our subconscious to assess how well or otherwise we fit into the world. *It is easy to see that the more that 'as-is' template becomes separated from the 'basic-ideal' that reveals our instinctive selves, the more likely we are to notice possible threats to our security in one way or another. We subconsciously recognise that we do not have the right resources to deal with the situations in which we are likely to find ourselves.*

In short, we start to suffer anxiety neurosis. Then, events may not be seen in their true form, but in the form that we are frightened we will encounter and not be able to survive. This can cause a bias in the perception of an event that is peculiar to that particular individual, which is why truth is very seldom, if ever, the same as fact. In some cases, there can eventually be such perceptual distortion created in this manner, where emotional upheavals and disturbances have been particularly profound, that an individual is simply no longer able to view events in the same way as other people and yet has no recognition of this fact. Perception has become distorted to the point that it can quite easily be mistaken for psychosis.

The New Fundamental Belief

The fundamental belief system is as secure and unassailable, in the normal way, as the knowledge that we must eat to live. It is something that the conscious critical faculty will protect most vigorously from change; anything that challenges information that is already an established and functional part of subconscious is instantaneously rejected, even if it is something that the conscious mind *wants* to believe.

So in those cases, we have to bypass that conscious critical faculty and introduce a new fundamental belief – or allow one to be introduced. Of course, what we introduce depends on the nature of the problem and is up to the ingenuity of the individual therapist, but it must be introduced at the right instant for maximum effectiveness.

The Moment...

There is a moment in any interactive style of therapy for such an introduction, a moment when the conscious critical faculty is naturally lowered, and that is when emotion *that has been generated by some event that is directly linked to the fundamental belief system* is being released. At that moment, we can help our client to make profound changes for himself.

It is always best to let the client give the therapist the suggestion. So we should ask him what he would have liked to happen, what he believes should have happened, at that point in his life. Or we can ask him what he would do if he saw a child in that exact situation right at that moment. In this way he will actually construct his own curative metaphor. There is actually no need to do much more than that, because by vocalising it, he has created it in his mind in the modality that is best for his psyche, in the format that feels best to him. All we have to do is feed it back.

Examples are:

Client: *"Somebody should have __told__ her..."*
Therapist: *"And then what might have happened?"*
Client: *"She might have told me she loved me."*
Therapist: *"And how does it feel when you __hear__ that in your mind?"*

Client: *"Why didn't she just cuddle me and make it __feel__ better?"*
Therapist: *"How does that __feel__ when you think of it?"*

Client: *"They should have __seen__ what was happening..."*
Therapist: *"And what might have happened then?"*
Client: *"They could have made it __feel__ better couldn't they?"*
Therapist: *"And how does it __feel__ when you __see__ that in your mind?"*

Any of these situations can be used to create a success metaphor that you could feed back to your client at the next session and this can be astonishingly effective, because you are actually telling him a story that is a perfect match to his own thought processes. The metaphors we use need to be carefully constructed and preferably indirect, to fire the imaginative process; warrior stories for Warriors, dramatic/novel stories for Nomads, 'getting there by work and patience' stories for the Settlers.

Another way of working is to help our client create a 'virtual parent' in his mind, a parent who responds to the client's personality type in a way that is supportive and encourages the development of his natural positive attributes.

Memory

It is not an exaggeration to say that one the biggest problems of psychology the human species has to deal with is the effects and affects of long term memory. Because it is not the actual events of an individual's life that shape and reshape personality, not even *just* the way he reacted to those events, but the way that he remembers them. If somebody remembers that he fell off his bicycle when he first tried to ride it, there is negativity. If he remembers that he actually managed to ride it for one hundred yards before he fell off, there is positivity. What he actually remembers will depend on his personality type and the influences of life.

Memory plays a huge part in everyday behaviour and an even bigger part in therapy. It is a function of the brain, rather than the mind, a chemical reaction of sorts which is simply not well understood at all. It is the reaction of the mind to those memories which causes us problems, rather then the memory itself. It follows that if we can help somebody to change the way he reacts to his memories, how he perceives them, then we are helping him to produce change in his life, because we are all the product of experience and our memories are the map of our experience.

Continuance of Improvement

The theory that memories, or, more precisely the psychological experiences that are produced by memory, are created afresh each time is a very useful circumstance which accounts in part for the effect whereby an individual often continues to find improvement in his life long after therapy has finished. We help clients to generate a change in their personal belief system, if we do our job properly, so that from that day on, every memory that comes to mind will be viewed in a more positive light. And since every experience is instantaneously compared with all like past experience, and therefore serves as a reminder of it, it seems likely that our client's personal belief system is being continually upgraded, day by day, those emotional stacks continually being modified for the better.

But we should remember that the emotion is not, itself, responsible for our ills. *It is any subconscious programme that was set up by that emotion the first time around that **must** be dealt with to create profound change.* There may be a programme for failure, for instance, and we will need to do some detective work with our client to identify exactly what that programme is trying to achieve.

It is here that Archetypal Parts Imagery can come into its own, providing insight and enlightenment for our client, as well as laying the foundations for lasting change.

The Therapist's Dilemma

As we help the client to become aware of those limitations that have been placed upon him, aware of his *true* instincts and urges, it can sometimes appear that we are achieving an opposite effect to that which we might have intended. The enforced Settler starts to show his true Warrior self, for example. But if being Settler is putting pressure on the psyche, then for that individual's emotional health and eventual happiness, it is necessary for them to *stop* being a caring Settler.

We will have helped him to realise where his true strengths lie and she will become more useful to himself and others once his potential is able to be realised.

Once you have fully grasped the concept of Ancestral Instinctive behaviour and how it affects our lives, you have a tool of inestimable power for good. Now read on to discover how to use it...

CHAPTER SEVEN
Parts Imagery at Work

Selfish Parts

Thorough reading of the personality outlines and other material in Chapter Three will have given you a working grasp of each of the three 'selfish' Parts and how to identify their activity within the psyche of your client – and that of your own.

The reference to 'selfish' here really just indicates that each part will seek to make your client's world work the way that the Part does, which is where conflict so often arises within the psyche. Sometimes, you will be fully aware of the influences or a particular Part, while at other times, it will be an entirely subconscious process. In any event, an individual will always be far more aware of the urges from his predominant Part than from the other two – but you can rest assured that all three are active, one way or another.

Functions

Here is a list which shows the function of each – how each part does what it does, or how much of it an individual might consciously be aware of, is not important; for the moment, just accept that these are the functions of each part in the psyche:

Warrior is concerned with all issues of control and getting your own way. It is the part that will rebel if you get a parking ticket, for instance, or get angry if somebody will not do what you want them to. There is no patience or tolerance here – it is all about getting the maximum take for the least give and about keeping you as near to 'the top of the pile' as possible. It is guarded and watchful for threat of any sort and will seek to gain control of, or advantage over, anybody with whom you are involved.

Settler is the part that seeks to be liked and accepted as part of the crowd or group. It is concerned to be seen as caring and conscientious, reliable and trustworthy, supportive, tolerant and 'nice'. It is the Part that wants to help others and feels upset if they seem not to notice or care, the Part that feels sentiment and deep-seated emotion. It has a high moral code with a strong belief that you should always see the best in people and never seek to take advantage of their weaknesses.

Nomad is interested in having fun and looking good. There must always be something going on and it does not matter whether it is something good or bad, particularly, as long as it is exciting. This Part needs stimulation. It is basically pleasure seeking, totally self-centred, has hardly any interest in moral codes at all and abhors any form of unpleasantness. It is the child Part with child values and attitudes, and also the Actor Part who will adopt whatever stance or attitude seems to fit the occasion.

The Sub-Parts
Each personality type has three sub-parts, really just variations, which will exhibit different facets of the major

character traits, though the types are still clearly recognisable. The main 'drivers' are still the same but may be expressed in different ways. Here is an outline of each, which will give you sufficient information to readily recognise them.

Any one of these modes may be evident during Parts work and it can be helpful to your client to recognise the ability to 'fine tune' his automatic responses to the challenges of life.

Warrior

Dictator – everybody must do his or her bidding, or there's big trouble. The Dictator is given to huge rages/outbursts when others transgress and seeks to control by fear and intimidation. It is more selfish than the other two and will often have double standards of behaviour. This is one of the most difficult of individuals to deal with and often actually *proud* of that fact.

Leader – firm, often quiet and unyielding insistence on having her own way and will not be easily deterred from any task. There is a moderate degree of selfishness which increases drastically if it begins to look as if control may be at risk. The Leader is impassive in the face of adversity and ultra-stubborn. They are often admired for their achievements and their lack of boastfulness.

Crusader – the planner and goal-setter who also tends to vigorously defend the rights of others and what he believes is right, though has great difficulty in accepting the views of others if they contradict his own. High standards and moral code, and less inclined to selfishness than the other two subs.

Ruthlessness is still there though, as also is the need for control.

Settler

Artisan – this one can quite often go unnoticed in the crowd; they are quietly conscientious, do not ask for much, and simply get on with the process of living their life the best way they can. They are often community-minded though somewhat low on charisma and will work in jobs that reflect this. Carpenter, Farmer, Mechanic, Shopkeeper, etc. are common occupations.

Carer – the 'typical' Settler mode, caring at least as much about the welfare of others as for that of self. There is a natural tendency to try to 'make things better' wherever problems of almost any sort are perceived. This is the individual who so easily feels inadequate, however successful others may perceive their efforts to be. He is unselfish in the extreme.

Philosopher – the thinker and teacher predominate here. Even when teaching is not the chosen profession, there is a powerful urge to spread information, especially when it is about people, Nature, or The Universe. They are excellent communicators and can usually find solutions to the difficulties and worries of others. Not so easily for their own problems, though.

Nomad

Entertainer – the joker and prankster who loves to role play and tell jokes with much gusto and mimicry. You can never be sure whether or not you are seeing the real person or a personality which has been adopted for the moment; they are often not too sure themselves, though will not waste too much time trying to figure it out. Usually, much charisma exists here.

Traveller – the original Nomad, the wanderer. The modern version of this type does not *necessarily* wander the land in search of adventure (although they might) – they are far more likely to substitute that urge with frequent changes in jobs, houses and even partners. Low on responsibility, they can walk away from situations leaving mayhem in their wake. They are inclined to be less ebullient than the other two subs.

Trickster – this is the realm of the con man, albeit a legal con-man – there is often too much fear to do anything illegal. This type can often be found among salesmen, bankers, accountants and insurance industry workers; any occupation, in fact, which directly involves separating people from their money as the main part of their job. The Trickster is almost always extremely personable.

The Inner Advisor

The Warrior, Settler and Nomad Parts, and their sub-parts, can be thought of as the 'major players' in this style of therapy. But there is a fourth Part that is of immense importance for the sort of work we are going to embark upon and this can be thought of as the 'Inner Advisor', which is a term that you may already be familiar with, since it has been in use in other 'parts' type therapies for some considerable time. Another good title for this part is 'Oracle' for it is the part that knows everything about you, including your strengths, limitations, values, capabilities, etc.

This is the impartial part who can weigh up the consequences of all that you do and all that you plan, taking into account all that you are and all that you can achieve. It knows what is good for you and what is not, what will be easy for you and what would be more difficult. It will always advise you infallibly, but seldom, if ever, let you know why the advice is what it is; you can ignore the advice and yet this paragon will always seek to get you back on the right road, no matter how far you stray.

To some, it is the still small voice of conscience, though it is not really that. To others it is their deepest instinctual self. Whatever it is, if we could only bring ourselves to *always* heed it, though very few do, we would all have a more comfortable and successful life. We would find as much contentment as we could possible achieve, for this Part takes account of that 'basic-ideal' template and the difference between it and the 'as-is' model that is the result of our life and experiences so far. The problem is that the urges from the other three Parts often completely drown the voice of the Inner Advisor; and, as with so many things in life, it is what is bad for us that seems the most attractive.

Evolution of the Inner Advisor

There may be more than one Inner Advisor, though they will seldom, if ever, be present all at once; more often, it is though there is a steady 'evolution' of this part from the moment that he/she/it first appears. The form it takes then is not necessarily human and we should never challenge this with our client, simply go with it. Their subconscious has created whatever form appears and the client's subconscious mind most definitely knows better than the therapist's conscious.

The first appearance of this part is often in the form of an animal, and it will frequently have some quality or qualities that our client perceives as lacking in him or herself, though she may not necessarily be aware of that fact. Hence the timid or fearful person might find a Lion or Tiger; the compulsively unfaithful, a Dog, since this is 'man's best friend' and determinedly loyal; the gullible or naïve, a Fox; the foolish, an Owl; and so on.

Remember, this is based solely upon the client's own opinion of self and nothing else, so we should listen carefully and think about what is found; it can tell us much about our client's self perception.

It is not just animals that may appear; it can be a cartoon character or even an inanimate object, though this is rare. Whatever is chosen though, human, animal or otherwise, it almost certainly has some quality that our client perceives as admirable or desirable. Quite often, there will be a rapid evolution, even a sudden change, in the way the Inner Advisor is represented; this is almost certainly the result of the client seeking multiple changes. While this evolution might catch the unwary therapist by surprise, it all seems perfectly rational to the client. The Golden Rule of this sort of therapy is: **Go Along With The Client.** There is more about this Part in a later lesson, covering techniques of working.

This completes the overview of the Parts and how they work; now it's time to discover how to use them in therapy with our clients...

Working with specifics

This type of therapy really comes into its own where there is a specific issue to be resolved for which it is not easy to frame suggestion, or where such work is likely to be ineffective, due to underlying causes.

It is worth understanding, at the outset, the major difference between this work and other forms of therapy designed to deal specifically with such situations, most notably any of the various forms of hypnoanalysis. Usually, we seek to uncover the Initial Sensitising Event (ISE); this, as most therapists are aware, is not always sufficient for the client to find relief from his symptoms. Often, the subconscious programme that was set up as a result of that ISE needs to be consciously recognised, understood and rejected if it is not to remain as an **Acquired Behaviour Complex** – that is, almost, but not quite, a habit. An **ABC** can cause a symptom pattern to remain long after there is no psychological reason for its existence.

With Parts Imagery, we do not set out to work this way, though we do sometimes 'bump into' the ISE anyway, especially when we timeline with a part. What we seek to do with this form of therapy, though, is essentially a reframe of subconscious thought processes. We seek to discover an understanding of which Part of the psyche is running the programme and why, then find a way to rechannel the needs and requirements of that Part into a more constructive and useful behaviour pattern. There are many and various possibilities:

An agreement is reached between the conflicting Parts. Here, the conflict will usually have been between the urges that are relevant to two of the Ancestral Parts. For instance, after working through the presenting problem, we arrive at the realisation that Nomad is using food as an offset to the boredom of the Warrior working all the time. So an agreement could be reached that the Warrior will take a fun break every so often and the Nomad agrees to clamour less for food stimulation.

The behaviour/symptom pattern is recognised as being out of date and no longer relevant. This is likely when the pattern has existed since before some major change in the client's life and is only persisting as a matter of habit. Examples are: the Nomad Part who wanted to go to the pub a lot to avoid his bitchy wife but who has now remarried; the Warrior Part who, as a child, had to maintain an emotionless exterior to avoid ridicule; the Settler Part who, in early adulthood, learned that subservience avoided the aggression of a particular peer.

The behaviour/symptom pattern is accepted as ineffective and a new and better solution is encountered. Here, the Part that is running the programme can be guided to the recognition that there is a better and perhaps more relevant way of achieving the objective. The Settler Part who learned in childhood that being miserable led to attention and care from parents can be helped to accept that being cheerful gets more positive attention in the adult world. Here, of course, the old plan has been sustained because it has been achieving its objective of getting attention, though the subconscious has not differentiated between pleasant and unpleasant attention.

A Part agrees to a compromise arrangement. A Part accepts that a wish or requirement in its entirety is either not possible or not desirable and agrees to 'give a try' to a compromise. For instance, the Warrior Part may agree to be less rigid with self as long as the Nomad will agree to settle down to work without constantly seeking diversion.

Acceptance of a situation that cannot be changed, allowing peace of mind to be brought about. Here, there is a situation which, though not ideal, cannot be altered without too high a price being exacted. The Nomad Part might agree, for instance, to stop energetically seeking so much sexual excitement in order to safeguard a relationship, on the basis that the current behaviour pattern might result in no sexual excitement at all.

Recognition of a constructive way to achieve a desired result. Here, it may be realised that a different Part would have a better chance than the currently active Part in achieving an objective. This would be true in relationship or people-orientated issues, of course. As an example, the Warrior Part might agree to allow the Settler to be more active, with the proviso that Warrior be allowed to assert him/herself if the occasion demands it.

Conscious awareness of a conflict which had previously remained 'invisible', allowing resolution. Any 'Aha' moment fits into this category and can be the agent of sudden change. Often, these conflicts are related to the formative years and have much to do with parental urges or control.

Recognition of a learned behaviour pattern. This one is self-explanatory; any Part may recognise that a behaviour pattern has no purpose and only exists because it has been learned, perhaps in the formative years. Typically, the behaviour will have been useful in the past but is not now.

In addition to the Warrior, Settler or Nomad Parts, any of the above situations may involve other human or non-human Parts as well as logical or abstract imagery. As therapists, we continue to work, without judgement or criticism, with whatever the client gives us to work with.

Workable conflicts.
There are many areas in which Parts work can be of inestimable help, especially so if it is employed *after* effective analytical work or regression. They include:

- **Binge Drinking/Eating**
- **Low libido**
- **Concentration/memory problems**
- **Many physical ailments**
- **Lack of motivation**
- **Failure syndrome**
- **Lack of tenacity**
- **Continually losing employment**
- **Inability to show affection**
- **Excessive sex-drive**
- **PTSD**
- **Catastrophic/invasive illness**

There are, of course, many more. Much of the time, the work can be completed within one or two sessions, if it follows some form of analysis; when it is employed as a primary methodology, it can take longer, though it *may* not be so profound, under those circumstances. There are several reasons why it might be employed as a primary therapy:

1. It does not rely on 'formal' hypnosis, making it useful as a methodology with hypnosis-resistant individuals
2. It does not rely on the client recalling *actual* memories
3. Because the work is frequently imaginative and non-logical, it helps to by-pass resistance
4. It can be used to work at resistance issues
5. It can be used to help a client who feels 'stuck' in some way

Defining the problem

When working with broad issues, we need to 'narrow the field' somewhat, where we can. To do this, we need to define the problem in as much detail as possible and with precision. As an example, if we <u>listen</u> to a client who presents with "Personal confidence issues" we might discover:

- *"I think other people look down on me."*
- *"I think other people think I'm stupid."*
- *"I feel different from everybody else."*
- *"I think I look ugly/stupid/awkward."*
- *Any one of a number of other negative beliefs.*

This is true of almost all presenting problems, be they psychological or physical. Even when working with catastrophic illness, you will hear over and again things like:

- *"I always knew that something like this would happen"*
- *"I think I'm being paid back."*

- *"I might have guessed it'd happen to me."*
- *"This is just my luck."*
- *"It's always seemed like I was jinxed."*

All of these statements, of course, will hinder the success of any therapy that we employ, since the client's subconscious believes that it is natural that the illness should exist within his body. We need to dissolve this form of resistance rapidly by following up those statements, asking questions until we either find a good starting point to work from, or that particular strain of resistance fades away.

Having established an area in which we will work, we need to know exactly why the client wants to be free from it; this information allows us to reframe what was presented as a general symptom, into a specific conflict. A good question here is: *"What is it that you would like to be able to do that this* (symptom) *stops you from doing?"*

If this question is inapplicable, because the symptom is physical, for example, then you could ask: *"If you didn't have* (symptom) *then what would you be able to do that you don't do now?"* Here, you should not accept 'Just feel better' as an answer; symptoms are there for a purpose and we need to discover a little of what that purpose might be. You can also ask: *"If you didn't have that symptom, then what would you have to do that you don't do now?"* As a follow-up to this, of course, you would pursue a *"And how will you feel about that?"* response – note the use of 'will' as opposed to 'would', the reasons for which should be obvious. Another useful question can be: *"If you lose this symptom, what else will you lose with it?"*

Of course, you need to ensure that what ever it is that your client wants to happen as a result of therapy is both plausible and possible; when there is something obviously amiss then there is a need for some work to be done in order to produce a practical goal. It is there that work should start. A client who says he wants to 'be a real hard man', for example, or who would not want to go to work clearly has issues which need working at *before* we even start on the symptom pattern itself.

Seeking to Avoid

Most symptoms are designed for avoidance; discover what the subconscious is seeking to avoid and we are well on the way to beneficial change. A stomach ulcer, for example, might be to stop the client from having to go out to eat; to have an excuse for not having sex; to avoid looking foolish if a failure occurs in some area of life (*"It's not my fault; if I didn't have this damn' ulcer..."*) or many other reasons. Sometimes, just asking the question alerts the client to the underlying difficulty and then our work is almost done, so you should always pursue this line until there is agreement with the client that you now have a focus of how the symptom most affects your client's life.

Where the client seem unable to focus upon anything relevant, then you can usefully ask in what areas of life there *is* discomfort or reluctance, then investigate how the symptom or its removal is relevant. It is odds on that there will always be *some* connection. A few useful areas to search are:

- **Social issues**

- **Work-related issues**
- **Relationships**
- **Sexuality**
- **Attitudes to food and eating**
- **Compulsive or obsessive behaviour patterns**
- **Jealousy issues**
- **Personal confidence and self-worth**

There are obviously plenty of others, but this is a good 'starter' list – you will quickly discover that as you ask the questions they will tend to lead you into many other areas. As a matter of interest, if you encounter evident resistance here, it is usually easy to diminish. All you will need to do is to point out to the client that when he starts to be able to do that thing, it is a fair indicator that, between you, you are getting to the root of the problem.

Client response

As an example of the need to get the right 'point of focus' we will take the situation where the symptom negatively affects the sexual life of the client; if the client *wants* to have sex but is unable to because of the symptom, then we are looking at the thing that needs working on. If, on the other hand, the client *does not* want to have sex even if the symptom did not exist, then we have not yet found the conflict. We need to discover the deeper conflict that has the client not wanting to have sex – but, of course, the client must agree to search for that conflict. Sometimes, he would rather put up with the symptom than develop a need for a good sexual life, for a variety of reasons; then resistance may make further work impossible. The client may well have

136

difficulty in understanding why his symptom cannot be alleviated without resolving the deeper problem. Probably, the best way to deal with this situation is to point out that it looks as if the symptom is creating a valid excuse to avoid sex and if you remove the symptom there will no longer be a valid excuse. The response from the client depends very much on the personality type:

- The RO will insist that, no matter what, he would just refuse sex, symptom or not. Resistance here will be minimal, now that the subject has been broached.
- The IA will be anxious and ask if there is not another way to work. Resistance will be high and the tendency to 'cut off the nose to spite the face', or the 'all or nothing' reaction may well come into play, producing a sudden exit from therapy.
- The CE will quite often suddenly – spontaneously – decide to either (a) forgo therapy altogether, or (b) go into it with huge enthusiasm, maybe with the decision that he will be the 'absolute best' at sex once the problem is resolved. In the latter circumstance, of course, resistance will be non-existent; the subject has been broached and the CE is giving a typical reaction – embracing change and going to extremes.

Whatever the response, as long as we have approached the true 'point of focus', therapy can proceed successfully.

The Parts Work Hierarchy of Needs

Related to the above situation, it can be a good idea to create a hierarchy of needs in the client's life, where he positions certain elements of life in order of importance. It might look like this, for example:

- **Affection**
- **Sex Life**
- **Relationships**
- **Popularity**
- **Independence**
- **Determination**
- **Control**
- **Image**
- **Admiration**

If he wants to change one of the elements before placing them in order of importance – for instance, image is unimportant, but money is – then that's all right, though you should always work with at least eight elements. There are nine listed here and they provide a good starting point.

The list complete, the client now has to place the wish to be free from the presenting symptom in the relevant position – and this is where the clever bit comes... everything that is above *that wish to be free will possibly be hindering therapy, since it is of greater importance in his life than the wish to be free from the symptom. In other words, if he had to choose to keep the symptom or lose one of those elements,* he would choose to keep the symptom.

It should now be obvious that our task is now to find out how the integrity of those elements that are higher up 'the tree' might be threatened by the removal of the symptom pattern. Usually, conversation will reveal the difficulty, after which we can reappraise our client's requirements, which may very well now be to find some way of coping/coming to terms with the original presenting difficulty.

Working with Abstracts

We can often employ abstract imagery to overcome the problem in imagination – use anything the client can come up with, helping only in the most general terms in order to illustrate that it may be absolutely *anything* he can think of. **Crystals, magic jewels, suits of armour, transforming devices to change a threat object into something useful, weapons, Merlin, Jesus, and other mythical or supernatural entities, fortresses, force fields...** anything at all that can be effective within the realms of imagination. We just have to make sure that our client explains with total clarity how he will actually use this item to overcome his problem.

It's definitely better if your client comes up with the imagery, since it will be directly related to their subconscious processes and resources – or lack of.

Explore whatever is given as a representation of the problem. A hole – go into it, around it, get the texture, temperature, depth, width, purpose, etc. Eventually your client will give you a lead.

A scream – follow that scream all the way to its source.

A rope/string/cable – follow it to find out what it's fixed to.

A circle – are you inside or outside it? What does it mean? What is it for?

A moving vehicle – where is it going? Who's inside it?

The Negative/aggressive, non-integrated destructive part

We can occasionally find the sudden appearance of a negative Part that is not really integrated with our client's 'way of being' at all – maybe a violently aggressive Part within the psyche of a benign and kindly individual. This is where Parts therapy departs radically from many other working methods; often, that 'dark side' would be considered as evidence of unreleased trauma, something to be worked through and released. In Parts work, we simply seek to communicate with whatever our client's mind has conjured up, which might even take the form of ogre/monster/alien/demon/Satan etc. For reasons which should be obvious, this is very common when working with catastrophic illnesses such as cancer.

Ask what the client would need to be safe from this creature while he talks to it, to discover what it wants. Maybe he will need a shield of some sort, or a safe refuge where the negative Part cannot go; perhaps he needs to hover above the scene for a few moments, or to be safely encased in a cocoon of some sort; or perhaps he can find a way to kill it, so that it can be resurrected as a strength or resource. We can even use a transforming 'gun' or other device. The important thing is that the client (never the therapist) must always think of/invent the intervention and not simply allow chance to take over in the form of some external 'miracle'.

It is important that we should never seek to simply destroy any Part that surfaces, if this can possibly be avoided. Most of the time, your client will find a way to transform the negative Part into something useful. If we destroy it, the client will simply not be able to find any way to deal with whatever part of life the symbol is representing.

140

Getting to the point

Whatever symptom pattern or symbol our client comes up with, we have the task of narrowing things down to the smallest particle of psyche that we can. In this way, being frightened of arguments may eventually become an anxiety about never finding another partner – or a fear about never having sex ever again. Somebody with Cancer *might* be frightened of dying <u>or</u> frightened of recovery and having to deal with the world again. And the individual who claims to be depressed could just be fed up with living but might just as easily be furious that his partner does not recognise his true worth. In this last instance, it would not matter if the individual was totally unjustified in his belief – it was he *feels* that is the object of our endeavours.

There's no right/best way to work – the client will eventually find the answer, no matter what path is pursued. As you become more adept, though, you will get there faster. A lot of the time, resolving one issue reveals another conflict to be worked on and this will often continue to happen until you reach the 'core'.

It is not unusual for an individual to 'meander' from the original presenting problem, into a kind of 'sub-problem' that has been hanging around for years, then into a memory of an unresolved difficulty that can now be solved, a recognition that a repetitive programme seems to exist and a subsequent exploration of that, before coming full circle to the original presenting problem – with an 'instant' solution available and ready to go.

Two simple work methods

We are going to have a look at two of the simplest methods of working within this style of therapy, something you can do with very little practice, either for yourself or your clients. It is also quite possible and permissible for you to work with your friends and family, unlike most other forms of therapy.

Both methods are somewhat limited, in that you are unlikely to be able to use them to deal with complex problems. This is an excellent starting point, though, and it is to be recommended that you begin practicing immediately with any volunteers you can find, whilst keeping away from any deep-seated or possibly serious symptoms.

Method one.

This is excellent for minor social difficulties (speaking in public, interacting in gatherings, talking to strangers, etc.) or for anything that involves being able to complete a fairly straightforward task like complaining about faulty goods, passing a driving test, attending a job interview, etc., where the symptom pattern is of moderate severity. It will not work well, if at all, for phobias or other severe disorders like panic attacks or depression.

First of all, you will need to briefly outline the Warriors, Settlers and Nomads concept, describing the types, but without necessarily going into great detail at this point. Then settle your client down, much as if you were going to give a hypnotic induction – which you are not, because we don't need it.

Once settled, ask your client to visualise the symptom and the way it feels when it is active, and to tell you what he is experiencing. You need to help him create this image as vividly as possible. Now ask which of those three archetypes he believes would have the resources to deal easily with the problem – if the problem were speaking in public, it would probably be the entertaining Nomad. Now ask your client to imagine that Part presenting in an appropriate manner and visualise how the task would be achieved. Go though the imagery several times, reminding the client from time to time that this is a part of his own psyche that he is observing, that these resources, this pattern of behaviour, has originated in his own mind.

When there is evident familiarity with the image(s) then that is the time to end the session, after telling your client that all he has to do to be successful in whatever he is seeking is to visualise that image just before the event.

Practical Work – finding the most useful part.
- ➢ Work in groups of two or three, therapist, client and optional observer
- ➢ The 'client' will think of a difficulty he experiences
- ➢ The therapist assists the client to test the difficulty being performed by that part that is decided is the most suitable. For the purposes here, test it also with the other two parts and notice how it feels each time.

Method two.
This is somewhat different in that its greatest use is in finding the source of a difficulty within the psyche, though it will not necessarily lead to a resolution of the problem without further work. It is particularly effective in those situations where somebody consciously wants to do

something but feels as he is being held back by some subconscious force.

Here, you would briefly explain the idea of parts therapy, again without going into great detail. Something along the lines of: *"The subconscious mind can actually visualise separate parts of ourselves, so that we can isolate the very bit of our mind that is causing the problem... does that make sense?"* Wait for agreement and go through the concept again if necessary, then continue with: *"Good. So if we examine your problem, your subconscious will allow you to see, in your mind's eye, a representation of that part of you that's not happy with what you want to do. It may even look like you in some way, though it might well look like something completely different. Whatever you find is fine. So shall we begin?"*

Having got the client's agreement, we ask him to visualise the problem, difficulty, or symptom, as in method one, and tell us about it. Once the image is properly clear, then we tell him to ask the part of his mind that's responsible for the problem to come forward. It is usually only a few seconds before the client finds an image and often understanding at the same time.

For the moment, you could just ask the client what he believes that part wants and work with that. Later on, you'll see how we can use this simple method of working to explore the problem further.

Practical Work – finding the source
- ➢ Work in threes, therapist, client and observer
- ➢ The client focuses on a difficulty

> ➤ The therapist assists in completing a clear image or images that are associated with the problem
> ➤ When the image is clear, the therapist asks the Part responsible for the problem to come forward
> ➤ Therapist and observer assist client in discovering what that part is seeking to achieve with the difficulty – what the Part wants the difficulty to do **for** the client.

CHAPTER EIGHT
Doing it – part one

Although there is much important information given in this and the next lesson, and the working techniques explained, you will need to study the chapter on case histories to fully understand how to implement this style of therapy at its best.

There are many ways to begin a session of Parts/Guided Imagery session but the one thing that is probably the most important is the pre-talk, just as in more 'standard' hypnotherapy sessions.

The Credulity Factor
We should never lose sight of what we are asking our clients to do here. It might seem normal to the therapist to use imagination and creativity to achieve an objective but for many of our clients, it will be the first time they have even heard of the concept. When therapy starts, we are going to be asking them to create images in their mind that have no reality, as far as they are concerned; and then we are going to ask them to *talk* to these images which might not even be in an animate form. More, we need them to believe that this peculiar idea of working in an unreal world can help them find relief from something which *is very much part of* what they perceive as the real world. Essentially, we are asking them to believe that an imaginary fantasy can help to heal a

harsh reality. To do this, we have to somehow by-pass the **Credulity Factor**, that part of our mind and brain which tends to cause us to dismiss that which we do not find believable.

This Credulity Factor exists in all of us, to a greater or lesser degree, but it can always be by-passed. Even the most left-brained and unimaginative individual can still feel excitement or fear which means that the imagination works perfectly.

We will digress for a moment, to examine this concept further. When our logical and analytical client is about to have an operation in hospital, she may well feel anxiety. It is not about the operation but about the possible *outcome* of the operation; death, maybe. The imagination can create all sorts of uncomfortable feelings here, even when the operation is a minor one. If an individual has been waiting for a longed-for event to take place – getting married, perhaps – then her excitement levels will rise as the day approaches; but the excitement is brought about not by the fact that the day is approaching but by the imaginative part of the psyche projecting forward and assessing the joy that it is believed may be felt. And that belief is only brought about by imaginative processes!

Emotional Reaction

Put another way, it is not an event or circumstance which causes joy or difficulties in life, *but our emotional reaction to that event or circumstance.*

So, to return to the point; we have to by-pass the Credulity Factor if we are to be successful in this style of therapy. We have to do this in two stages, in fact; the first

147

stage is to explain clearly what we are going to do and then convince our client that the process actually can work and will work for her. The second is on the first working session. After that, we're home and dry!

The first stage will normally be accomplished during the initial consultation and all you really need to do at first is illustrate to your client in some way how imagination and belief systems work. First, we need to get her to the point where she can recognise and accept that what she *believes* or *imagines* might be the outcome of an event actually governs the way she functions and feels *around* that event. Then we need to get her to realise that beliefs can be easily changed and that once those beliefs *are* changed, she can function and feel differently from how they did before.

A good analogy to use is that if a shy man subconsciously believes that girls will laugh at him, then he will feel uncomfortable around them and behave awkwardly – and the girls may well laugh, thus strengthening his belief. But if his subconscious belief about self changes to a more positive viewpoint, then he will begin to feel comfortable and behave more naturally. And life will change in that respect.

Working with Reality and Imagination

All we have to do then is to point out that negative reactions exist in the first place because the subconscious does not easily distinguish between reality and imagination. It has perceived a concept as a result of the interpretation of an event or events, creating fear, guilt, or some other type of negative emotive response. It is not the event which causes the problem of negative emotion, but what the imagination has believed would be the outcome; this process actually

148

makes it easy for us to reverse the situation and we can do this in several ways. One way is to reinterpret the original situation, if it is known or once it is discovered – and Parts work *does* uncover 'secrets'; we can find resources (parts) to reinterpret the belief itself; we can gain an understanding of the reason for the existence of the belief and use a resource to render the belief unnecessary; we can remain entirely in abstract mode and use a resource to destroy the belief. There are many other ways to work; in fact, many therapists discover that there as many different ways as there are clients,

Of course, you will need to adjust what you tell your client to the nature of the presenting symptom; if it is physical problem such as alcohol addiction or psoriasis, you will need to spend a little more time on this next concept...

Symbolism

The subconscious works not with words, as such, but with symbols and will therefore produce a symptom which is symbolic of the conflict that exists. In this way, obesity brought about by over-eating, for example, might symbolise a perceived lack of affection – and overeating is a compensation, or represents attention from self – or a need to *not* have attention (perhaps sexually) and the fat is 'designed' to deter people. It may express a great many other things instead, but these two suffice to show the diversity of subconscious response and also how a symptom can actually *worsen* the situation that has created it. Think particularly about the first of those situations outlined here and you will be able to see that this is certainly so.

It is fair to say that, to an extent, *every* symptom is symbolic, being an expression of a need to discharge, via some form of motor action, an idea 'taken on board' by the subconscious. But what we are talking about here is particularly those symptom patterns which have physical quality to them, rather than a purely psychological or thought process. In other words, symptoms like alcohol/drug dependence, psoriasis, eczema, asthma, IBS, migraine headaches, OCD, even catastrophic illnesses like cancer and multiple sclerosis.

This ability of the subconscious to express itself effortlessly via a symbol actually works to our great advantage. It is a fact that if we energise an idea or concept in our conscious mind, then 'push it to one side', the very next thought or concept will in some way symbolise the original idea. So if we energise our client's symptom, then ask her to create a symbol that in some way represents that symptom, we will have something tangible to work with. We will be returning to this particular concept later on. First, though, we will have a look at the easiest way to get our client past the Credulity Factor.

Parts and Warriors, Settler and Nomads

Most versions of parts therapy work at the symbolic level outlined above and the client will often struggle to find something which she can recognise, rather than tell us the first thing that comes to mind. So, to help her along, we actually give her the first set of symbols, something she can easily identify with because she can easily recognise the concept of parts of personality represented by the **Warriors, Settlers and Nomads** concept. Often, the problem will be solved at this level, especially if it relatively minor; confidence with public speaking is a good example. Motivational difficulties and career enhancement issues can often be resolved at this level, too.

The first part of this work is easily done without any formal hypnosis. On our first working session, we simply introduce our client to the concept of conflict in the subconscious and how this generates symptoms. We can also touch upon the idea of erroneous belief about self and explain both of these ideas clearly. This will help:

Conflict: our conscious mind wanting to do something that our subconscious has, for some reason, taken on board the idea that we should most definitely *not* do. If we had no interest in whatever it is our conscious mind wants to do, *then we almost certainly would not have the symptom.*

Erroneous belief: unquestioned acceptance of information about self, given to us in our formative years by somebody else, who may have had an ulterior motive, or a conflict of their own, that led them to give us this information.

It is important that we explain clearly the concept of part of the psyche restricting that which we consciously wish to do; we need, too, to make the point that we are going to find a way of keeping each part happy – we are not going to ride rough-shod over the objecting part but find a way to achieve complete harmony. There may be a need for compromise of sorts, sometimes, but as long as the client is happy about that, the symptoms will be alleviated. We will find beneficial change.

Gaining credibility

We can tell our clients about the inherited instincts hypothesis, as given in Chapter Five, and outline the three archetypes. The scientific and evolutionary 'feel' to this concept will lend credibility to what we are doing and will tend to reassure our client that we really do know what we are talking about. Of course, you may choose to use the speedier 'Three Primary Colours' concept from Chapter Four, in which case you must make it sound *exciting.*

Now, this is most important: *we must get agreement from our client that she would like to create the imaginary images of the archetypes before progressing, because it is essential that the client feels in total control of the process. This also helps to build a 'yes set', which will help us no end.*

On the rare occasions when we get a 'No' at this point, we have something to work with, using your 'standard' psychotherapeutic skills to explore the reasoning. There is usually a fear of some sort present in the psyche and it may even be the cause of the client's presenting problem; sometimes, it is fear of the concept of one of the parts (often Warrior); in other words, our client is frightened of herself! Of course, this is not uncommon in a timid individual who may well be anxious about her own suppressed or repressed feelings of aggression. Whatever we find, it is essential that we release the resistance before we proceed.

Conversational Working

Having got a 'Yes' from our client, we work in a conversational manner, encouraging the development of each Part to a reasonable level, remembering that Parts can be of a

different gender from the client and asking questions to
ensure that she is focussing sufficiently:

- *"Tell me what this person looks like."*
- *"How does s/he sound?"*
- *"How tall is s/he?"*
- *"How is s/he dressed?"*
- *"What is his/her name?"*

Some clients – and some therapists – may well want to
refer to these parts simply as 'Warrior' or 'Settler' or
'Nomad'. This is perfectly in order and will not affect the
outcome; a good way to discover what works for your client
is to ask: *"Does he/she have a name?"*

You should always ensure that your client seeks to
develop a <u>positive</u> version of the particular part; it is
sometimes necessary to find a way to despatch one that
shows more of the negative characteristics of the type than
the positive – for instance, a 'shifty' and/or unreliable
Nomad, or an aggressive and tyrannical Warrior. This
exercise, in itself, can result in a much improved 'way of
being for your client.

Usually, by the time you have done this with the three
parts, your client will have entered into the spirit of it all and
will begin to volunteer extra information. Keep going until
you have a clear picture of each of the archetypes. This is
probably a good time to introduce the concept of the Vivid
Mental Image – the VMI; you will be using that concept
quite frequently and it is something that the vast majority of
your clients will love to do. The VMI is simply a mental
image that is as complete is it could possibly be; there is an

awareness of the height, weight, shape and bearing of the archetype, the way he or she moves, clothes, voice, body scent... everything, in fact, that you could become aware of in a living person who you knew very well. It is possible to develop this VMI to the point where the behaviour of a Part can be confidently predicted for any given circumstance.

A True Part of the Psyche

If we now encourage our client to recognise that the personality she has 'created' is actually a *true part of her own psyche, a part that actually exists in her mind and can be accessed whenever she needs it*, this is a confidence-boosting therapy in itself. You will need to emphasise this and be sure that the client takes it fully 'on board' that this is a part of *her*. Many clients will be astonished that they can develop such a clear image of a type of personality that they have always believed was not part of their 'way of being'; it is useful to point out the concept of: 'if you can see it, you can be it.' Sometimes, this is all that is needed, as one of the case histories, later on, illustrates.

The VMI task complete, we can begin to use hypnosis (this may not be until the second session), though it is not necessary to name it as such. I usually just say something like: *"Ok, in a moment or two, we will start to see just what those parts can bring to bear on your difficulties... Just allow your eyes to close and steady your breathing for a moment or two... that's right... just let your body relax as much as you want to."* After this, you should allow maybe a minute before starting with the therapy itself.

Getting involved

This is where the work proper begins, when we get our client actually communicating with each Part, either separately or together. It really is most important that we give her total control – we only act as a guide, somebody who knows how to help the client create her own symbolic world from her own imaginative processes. It is easy enough; we simply ask the client if she *wants* to talk to whichever part is relevant or present, then wait for an affirmative before proceeding. The next thing is to instruct the client to ask the Part if it will agree to talk to her.

Sometimes, this is where we hit a small stumbling block, where the client 'feels silly' or for some other reason does not enter into the spirit of things. The best way through this is to allow her to be as dissociated as she needs at the beginning then gradually increase the amount of involvement.

This is actually quite easy. All we need to do here is ask the client to imagine what the Part *would* say about the situation, if it was in the real world. We can go a little further by explaining that all solutions come from the creative part of the mind and what we are doing here is to let that creative part work without restriction for a little while. Most clients will go along with this and once they start talking, they will gradually become immersed in the concept, many of them becoming noticeably enthusiastic as they become aware that they *do* have answers, even if those answers are not yet workable in reality. They learn that they can be creative and if they can be creative, then they can find an answer.

It is worth recognising that the Nomad Part can present in many guises and can even appear as the child part of self. This Part may actually change during the session, allowing us

155

access to some of the deepest and darkest corners of the psyche. Much expression will be carried out through the Nomad Part, and it is a good idea to teach your client about this ability to change and the inherent expressiveness. Generally speaking, the Nomad is associated with the child within; the Warrior with parental or other influences; the Settler with the sense of self.

Now we will have a look at a two more working methods. You can try talking to the parts if you practice these, though communication will be covered in detail in the next module.

The Meeting

As shown, method one works especially well for the logical and analytically orientated personality, especially if she is familiar with an environment in which she has meetings. Method two works better for the 'softer' type of individual, or those who might find formal meetings threatening or otherwise uncomfortable.

(1) Client Associated

Here we get our client to imagine a meeting around a circular or triangular table where she is one of the parts having a meeting with the other two. We then ask our client which two Parts they can see. We can safely assume that our client is functioning in the role of the other Part. This is probably the best method to use, most of the time. The major contra-indicator is when your client feels great anxiety about the prospect of exploring their problem, when you would then use the dissociated method.

When your client tells you which two parts she can see, follow with: "And how do you feel as you sit there?"

There are two main answers:

(a) The symptom is mentioned in some way, or our client feels uneasy or uncomfortable. This is the usual situation when the symptom is **Reactive,** creating a behaviour pattern which is triggered and which feels uncomfortable for the client. Examples are panic attacks, anxiety, blushing, obsessive disorders, and most physical symptoms.

(b) The client feels comfortable. This usually happens when the symptom is **Resistant** or resistance based – alcoholism, gambling, excessive smoking, philandering, etc., or any symptom pattern for which the client has a hidden agenda to avoid change.

If the answer is (a), then the Part is likely to be the 'owner' of the symptom. The symptom is likely to be 'anchored' in some way to the primary characteristics of that Part – control issues for the Warrior, personal issues for the Settler and freedom of choice/movement for the Nomad. We need here to help our client to the recognition that the other two parts may have the resources that are needed to resolve the difficulty.

If (b), then the Part is likely to be the one who is causing a 'stuckness' that is at the root of the symptom pattern. We need here to negotiate an awareness of this fact and gain an agreement to allow compromise.

(2) Client Dissociated

In this scenario, the client observes all Parts and will converse with them individually or together. This method works best when seeking to access hidden or dormant resources. When working in this way, we get our client to describe the situation in which the meeting is taking place and how she feels as she communicates with each of the Parts. Subsequent communication will help our client to recognise strengths within him or herself. The advantage here is that the client can remain detached from any problem issues and may therefore view them more objectively. The disadvantage is that the lower involvement can lead to lack of stimulus of the imagination or emotion – though this can actually be useful when dealing with any form of Post Traumatic Stress Disorder (PTSD).

Whichever method you use, the trick is to attempt to find a situation which is agreeable to all three Parts, even if one or two of them are only prepared to 'give it a try' – then, of course, there will be a need to re-evaluate the situation later on.

Reintegration

After you have finished, it is extremely important to reintegrate all three Parts into the client's psyche. Failure to do this can result in several hours of discomfort and internal argument. The easy way is to have the three parts joining together in a kind of 'group hug' and becoming as one before being totally absorbed into your client's psyche. Allow your client to perform this task on his/her own; there should be no need for guidance from you at this point, other than to outline the procedure as you have just read. The last thing that you should say in the working part of the session is something like: *"When you are quite sure that you have absorbed all those parts back into yourself, and not before, then you can allow your eyes to open. Don't rush, there's plenty of time. Only when you're sure you're quite ready..."* Then just wait for as long as it takes, within reason. If you <u>should</u> feel the need to hasten things a little – and this should not be until at least 2 or 3 minutes have passed – you can say: *"Ok, in your own time now... just getting ready now to... open your eyes... and be awake and aware..."*

Although this is essentially a logical style of working, as long as your client 'plays the game' and tells you the first thing she thinks of each time you ask a question, much subconscious work will surface, as one of the case histories will show you.

Some problems will be solved by this direct method; others may need more advanced ways of working, including symbolism and fantasy work, both of which are covered in the next module. Whatever method of work you employ, it is essential that you become totally at ease with the concept that follows...

Communication

This is sometimes the tricky bit unless you handle it confidently, for this is where some clients will become inhibited. Probably the best way to handle this is to have your client converse – always remembering to get agreement first – with the part in her mind, and then tell you what has been said. We can and sometimes *should* <u>guide</u> the conversation, especially at the beginning.

<u>It matters little whether we are talking to a Warrior, Settler or Nomad Part, or to an animal or even non-human Part.</u> Never forget that the Part is simply the communicator for the creative and imaginative part of our client's psyche and whatever representation it has, *we are communicating directly with our client's subconscious mind.* So our first task, as therapists, is to ensure that the right questions are asked in order to guide our client to a solution, or at least an off-set, for the presenting problem. There are many ways to work, but the important thing is to get dialogue going.

Sample questions to Client:

- *"Do you want to talk to (Part)?"*
- *"Is there anything you want to say to (Part)?"*
- *"Is there anything you'd like to ask (Part)?"*
- *"Is there anything (Part) has to say to you?"*
- *"What does (Part) mean, to you?"*
- *"How does (Part) fit around your problem?"*
- *"How do you feel in the presence of (Part)?"*

Assuming that the client is in agreement with the idea of conversation, we can suggest that she asks the part:

- *"Will you talk to me?"* (This is an essential question)
- *"What is it that you want?"*
- *"What are you here for?"*
- *"What are you going to bring into my situation?"*
- *"What do you need?"*
- *"What stops you from having that?"*

160

- *"What do you try to do for (client)?"*

And wait for the answer.

You should be able to see how you can apply the above questions to the simple method of working (method two) in lesson three.

If you have temporarily finished communication with a Part, but now need to access another Part, always ask the client to ask the Part if it will 'wait there' for a little while. You will be surprised how often there is a sudden recognition that this Part does not want to wait and is in fact most anxious to resolve something – and in those circumstances, the answer you and your client are seeking is almost to hand.

It's ok to help a little if the client seems to be struggling but, in general, we must let the client do most of the association work. You can't get this wrong. Just follow your own instincts as to the sort of conversation your client has with the Part and be ready to observe the 'sub-personalities' – parts of the Part. (These will be different from the sub-personalities referred to in lesson two, which are really just variations.) They often represent issues that had lain almost hidden. When working with the 'Warriors, Settlers and Nomads' concept, you will quite often discover a negative Part or sub-part that needs to be changed or accepted in some way. It is your client who must decide the course of action and how to carry it out – your job is to ensure that she works at this until there is a feeling within your client that this task has been completed. This is the signal of subconscious change, of new and more positive resources being accessed.

The Most Important Element

Because we need to ensure that the limitation of logic is not brought to bear, we must insist that our clients tell us the first thing that comes to mind as an answer to the question, without judgment or criticism. This is probably the most important element of this style of therapy, since it is that first response to a question that is most likely to be from the workings of the non-critical subconscious, the objective part of self that 'knows' the best way forward, taking all elements into account. The client ignoring this first thought is a form of resistance, possibly stemming from the fact that the best solution, which may be some form of compromise, is not one which immediately appeals to conscious logic for a whole variety of reasons. Some examples of this are given in the next Chapter of the book.

When the client 'double-takes' or spends more than a couple of seconds finding a response, she is almost certainly being selective with the answer, perhaps seeking to avoid an uncomfortable truth. Whatever surfaces, *we must always accept it as the right answer;* our own lack of judgement and criticism is just as important as that of our client. We work with what we are given, helping our client to discover the workable truth of the answer.

What we want the conversation with any Part to do, is to move our client away from negative towards positive responses. Where something apparently negative surfaces, then we need to deal with it, either to get rid of it by converting it into something useful. Some of the case histories show exactly how easy that can be to do.

Whatever method of work is chosen, something that is most important is that <u>your client *must* be able to relate what</u>

transpires to their presenting problem. Often, they will find this understanding as a matter of course but sometimes you will need to offer encouragement by asking something like: *"And what sort of sense does this make to you?"* at the right moment. This is the point at which she may well realise that she has been creating her own obstructions for years.

Practical Work – Exploring the Meeting
> ➤ Working in threes, therapist, client, observer
> ➤ The client chooses a minor situation on which to work
> ➤ Ensure conversation with each part
> ➤ Compare emotional/physical responses to both
> ➤ Ensure reintegration of the three parts before completing the session
> ➤ Explore both **Associated** and **Dissociated** methods

If all you managed to master was the foregoing, you still have enough knowledge to work with Parts Therapy. Read on, and you will eventually be able to assume mastery over the method – and since you can use this on your own, you can even use the method itself to increase that mastery!

CHAPTER NINE
Doing it – part two

In addition to some general issues that are important within this style of working, this lesson covers some rather more advanced aspects. We will cover resistance issues and how we might overcome them, and also the idea of regressing a Warrior, Settler, or Nomad part to a time when they learnt a behaviour pattern.

In this advanced work, it is still <u>essential</u> that input from the therapist's psyche is kept to a minimum – zero would be even better, if it were possible. We are guides who ask questions that encourage the client to explore his own mind; we are NOT individuals who show how clever we are and what a grasp of human motivation and thought process we have!

First of all, we will explore an aspect that the client can easily access for him or herself at any time, whether or not their therapist is present or available.

Inner Adviser

The Inner Adviser is a very special Part. Ageless, non-critical, non-judgmental, completely objective yet compassionate, and with the profound wisdom of an oracle or a sage. This is the Part that knows everything about you, everything you can do and everything you cannot do;

everything that would be good for you and everything that would not be good for you; everything you should do and everything you should not. The Inner Adviser will always counsel soundly, though is not offended when the advice is not followed; if you decide upon a different course of action to anything advised then there will be more counsel when it is needed and for whatever or wherever your chosen course has led.

This part is our own personal and infallible guide to the jungle of life.

We all have an Inner Adviser. It is evidenced in that uncomfortable feeling you get when you embark on a course of action that you want to follow yet have vague misgivings. Most of the time, those misgivings turn out to be well-founded! It is revealed again when we give someone advice that we know we may not follow for ourselves; if it is good advice, then we may be surprised when it works; if it is not sound, then we feel guilty when everything goes awry. It sounds like conscience, but it is not – though conscience can be mistaken for this Part. It is that Part of you that is able to project forward and assess outcomes of actions and knows how that outcome will be affective upon your life and happiness. It can help you over-ride instinctual urges *where necessary* (and if you doubt the wisdom of this, just think about the sexual urge and the trouble it can cause!) as well as materialistic and hedonistic pursuits. It can take account of your age and social situation, culture, relationships, career prospects and illness, among many other things. In other words, it can get you the best in life that you can have.

165

Perfect Wisdom

We all have it – but most of us have no idea how to access it.

Once you have learnt how to access this perfect wisdom of your subconscious mind – and that is all the Inner Adviser is, of course – you can use it again and again. If you were to always follow the advice you gave yourself, you would make few serious mistakes in life, though there are very few who actually manage to do this! A lot of the time, conscious wish over-rides our subconscious wisdom. This Part cannot *make* you do anything and the trouble is that our imagination will so easily lead us astray and into a path of action which does not pan out the way we thought it would.

Interestingly, the Inner Adviser will often embody something that the client perceives himself as lacking, so the man who feels that he may be foolish might find an Owl; the faithless wife, a Dog (man's best friend); the one who is timid, a Tiger or Lion. It may be a futuristic human, a goddess, or an ancient wise man or hermit; it can just as easily be a mountain, a cloud, or a piece of office equipment. Whatever it is, we always treat them the same and give them the same credibility, as well as ensuring that our client identifies himself *totally* with this part of his psyche. This is the part that he can access to help with the process of making important decisions, the infallible part of his psyche that will always 'get it right'.

It is not unusual for this Part to change form from time to time and there are many individuals who find themselves with a whole series of Inner Advisers, even multiple Advisers, over a period of time. It is very likely that this is to

Advanced Hypnotherapy and Hypnoanalysis

do with personal development creating a more efficient form for communication.

Finding the Advisor

In a session, there are many ways in which you might help a client to discover his Inner Adviser, and many ways to work, but probably the easiest is the one illustrated here. First, you would need to explain the concept as given above and be sure that your client understands it – so it goes without saying that you, yourself, must be fully conversant with the concept before trying to employ it in your work with a client. You should use the method for yourself exactly as it is given here; it will be easier if you can find somebody to talk you through it. Here is how it would be delivered in the therapist's office, after a short 'settling down' routine, as given in the previous lesson – <u>and after getting that all important agreement from our client that he wishes to actually meet his inner adviser.</u>

"Now just imagine yourself in a comfortable place that is exactly right for you... a place that feels totally safe...it might be an orange grove, or almost a void... it could be an ocean, a valley, or a grassy plain with hills in the distance... or just a place of light or dark...and I'd like you to tell me what you can see."

Here, we wait for our client to describe 'his' place and the only prompt we should give at this point is something like: *"Just tell me what you see... tell me what comes to you..."* If he says: "Nothing," just wait – there will often be a description very shortly after that. If he says: "Nothing," again, then you can proceed with: *"Tell me about the nothing... what sort of place is the nothing, what does it feel*

167

like?" This might seem a little odd, but it sets the scene quite well because we're going to be working with whatever our client produces – so he is about to discover that there's no way to avoid telling us what's in his mind! If wants to produce a 'nothing', then we'll talk to the 'nothing' to find out what it wants and what purpose it has.

Whatever image our client comes up with, we need him to describe it and tell us the colour, lightness or darkness, and so on. He should describe it clearly enough that you have a clear image in your own mind, and you should keep on developing it until this is the case. Surprisingly, even a 'nothing' can be described in this way.

Then continue:

"Good...now I'd like you to stare into the distance – your mind knows exactly in which direction – and keep on looking until you can see a small dot, in the distance, coming towards you...tell me when you can see that."

Wait for a positive response, then:

"Ok – now this is your Inner Adviser...and I don't know whether it's approaching quickly or slowly... I don't even know if it's a human or an animal or some other form... it could be anything... but I'd like you to tell me when you can begin to see what it is..."

Again, wait for a positive response from your client, then:

"Good, that's fine...tell me what you see..."

Get the client description and develop it as far as he or she can. Then:

"OK – is (Part) with you yet?"

Wait for affirmation, then:

"Good...would you like to talk to the inner adviser?"

Wait for a 'Yes', then:

"Ok, now I'd like you to ask (Part) *what* (it/he/she) *has to say to you... it'll be just a symbolic thing, or a word or two...but just tell me what you find...the very first thing that comes to your mind..."*

One Piece of Advice

Of course, if you're working with a specific situation, then the symbolic advice will be associated with that, but if you're just introducing your client to this Part, then the advice will be for a general thing in the client's life. It is a good idea to indicate to the client that this Part will usually only give one piece of advice on any one 'visit', since this can have the effect of focussing the subconscious so that the advice is truly profound.

Now you continue as for other aspects of Parts work:

"OK – now tell me what that means to you."

From then on, you simply pursue the client's thought patterns, always seeking to guide towards positive outcomes. Useful responses could be: *"And how does that idea seem?"; "Is that something you could do?"; "How easy would it be to do that?"; "What would be the best thing about that?"; "Have you ever thought of doing that before?"* and so on.

To get the best from this Part, we need a total suspension of logic and though this can be difficult for many, it is essential if we are to work with the impartiality that can be available. The first thing that comes to mind as a response is what we should take notice of. Some therapists seek to reduce all problems to a 'Yes or No' situation, and there is something to be said for this, since the answer needs little interpretation. But there is also much to be gained from working in a more open-ended manner, when the answers may be purely symbolic or take the form of a cryptic remark. Then, we simply pursue the answer with the same sort of questions as shown above, allowing our client to find their own truths.

Emotional Values

The most important thing to remember is that we are seeking the Part that will be totally objective about the client's situation, *not necessarily* a Part that has total logic. Our clients need to take emotional values into account. It would be logical to leave a job where the hours were too long and the boss was a bully; but if the boss was the client's life partner... It would be logical for somebody to avoid the places where panic attacks occur, but this would not be solving the problem; it would simply be putting the problem 'on hold' for a while, until the subconscious finds another trigger, another anchor, to discharge the motor action of panic. Not only that, the chances are high that, the next time, it will be worse...

Practical Work – finding the Inner Adviser

Workshop guide:
- ➢ Working in threes; therapist, client, observer
- ➢ The client thinks of a personal difficulty/problem
- ➢ Using the method outlined above, find the Inner Adviser
- ➢ Therapist and observer assist the client to assess <u>why</u> that particular Inner Advisor has been chosen (this is for this exercise only and not to be used with a client)
- ➢ Get the symbolic phrase

> ➤ Therapist and observer assist client to assess what this phrase means.

The Fake

Just occasionally, the Inner Adviser will turn out to be a fake – what appears is actually Conscience or Superego, and there is a danger here. Either of these Parts is concerned about doing *what other people would agree with* or doing what the client *consciously believes* is the 'right thing' to do, and not necessarily what is best for the client. What a wonderful bit of subterfuge and sabotage that can turn out to be!

This Part will be based upon the existing fundamental belief system and conditioned response patterns and will seek to resist change. It is not difficult to observe when this has happened, because every bit of 'advice' will simply point at the client continuing to do, in some way, what the client is already doing. We should treat this impostor as a negative Part and deal with it as such. Probably the simplest way is to get the client to find the Part that *disagrees* with this impostor (though we do not tell the client it is an impostor at this stage.)

Of course, what we are looking for here is the source of conflict. There is no doubt that there *is* one, since conscience and superego are based upon the moral code that we are taught, a code that is not congruent with our base wishes. As soon as any dialogue between the two ensues, it should become evident that this is not the totally objective Inner Adviser but just another negative Part seeking its own way. The game is up! We have not finished with it, though, because we need to discover its purpose and how we can get agreement with it. Always remember – the major object of this work, wherever possible, is not to attempt to defeat or overrule a part, but to find a way to satisfy its requirements whilst still getting agreement from it to allow the formation of a more desirable behaviour pattern for our client.

A good example here is when the Conscience Part suggests that staying in a relationship that just does not work for our client is the 'right thing' to do (an idea possibly implanted by a parent). The Part that disagrees – we will assume Warrior for this example – might argue that there is no need to live with past mistakes and that anyway, the partner must be unhappy too. The agreement could be that dissolving the relationship in calm and respectful manner, suspending Warrior attitudes, would be acceptable. If the dissenting Part was Nomad, the agreement might have been to ensure a responsible and fair conclusion; the Settler might well have agreed... no, come to think of it, the Settler would be the one resisting leaving!

The Messenger

From time to time you will discover that just when you believed that the Inner Adviser was about to make an appearance, it becomes evident that this is not the case and that a messenger of some sort has arrived instead. The evidence is in the lack of meaningful symbolic or emotional communication; there may be just a distinct feeling within the individual that she or he is being required to wait, to mark time, for a while. This is possibly a trick of the subconscious playing for time, maybe because there is an awareness that more information is needed or that there is other work to be processed. Sometimes, there is a feeling that this part should

172

be followed, in which case let your client follow, and just 'play it by ear'. It may be that the Inner Adviser will be in a different place in the client's mind, in different surroundings perhaps. Whatever happens, let your client feel what he or she feels, and confirm that it is exactly what should happen at this time.

The Inner Adviser and WSN

Sometimes, when working with the 'WSN' concept, it becomes apparent that the client's plans are being repeatedly sabotaged by one particular Part (and it is just as likely to be any one of the three). This is more than just one Part 'getting in the way' – it is an apparent determination that a certain type of plan or objective should not be completed. When no help from, or compromise with, the other Parts can be found, and when the obstructive Part refuses to communicate reasons for the sabotaging behaviour, there is usually a fear that something that is important to the individual may not receive full credibility.

We obviously need some easy way to by-pass such resistance and a fairly effective method is to introduce the non-judgmental, all knowing, Inner Adviser into the conflict to talk to the Part. Oddly, perhaps, the individual's awareness of the non-critical attitude of this part of his own psyche often allows the difficulty to be expressed – and then, of course, we have something to work with.

Quite often, this sort of thing will happen with a Part that does not appear to have anything to do with WSN – it is just a Part, an image, which is evidently preventing our client from making progress. We will often have been talking to one or all of WSN when this other Part spontaneously appears. It is always a weaker Part than the three 'main players' but must still be taken seriously; we must communicate directly, via the Inner Adviser or one of the other three, but we must find out what it wants and get that all important agreement to allow change to take place. There is an example of a completely non-communicative 'extra' part, and how it was dealt with, in the case histories section of this course.

Now we are going to investigate some of the more novel, and often exciting, ways of using this style of therapy.

The Fantasy World

It is true to say that one of the most fascinating ways to work with the right sort of client is to create a fantasy world. This fantasy world is identical to the real world, including the existence of her presenting problem, except for three important concepts:

1. The problem is most definitely one which can be resolved, though this cannot happen except by direct intervention. In other words, the client cannot simply rely on some outside force entering the scenario and creating a 'miracle'.
2. The client definitely has the resources to create the change that is needed, either by destroying the problem or converting it into a positive resource.
3. The only limitation on resources is her own imagination; if she needs a ray gun, she has one; if she needs a computer implant in her brain, she has one of those; whatever she can imagine as a way of solving the problem, that's what she has.

174

The outline for this sort of concept is simple; we explain to our client that in the fantasy world there is *definitely* a solution to the problem and that she *definitely* has the ability to apply that solution. So we define the problem, and let each of the three parts have a crack at resolving it. The Warrior may well seek to destroy it or possibly control it; the Settler will perhaps seek to in some way find a benefit within the problematic situation whilst easily understanding the reasons for the existence of the rest of it and therefore adapting to its presence; the Nomad will try to find a way to escape it in the easiest way possible.

Your job here is partly to *gently* explore the suggested behaviour patterns where it is necessary to focus our client's mind towards a final solution, and partly to assist our client to find the resources they need to produce the needed change, however outlandish they might at first seem. We follow each idea through to a conclusion that is satisfactory or acceptable. It is important that we only guide and do not lead; our clients have to find *their* solutions, not ours. Ideally, we will find three different approaches and three different solutions and what we have to do then is to evolve a 'game plan' in which the plans of one of the parts does not sabotage the work of either of the others. In this way, we might often discover that there is a need to use a part of personality in a different way, or maybe subdue the reaction of one of the parts, in order to find success.

An Example

An example might help. We will look at a predominantly Settler male with a problem of being bullied in the work place and who is now unable to even go to work. The Warrior may decide to fight back in some way and we could pursue this line; but physical fighting is not a good option for the Settler, so we would need to encourage the use of Warrior guile, perception, and the ability to manipulate.

The plan does not have to be logical – the Warrior could, for instance, have a helmet which allowed him total insight into the aggressors mind so that he could outthink his 'opponent'. That would only be an allusion to Warrior perceptiveness or simple heightened awareness.

The Settler might decide to make a friend of his enemies; but this may not be influential with those who are inclined towards bullying – in fact, it could lead to advantage taking, thus worsening the situation. Following up and investigating the suggestion of making friends with simple: "And what would happen then?" type of questions would soon reveal this. Here, we may eventually come to the conclusion that the best part of the Settlers attributes in this situation is simply that intuitive instinct about the intentions of others. The Settler may well need to stay out of the conflict.

The Nomad would almost certainly elect to run away – but that would only shelve the problem temporarily, as pursuit of that answer would probably soon indicate. We might then discover that the Nomad ability to act a part and to be expressive comes in very handy; from here, it is a short step to combining the activity of all three parts into a workable plan. The Warrior and the Settler both perceive what the aggressor is thinking or feeling, the Warrior can perhaps observe the Achilles heel, and the Nomad can put the whole thing into evident action. Again, *it does not have to be logical!* We are looking for a fantasy answer in a fantasy world, and any answer our client comes up with comes from his mind and is therefore symbolic of his thought processes and his resources to deal with the problem.

We can also use this style of working in a way that other versions of Parts Therapy or creative visualisation tend not to do so well; we can set a process in motion that is designed to find *gradual* change – which can be a far lot more acceptable, on occasions, to a client than a rapid upheaval. This is especially likely to be so when we have identified a part that has been lying dormant for many years for some reason or another. Under these circumstances, the client quite often needs time to adjust to the new resources that are presented before being able to use them to the best effect – the old adage, 'practice makes perfect' is very true here.

Once the symbolic solution has been settled upon, we can ask the client what that might mean to him or her, how that might be translated into action in the real world. Almost always, there will be a need for a little help and almost always, a workable solution will be found. We may even be able to use the solution as a hypnotic suggestion, since this solution will be from our client's own thought process and therefore very likely to be accepted by her subconscious.

You will see this process in action in the lesson on case histories, in the case of the man who had been terrorised by his wife for many years. Also in that lesson are a good few examples of translation of symbolic representations into practical solutions – an essential if our client is to get the best out of this style of work.

Practical Work – the Fantasy World
Workshop guide:

177

> ➢ Working in pairs, therapist and client
> ➢ The client defines a problem or difficulty
> ➢ The therapist assists in examining all possible solutions from all possible angles
> ➢ Assess which solution is likely to be most effective

Permissive World

This is somewhat similar to the Fantasy World, except that the fantasy does not have to remotely resemble the real world at all; it can be a foreign planet, an exotic beach, outer space, a journey inside her own mind/brain, a journey inside somebody else's mind/brain, a void... there are literally endless possibilities. Neither do we work necessarily with the WSN concept (although I almost always introduce this in the first instance, since it gets the client into the idea of communicating 'inside her head'), because this method is completely 'open'; we help our client to focus on the problem then ask her to find a symbol that is in some way representative of it. The focussing may be done in or out of the session, with or without accessing the WSN parts first.

Generally, in this method, we seek to solve the problem *by proxy,* in a way, by working with the symbols and concepts that represent it or are otherwise brought into our client's realm of thought. We also follow up the negative emotional responses we hear from our client and turn them into symbols, making sure that our client has a clear understanding of how and why the symbol represents the emotion.

Here is an example. A young man had presented for general feelings of inadequacy and mild depression, along with a sense that he was a disappointment to his parents, through not following the career that they had wanted for him. There had been much before what is shown here, but this fragment is particularly descriptive of how this type of therapy can work:

Client: *"I feel sad..."*
Therapist: *"Find what represents sad. The first thing you think of."*
Client: *"A football – but it's flat. You couldn't kick it."*
Therapist: *"Tell me what football means to you."*
Client: *"Oh, I know what it means! I HATED football but my dad always insisted I had to play it. I tried and tried but I was useless. Completely useless. Like that football, I suppose."*
Therapist: *"Tell me about useless. The first thing you think."*
Client: *"Useless is what I feel most of the time, actually... but I've just realised that I was actually very good at science."*
Therapist: *"And what does that feeling of being very good at science do?"*
Client (grinning): *"Well, I don't <u>have</u> to be the way dad says. I don't even **want** to kick a football!"*
Therapist: *"So what would you like to do with that flat football?"*

(This is important if we are to resolve the conflict between what the client wants and what he feels he should be.)

Client: *"I'm going to pump it up and give it to my dad!"*

(The client was quiet here for a few moments, then grinned again.)

Client: *"Done!"*

Therapist: *"How does that feel?"*

Client (nodding): *"Yes – great. Dad took the ball and now he understands. It's ok if I'm different from him. It's ok if I'm different from either him or mum, come to think of it…"*

Inflating the football and giving it back to his father is a symbolic act of ridding himself of the sadness, as well as of forgiveness, and of relinquishing any need to emulate father. Obviously, there was more to the case than this, but the work shown here is pivotal.

Practical Work – permissive world

> ➤ Working in pairs, therapist and client
> ➤ Client defines a problem
> ➤ Therapist encourages symbolic representation of problem; this may be absolutely anything at all, even something completely outrageous
> ➤ The therapist and client jointly explore the symbolism
> ➤ Attempt to make <u>logical</u> sense by translating the symbols

It is important to realise that you cannot hurry this sort of therapy, any more than you can other styles; you will sometimes find yourself going down 'blind alleys' or wandering off into a kind of mental maze which just goes round and around without ever getting anywhere. When you feel this sort of thing is happening, it is as well to create a shift of some sort. Here are four ways of doing that, though there are many more:

1. Ask your client to let his/her mind drift back to a previous 'scene' which was relevant to the presenting problem, then continue in a different path.
2. Ask your client if he would like to become a third person, an observer, watching herself working and giving guidance on what path she should pursue, what she should be looking at, etc.
3. Begin some 'inner advisor' work.
4. Ask the client if she can imagine that she is suddenly flying through time and space to a time when something feels different about the presenting problem, and ask her to tell you what she finds – what it is that's different, how did the changes occur, and so on.

Non-human Parts

There will usually be many more Parts entering the session – sometimes referred to as 'sub-personalities' – though you may choose whether or not to work with them. Sometimes it will be another humanoid character, possibly in cartoon form, though it is not at all unusual for parts of personality to be expressed in other than human form. Other than animate form, in fact. The case histories shown later illustrate this point very clearly.

In the fragment shown above, it would have been possible to have communicated with the football and, indeed, that would have been a good course of action had the client not gone so immediately to the understanding of the symbolic meaning. We would almost certainly have arrived at the same end result.

Always remember that every part that appears is there for a reason; it is telling us something about our client and our client's relationship with his or her presenting problem.

To summarise this permissive method: we simply get our client to describe the nub of the problem in some detail, then ask for something to be there in her mind that is a symbol representing the problem in some way. The client should tell you the very first thing she thinks of and it can be literally anything at all.

Symbols

Here are some examples from cases:

- *A purple cloud*
- *An animal (sheep, goat, elephant, alligator, worm, snake, tiger... etc.)*
- *A box*
- *A house*
- *A ghost/phantom/spirit*
- *A boat/car/plane*
- *An amoeba*
- *A flash of light*
- *A planet*
- *A lake*
- *One of the Warrior, Settler or Nomad Parts.*

Whatever is nominated, it is simply a substitute that is more easily able to express part of the problem than the client can in the normal way. At this stage, the client will usually not be aware of why she has chosen this particular image. Since the mind is most definitely *not* a random device, though, and because there will have been a fair amount of discussion of the problem or issue, it is certain that the image will be related in some way to the presenting problem.

Ask your client if she wants to give a name to the image – again the first thing that comes to mind. This might be a proper name, or an abstract label, like 'Midnight', for instance. Whatever is chosen, work with that. Sometimes, animals are just called by their species – 'Tiger', 'Wolf', 'Lion' and so on. Not unusually, Parts are just referred to by their initial 'identifier'; Warrior, Settler, Nomad, Mountain, Cloud, Spark, etc. It is when we have two or three similar characters, or cartoon entities, that we find more names being used. The only problem we might have here is that the therapist needs to keep track of them and for this reason, we usually seek to avoid having too many Parts in the scene at one time.

CHAPTER TEN
Doing it – part three

The Theatre of Imagination

This concept is a great way of helping a client to discover how different scenarios for change might work in 'real life'. We literally create a theatre in the imagination where a play is about to be enacted – for some reason, an open-air theatre seems to be particularly effective for many people.

There are several ways to work with this. A good way is to have the client visualising the 'play' taking the course of events that he wants to achieve, with everything running perfectly from start to successful conclusion. It is important that we do not allow any objections to get in the way at this stage, simply insisting that if it was a perfect world, then this is what would happen.

Once we have this idea in place, we introduce one of the Parts into the auditorium and enact the play again, listening to the Part's objections, if any, and finding a successful resolution or agreement to compromise. We then bring the second Part in to observe the rewritten play with the first Part and again seek to find agreement or compromise to any objections that arise. Finally, we bring the last Part in to join the other two, repeating the exercise.

184

As to which Part to introduce first, this is usually the one which it is perceived would be most likely to find objections. As an example, it might be the Nomad if we were working at establishing routine in some area of our client's life, Warrior if it we were seeking to find harmony in a relationship, Settler if there was a need to gain control over a situation.

There are other ways to use the Theatre of Imagination, including having the Parts playing different roles, directing the play, writing the script, or even introducing a new character who has the answers that are needed to overcome any objections or difficulties.

It is quite likely that you will be able to think of yet more.

The Magical Arena

This interesting method can sometimes produce a very rapid resolution of a difficulty – when a very rapid resolution is available. We ask our client to find his own special place full of magic, and wait until he's found it. It might be a forest glade, a pentacle or other mystical symbol, or simply some place that feels magical to him. Then we ask whichever part is troubled to wait within that 'magical arena' so that it can absorb understanding and knowledge which is especially relevant to the problem. We assist the client to translate the symbolic work as we go.

Practical Work – Magical Arena
➤ Working in threes, therapist, client and observer
➤ The client defines a problem
➤ The client searches for his 'magical place'

➢ Therapist and observer assist client to link symbolism to the presenting problem.

Parts Regression

This is illustrated at the end of Chapter Four, under the heading: **'Regressive Progression'.** There is a useful workshop guide in that section which can be incorporated into any Archetypal Parts Imagery workshop or seminar.

Timelines

It is also entirely possible and fruitful to conduct a kind of 'Timelines' session using only one Part. This is especially indicated when the client repeatedly embarks on a destructive behaviour pattern yet cannot make sustained changes. Usually, this is evidence of either:

(a) One Part being partially inactive.

(b) One Part being excessively active.

In the normal way, it will soon become evident which of those circumstances apply and which Part is causing the problem, just by talking to the client, though we *might* need to carry out a bit of 'investigatory' work to establish the true problem. Identifications having been made, we regress the problem Part back to a time when life was working in satisfactory manner. There, we carefully observe what was different before coming forward to the present day to see how those differences might be introduced now, <u>always taking into account the reactions of the other Parts</u>; then, if everything is acceptable, we progress forward to the near future to see how those changes might cause life to pan out, again being sure that we achieve harmony between the Parts. We can repeat this regression/progression routine as many times as our client wishes or until all the possible resources are exhausted.

Once everything is as good as we can get it, then that's the time to progress forward to the far future to observe the successes that the new 'way of being' have created; this last step is important, since it gives the subconscious a long term goal to be fulfilled and, therefore, a purpose in maintaining the new behaviour patterns.

Sometimes *both* those circumstances shown above apply, to two separate parts. This is often the case with those individuals who are overpoweringly dominant with others – the Warrior is excessively active while the Settler is partially inactive. The only way to deal with this is to timeline each Part separately, using the same technique as above.

Reasons for resistance

Sometimes, whilst a solution that has been found appears to be perfectly plausible, it will conflict with the client's conscious interest – and you may well not know about this. We usually discover it when we ask the client how they feel about this new plan, this proposal for resolving their difficulty, but there may only be the merest indicator. This can be a hesitant answer, a sudden flurry of body activity, sudden foot movement or any other of the clients discomfort 'signals' with which many therapists are familiar. Of course, the solution has come from the client's own mind, so at some level of consciousness, he or she knows it to be a workable solution.

Here are a few examples:

Leaving an unsupportive/selfish partner, conflicting with a moral code that says "You've made your bed..."

Looking for a new job conflicting with the knowledge that the boss "was kind to me when I was ill" or similar.

Leaving home to be in a relationship conflicting with the fact that a parent is in poor health.

Telling a lover that the relationship is finished conflicting with the belief that the lover is dependent.

Moving house conflicting with the knowledge that friends feel as if they're being left behind.

And so on... there are very many such conflicts possible, concerning belief structures, personal codes, morals and ethics, etc., often based on falsehoods and sometimes associated with unfinished business or unpleasant previous experience. We can:

1. Help the client to find an alternative solution.
2. Examine the objection to see if there is just a 'wait state' being employed. In other words, we ask how long the client wants to stay in this situation, then, if applicable, work on a time scale for when the solution can be brought to bear.
3. Work at the client's acceptance of the existent situation. For instance, in the first example above, we could help the client to accept the way their life will be if they decide to stay with their partner. Quite often, there is an abrupt change of heart half-way through this sort of work!

You will probably be able to see many other possibilities as you become more practiced at this style of working; but it is important to remember that *all we do* is help the client to discover <u>their own</u> way through their problems. We help them to find the way, not find it for them.

Call a friend...

Sometimes, a Part just simply refuses to communicate; either the client cannot see the Part in the first place, or there is a refusal to speak. When this happens there are a couple of alternatives that you can employ. By far the easiest, and probably the best is to call on a friend of the Part to speak for him/her – and here, the Part need not give permission. When working with WSN, it is even possible to ask one of the other parts to answer; you should always point out to your client that all the parts know each other and know how each other think. Always remember, though, that it is distinctly possible that the friend will be unconnected with any of the three major Parts.

When using this 'call a friend' routine, suggest to your client that he or she should take notice of any comment being made by the original Part – this technique is sometimes enough to actually trigger an argument between two Parts and persuade the previously silent one to speak up for him/her self!

Allied to this, you can ask each Part who he/she/it believes 'owns' the problem with which the client has presented. Usually, there is a consensus of agreement but it is possible that conflict and disagreement will be shown here. When this happens, it is necessary to resolve the issue in some way before work can proceed. There are really only two possibilities:

1. One Part owns the whole of the problem.

2. The problem is shared between two or three Parts.

Obviously, we are referring here solely to working within the WSN construct, since the problem exists, it must be owned by either one or all of the Warrior, Settler and Nomad Parts. Disputes will usually centre on integrity issues, so that there may be an unwillingness all round to admit to owning a problem of, say, not coping well with an ageing parent, for instance.

In reality, what is happening here, of course, is that the client's consciousness is getting the way of therapy by seeking to maintain image and/or integrity in the eyes of the therapist and some talk may be needed about non-judgementalism and confidentiality.

A problem must be allocated, or allocated in the correct proportions, if we are to effectively help our clients to resolve it.

Practical Work – Call a Friend

This practical work is to allow observation of how powerful the 'talking to a friend' can be. Obviously, since the therapist is talking to a third party here, the pressure on the psyche is greater than it would normally be; nonetheless, this is an illustration of the energy that will be built up in the client's psyche in a 'normal' therapist/client situation.

> ➤ Working in threes, therapist, client, 'friend'
> ➤ The client defines a problem and allocates it to a Part
> ➤ The therapist talks to the 'friend' about the Parts difficulty

> ➤ The client grades the difficulty of non-response on a scale of 1 -10

A time for symbolic working

Just occasionally you will discover a total impasse when the 'active' Parts simply cannot or will not agree to any form of compromise or acceptance of ownership/responsibility for a problem; you have a stalemate situation and this is clear evidence of resistance showing itself. Here, we need to work in a specific way, by asking our client to find a symbol that represents the stalemate situation. Whatever is produced, that's what we work with, no matter how unlikely the symbol. We talk to it and constructively question it in exactly the same way as we have done with the other 'regular' parts; in this way we will either:

(a) eventually uncover the reason(s) for the resistance and can seek to resolve the difficulty, again working with abstract imagery or with WSN.

Or:

(b) discover that the resistance simply dissolves once it has been revealed and understood.

It is important that we give total credibility to everything that a Part 'says', remembering that the information is coming from the client's subconscious, which is neither critical nor logical. We are dealing with the causes for emotional states, rather than logically understood behaviour patterns.

What was the alternative…?

Another useful way to work is to provide a learning experience to help overcome a projected future difficulty. Here we ask our client to find a time in the past when they dealt unsuccessfully with a situation that had similar qualities to the one that they are anxious about. Once they have it vividly in their mind, have them recognise the mode in which they sought to handle the situation, which Part was most active; then have them go through it again using a different Part of personality, selecting that which seems to get, for them, the most comfortable result. This is not dissimilar to the 'Theatre of Imagination' technique shown earlier and you could, of course, use that method of working in this situation if you so wished.

This method can also be used to achieve 'closure' on a past situation that the client cannot seem to let go of. Proceed as above, and when it is recognised that there *are* other resources available, the subconscious can stop trying to solve a problem which is now obsolete.

Practical Work – Alternatives

Workshop guide:

➢ Working in pairs, therapist and client
➢ The client thinks of a recent situation which had an outcome different from that which was required
➢ Therapist and client explore how the situation might have been different if the client had been 'operating' in a different mode.

Unwelcome Images

It is not uncommon for an unwelcome image to form in your client's mind; it could be an ugly, horrific or terrifying person, animal or entity, or maybe just a pictorial scene that is in some way disturbing. These are all messages from the subconscious, of course, but their unpleasant nature increases client resistance to the therapy and makes it difficult to work constructively with them.

Obviously, we need a way to deal with this eventuality and probably the best way is to treat the image as evidence of resistance, then set out to convert it into something useful or even destroy it altogether. It can be dissolved, melted, buried, burnt, drowned, lasered, flattened, blown up, cut up, fragmented, strangled, dangled, dropped, popped... or anything else that would effectively get rid of it. We have to let our client find the way to do this, but you must always remember – and tell the client – that nothing can truly be destroyed; it is energy and energy will always find another way to manifest itself. For instance, something can be buried under a landslide and have a beautiful verdant forest grow in its place (although we must always let the client find the replacement image). Then we can discover what the forest means to the client – you would probably discover that it was a more acceptable representation of a difficulty that the previous image; a forest is a jungle by another name and it is easy to see how that imagery might work.

Wild Imagination

Sometimes, the replacement image represents something that the client wants but which has been out of reach – hence the resistance. Communicating with that image may reveal the resources your client can use to advantage. Always let your client's imagination be as wild as he or she likes because that is simply the creative part of the mind at work and it is from the creative mind's work that our client will derive their solutions. Translating the meaning of the images can take time, but it is your client who will do most of the work. Your job is simply to support and guide them on their journey. There are examples in the case histories which clearly illustrate this technique.

When all else fails, we can employ a rather more direct tactic by employing the invincible Warrior to destroy the destructive or unpleasant part or image, whilst still allowing the formation of a more 'workable' part or image. It is also possible for the Settler to confer 'niceness' – and don't forget that the Nomad is the *absolute master* of change! The possibilities are almost infinite and the skilled therapist will be able to guide the client smoothly to success.

When working in this manner, with the WSN parts, it is easy to get the client started: *"Which of the Warrior, Settler or Nomad could best deal with this?"* You can even offer the broad possibilities of how each might do it, as shown above, and let the client decide which to employ.

Looking at a life...
This is a very easy way to work for both the therapist and the client, though, since it does not move around a specific goal or circumstance, it can sometimes seem 'loose' or inconclusive. We always start work with the WSN concept here and then talk to each of the Parts in turn, asking what they want to happen in life and what they think about the life they are actually leading. In the hands of a skilled worker,

this can produce startling insights, especially if the 'mode' of each part is clarified – that is, the **Warrior** will be identified as **Dictator, Leader,** or **Crusader.** This identification allows for more precise interaction between client and therapist. This method is useful with (a) a client who does not know why he feels the way he does; (b) when an impasse of some sort has been reached; or (c) when other methods have 'gone all around the houses' without finding any resolution.

Practical Work – Looking at a Life
Workshop guide:
> ➤ Working in threes, therapist, client, observer
> ➤ The client discusses the perfect life for each Part
> ➤ The therapist and observer identify any conflicts between parts

Ending the Session
The work over, and our client understanding how what has transpired in the session relates to his life, it only remains to tidy up and leave everything ready for the next session. First, we thank the Parts for agreeing to talk to each other whether or not they have found an agreement. This sometimes feels a little strange, but it is an important element if we are to get continuous cooperation from our client – politeness costs nothing and your clients will appreciate it. It also lends a touch of credibility to the procedure in that we address the Parts as if they were individuals.

Finally, we need to reintegrate back into one every part that is still present separately. Have your client visualise all of them combining in some way until there are only the

Warrior, the Settler and the Nomad left, then continue as shown previously.

The second and subsequent sessions should be a lot easier, since your client will now know what is expected. Also, this is a skill for your client to learn and the more they learn, the better they get.

As far as the number of sessions is concerned, there is no particular limit, but you do need to remember the tenet: <u>if you do the same thing in the same way you get the same result.</u> Ensure that each session differs in some way from the last, approaching the problem from a different angle, working on a different problem, using a different Part, asking the Inner Adviser for advice or guidance, and so on. Generally speaking, if there is not at least some enlightenment or pronounced change after three sessions or so, then you and your client may be on the wrong track – either that, or 'Parts' is the wrong methodology for the client and/or the presenting problem.

CHAPTER ELEVEN
An overview of a therapy

To help carry you through this overview, we will deal with a hypothetical client, based on several different case histories. Although it is shown here as a two-session therapy, it is highly likely that more sessions than this would be needed, especially when limited to the 'fifty-minute hour'. Having said that, it is certainly possible to create profound change in just <u>one</u> session.

We will assume that we are combining initial consultation and first work session, something which is actually quite easy to do with this sort of work.

Session one
Gather client details:
'Dave' Male, age 28, single, living with parents.
Relationship with both parents is good; they are supportive.
No siblings living.
Brother died when he was 8 and client was 4. No memory of him.
Presenting symptom: Depression
Symptom existent for: 4 years
Before symptom: Frequently bored but otherwise ok.
Various medications employed, to no great effect.

Works in a factory 'because the job was available'.
Has few friends 'because of my moodiness'.
Heterosexual, with a casual girlfriend he sees 4 times a week.
Sex life is 'nothing exciting'. Can 'take it or leave it'.
Cannot sustain relationships – 'They always go pear-shaped'.
Hobbies include watching football, playing the guitar, and drinking.

These are the 'vital signs' and there is plenty there for us to work with – it is fairly comprehensive 'picture' of a long-term depressed individual (he was depressed before he recognised it, probably, being only aware of boredom) and even has a possible cause, in the deceased brother, though it is a matter of conjecture as to how this actually fits.

We would, of course, enquire as to the pattern of the depression to see if there was any indication of Bi-Polar disorder and would probably seek to ascertain the reasons why (a) Dave is still living with his parents; and (b) the nature of the 'pear shaped' problem in relationships. For our purposes here, we will assume that the answer to (a) is: *"I can't afford to move out."* and (b) is: *"They keep on trying to stop me doing stuff. Drinking and football."*

It should go without saying that we would not comment on, or attempt to work directly with, either of those responses, though there is much there that suggests subconscious resistance to the idea of making a 'normal' separation from the parental home.

A Surfeit of Information

We might feel that we want to know more but enquiring further will only slow down the start of therapy. If there is anything else which is important or relevant, we can be confident that it will become apparent during the therapy. Some workers, in fact, would say that we have a surfeit of information, because all we really need to know is the symptom pattern. We can ask any other question we wish during the therapy and there is much to recommend that approach. It is worth remembering, though, that the client will feel you have taken more of an interest if your questions at the beginning are fairly comprehensive. Having acquired those details, we now have the task of <u>not</u> assuming that they are in any way connected with the presenting problem; whether they are or not is something for our client to discover.

During this 'case' we will look at a fairly general way of working, rather than using any specific techniques exclusively. The case histories will provide further clarification and will show some of the other techniques.

Encountering Resistance

So, we have gathered our information and Dave is waiting expectantly for us to do some magic... so we'd better start to convince him that we have something for him. This is obviously where the pre talk goes; we could begin by explaining the nature of conflict and erroneous belief systems as shown in Lesson Four. You may well encounter resistance to the idea of erroneous belief, because many people will say something like: *"Oh, no, I think I know myself very well, actually."* Our response must always be to agree that this is indeed possible, then point out that this will make the therapy even easier and more successful, since we do not have to resolve that problem... he'll find out if he's wrong soon enough!

So we explain how symptoms are always a result of the conflicts that everybody has tucked away in the subconscious and maybe illustrate the way that imagination and belief work, as shown in Lesson Four. This is also a good point to introduce the idea of Parts with something like: *"Most people have had that experience where part of them wants to buy something, but another part doesn't want to spend the money."* Get agreement that this is the case before continuing with: *"That's how we work, actually, discovering which Parts want to do what and how we can find an agreement between them. You know, it's odds on that your depression is the result of one part of your mind wanting to something another part believes you most definitely should not."* We need to find some sort of acceptance of this idea, even if it is only that we are the expert and must therefore know best. Any dissent must be dealt with, or resistance will render therapy ineffective; the client would in all probability set out to prove the therapist wrong. When we have acceptance, we have started to bypass the incredulity factor.

The Personality Test

Now we get on to the description of the WSN concept, making sure to outline the extreme differences between the types and at the same time watching for signs of boredom, because some people will simply not find it interesting. In these cases, a brisk: *"Well, anyway, we don't need to worry about how the three major personality types came into being*

– shall we just find out which one you are?" There are very few people indeed, even those who are depressed, who will not be keen to know which they are and what that means. So now we can do a personality test; the one given in Chapter Three will be suitable here. In truth you don't actually *need* to do this, though it will tell you a lot about the degree of each Part, which will give some indication of where and how you will discover the best communication mode. The main advantage of it is that it involves your client in the concept more completely and will continue that all important task of reducing the incredulity factor.

We will assume, here, that Dave turns out to be mostly Settler and secondary Warrior with Nomad lagging behind. We describe the nature of each of the modern versions of the types, point out that there seems to be enough Warrior there for him to get control of his life but not yet enough Nomad to actually enjoy it. We can enlarge on that theme if we wish, or we can just say something like: *"You're going to feel a lot more comfortable when we can get those two parts to be a bit more active. That depression of yours will start to disappear. As a matter of interest, what will you do with yourself when that happens?"*

You probably noticed already that we are communicating with the Settler Part and also eliciting what the client is looking for as a result of therapy. We know already that he wants to get rid of the depression, but it helps us a lot more if we can see what he actually wants to *gain*. We should also ask what he might *have* to do that he doesn't do now. Whatever the answer, we ask him how he feels about that, even if the answer is 'nothing'.

We will assume that Dave's answers are:

1. *"I could get a better job, something more worthwhile."*
2. *"Well, I might get more pressure from my parents about the relationship thing."*
3. *"Awkward. They've talked about it a couple of times."*

As you can see, we are building up quite a bit of information about how Dave functions, and doing it in such an informal way that resistance will be minimal. In this particular instance we do not need to delve further into the symptom – as we might do if he had presented with lack of confidence, for example – since it is already specific enough to work with, and we have elicited several associated issues to help us on our way.

Getting to the Meat

Now we need to get into the 'meat' of what we are going to do; so we can tell Dave that his problem exists because of conflict between two of those Parts of personality and say that the easiest way to find it is to actually ask them. This statement is best delivered with a brief smile since that will carry credibility for all three types. We continue with something like: *"Before we can do that, though, you'll need to develop a picture of each part in your mind. You might be surprised how easy that is, actually. Would you like to try it now?"*

Get agreement, ask your client to close his eyes if he wants to (though it's not strictly necessary at this stage), and you're on your way.

Spend as long as seems necessary on developing each archetype, where possible creating an image that is ancient, rather than modern. It's best if your client does not choose to use modern characters from real life or fiction, since that would probably lead to role modelling which is a different style of therapy altogether. Nonetheless, if that's all he'll find, then we go with it.

Introduce the VMI idea here and test it by asking him to imagine his major character – Settler in Dave's case – performing some ordinary task, then to tell you how he perceives the part reacting. It may be that there will be comment about the surprise of modern day life but this is unimportant – it merely shows that the client is getting properly involved with the task, which is the object of the exercise. The archetypes created, the client brought to the recognition that each part is a real part of his own personality, the VMI 'played', we have one task left and it allows us to close this first session elegantly.

"OK, that's good. Now we'll finish today's session by showing you how differently those parts of yours react to your problem. First of all, tell me who you think is the one who's feeling the worst of the depression?"

If we have described the parts properly and our client has understood us, then the answer will almost always 'fit' the major personality trait – so we will assume that our hypothetical client, Dave, has indicated 'Settler'. When it does not, the chances are that the client knows about the origin of his illness than he is telling you; the reasons for this should be obvious; in this case, we have told the client that the Settler is inclined to melancholia or depression and yet he is telling us that it's another part that's feeling the worst of it.

He must know, therefore, what it is that is affecting that part. We can pursue this next time but for now would just continue: *"OK. Now tell me how the other two parts feel about it."*

Here, of course, we are exploring parts work proper and finding resources to help our client: *"Good. So, if your* (designated Part) *was more active, you would be feeling less depressed, then?"*

Get agreement, however vague, and follow with: *"Great! OK, now tell me what your* (designated Part) *might do to begin to change how things are for you at the moment."*

We must get some sort of positive response from our client here, before following with: *"That's very good. All right, now what I want you to do between now and next time you come to see me is to see the VMI of your* (designated Part) *in your mind's eye for a minute or so each day. As you're waking up is a good idea, though any other time is good, too. And you can do that more than once a day, if you like. As often as you wish, in fact – you certainly won't do yourself any harm. And next time, we'll see what those parts have to say to each other about the problem."*

Your client should be able to leave at the end of this first session with an awareness that some headway has been made towards solving his problem. At worst, he will have an understanding of the nature of conflict and will believe that some sort of improvement is inevitable once that conflict has been addressed. At best, there will be a distinct lifting of the depression which may well last until the next session. In either circumstance, we will be working in the same way.

204

Session two

A week has passed and Dave, our hypothetical client, is back. When we ask how he's been he frowns slightly and says that whilst he felt better for a few days, there's been a feeling of something 'bugging me', though he couldn't exactly say what. This presents us with an opportunity for some symbolic work and we can go straight into it: *"That's interesting. Tell me, if that 'bugging me' feeling were a person or a thing, what would it look like?"*

Many individuals will find an answer almost immediately, some will struggle for a moment or two, but almost all *will* come up with a symbolic representation of the 'bugging me' feeling. In truth, this is not nearly as much use here as it would be during the session, but it has the advantage of getting our client finding symbols. We should make a note of the answer, because it will be quite easy to introduce it into the work later on. We will assume that Dave has told us that it feels like somebody nagging him relentlessly about something – a dwarf, perhaps, or some sort of entity like that. This could well represent a child Part of self, but we will not jump to conclusions and must refrain from suggesting it. The feeling is a bit like he gets in relationships when 'they' start wanting him to stop drinking and watching football.

We have another small pre talk here, to explain that we are going to be communicating with the Warrior, Settler and Nomad. We can also tell him that sometimes we will be looking at other symbols, which might take any sort of form or shape at all, just as we did with the 'bugging me' feeling. After ascertaining that he is in agreement with this idea, we have to make it quite clear that he won't actually hear voices and explain that the response will always be the first thing comes to mind. It is probably a good idea to reassure him that it matters not one bit if he feels as if he's making it all up, as long as he tells us the *first* thing he thinks of each time.

That done, we settle him down and begin work. We will begin by seeking communication with the Settler Part, both because it is the main personality and because it seems to 'own' the problem. Conversation will not normally flow as it might seem to here – there will frequently be long pauses while your client processes revelations, or struggles to find his way when emotions become complex.

This is the sort of thing that might happen:

Therapist: *"Just let your mind drift and find a place where you might like to meet your Settler. Tell me where you find yourself."*

Dave: *"A football stadium. It's empty and I'm sitting on the benches, just looking at the empty pitch."*

Therapist: *"And is Settler there?"*

Dave: *"No. It's empty."*

This is a manifestation of resistance, the Part we need to talk to not being available. It does not present too great a problem.

Therapist: *"Call him. In your mind. He'll come, because Settler always tends to do as he's told, does he not?"*

Dave: *"Oh, yeah...He's here now."*

Therapist: *"Ask him if he'll talk to you."*

Dave: *"He says he will."*

Therapist: *"Good. What do you want to ask him?"*

Dave: *"What all this bloody depression is about..."*

Therapist: *"Go on then. And tell me what he says. It'll be the first thing that comes into your mind."*

Dave: *"He says it's not fair. They want too much."*

Therapist: *"What does that mean to you?"*

Dave: *"I'm not sure really... This seems a bit silly, but it* **feels** *like it's got something to do with the other two. The Warrior and the Nomad."*

In practice, we would probably not get this far this quickly, but the above conversation serves to give you an idea of how to work; the case histories will show you more.

From that point, we would have Dave exploring the relationship between the three Parts, maybe discovering that the Nomad was bored by the unexciting existence and the Warrior was frustrated at the lack of planning and structure in Dave's life. We might then get something else happening...

Dave: *"All this stuff with the Warrior and Nomad. It makes me feel... well, irritated, I suppose. You know, a bit cross."*

Therapist: *"OK, that's good. Now, if that 'bit cross' feeling were a person or a thing, what would it look like? The first impression that comes to mind."*

Dave: *"Uh... I don't know, really..."*

Therapist: *"Don't try to make sense of it – just tell me the very first thing you think of, the first thing that comes into your mind."*

Dave: *"Well, it's like a...stone statue or something."*

Therapist: *"And what does that mean to you?"*

Dave: *"It doesn't mean anything. It's just a stone statue."*

Therapist: *"Will stone statue talk to you?"*
Dave: *"No. It's just a stone statue. I think it's one I've seen somewhere. Don't remember it. It doesn't feel nice."*

Now, we cannot ask for a symbolic representation of something that "doesn't feel nice", since "doesn't" cannot be represented – the subconscious cannot accurately interpret "doesn't". So:

Therapist: *"Tell me how it **does** feel."*
Dave: *"Sort of... uncomfortable."*

"Uncomfortable" is not specific enough, so:

Therapist: *"What sort of uncomfortable is that?"*
Dave: *"I don't know...afraid, I think."*
Therapist: *"Tell me who afraid belongs to. Warrior, Settler or Nomad?"*

When we find a definite emotion like this, it's useful to attribute it to one of the Parts. We could just as easily have worked with a symbol for "afraid" and may choose to do so if our client was not able to apportion 'ownership' of it. Earlier, the work was with a symbol for "bit cross" and we could, of course, have sought to attribute "bit cross" to one of the major Parts.

Dave: *"All of them, I think... but Nomad hates it most. He wants to run away."*

It would be tempting here to pursue the reasons why Nomad wanted to run away and there would be nothing wrong with that direction; but because we're searching for conflict, something different might be more useful:

Therapist: *"What do the other two think of that?"*
Dave: *"Settler understands. But Warrior is a bit cross."*

This is why it is not particularly important, much of the time, which direction you take, since if something needs attribution, we will still find it. So here we are with Warrior feeling the "bit cross" that it is almost certain was mentioned earlier. So we could ask Warrior exactly what it is that is making him cross. It could be that Nomad wants to run away, or that Settler understands Nomad, or Warrior is simply cross about "afraid"... or any one of a number of other things. Remember, we are not working with logic here, but with the non-rational subconscious.

An Impasse

Now we will assume that some time has passed and we have now reached an impasse. Warrior is not particularly forthcoming about "afraid", Nomad is now refusing to communicate altogether and Settler is sympathising with both of them but does not have any particular feelings about the situation.

Time to change direction...

Therapist: *"Do you remember, earlier today, we talked about that 'bugging me' feeling and it seemed like it might be a sort of dwarf-like person nagging you? I want you to ask that Part if it will talk to you."*
Dave: *"Actually, it's like a bratty little kid... a horrid, bratty boy, whining on and on about something or other."*
Therapist: *"What does bratty boy want? Will he tell you?"*
Dave: *"Actually, it's a kind of small version of me."*

209

Therapist: *"And what does he have to say? What does he want?"*

Dave: *"He just wants some attention...he doesn't get enough attention. He doesn't understand."*

Again, it is not easy to work with a "doesn't" anything. So:

Therapist: *"Do you understand?"*

In view of the reply, there would in all likelihood be a long pause at this point, during which the therapist could sit quietly or repeat the question.

Dave: *"Yes... I think so... It's after my brother died. Mum and dad were very wrapped in it all. And I've just realised what that stone statue is, too – it's the angel they put on his grave. I didn't understand what it was all about but they were very weepy and I think it bothered me quite a bit. I think I felt as if I should look after them but didn't know what to do."*

There may or may not be emotional response at this point; if so, we reassure and wait, if not we simply continue working. We are not seeking abreaction but understanding. We will assume that, as a result of talking to 'Bratty boy' Dave now makes several recognitions:

1. 'Bratty boy' knows he must not desert his parents like his brother did.
2. Settler knows, therefore, that relationships are pointless.

3. Settler doesn't mind the dead-end job, because it poses no threat.
4. Nomad still feels like he doesn't get enough attention.
5. Warrior wants to just get on with things.

The final part of the session might be something like:

Therapist: *"What does Bratty boy want to happen before he could leave his parents?"*

Dave: *"He needs to be sure they're ok...Warrior <u>really</u> wants to get on with things now, though."*

Therapist: *"What do Warrior, Settler and Nomad think about that?"*

Dave: *"Warrior's fed up with the whole thing..."*

There, of course, is the depression!

Dave: *"Settler says he has to look after mum and dad."*

And there's the conflict!

Therapist: *"What does Warrior have to say about that?"*

Dave: *"He says we don't have to be around them all the time. Just looking out for them. They can cope."*

Therapist: *"And what does Settler think about that?"*

Dave: *"Well, if Warrior doesn't go too far too fast, he supposes it's ok..."*

Therapist: *"Will Warrior agree to that?"*

Dave: *"He'll give it a go, yes. As long as Settler doesn't start getting too soft."*

Therapist: *"And what do you think of all this? How does it seem to you?"*

Dave: *"Yes, it all makes sense. I can see what's been happening, altogether."*

Therapist: *"And does it seem as if you'll be able to solve your difficulties now?"*

Dave: *"Definitely. Absolutely."*
Therapist: *"So the Parts can agree, then? Will they shake hands on it?"*
Dave: *"They already are..."*

It's not unusual for a sudden smile or even laughter to appear at this sort of juncture, which you should take as a very positive response. Similar agreement would need to be found with 'Bratty boy' and Nomad, making sure that each Part is content with the outcome, how it affects them, and what is expected of them. You will often find the 'give it a go' response where it is evident that there may be practical difficulties surrounding any given situation. In practice, this seems not to matter, because a new behaviour pattern has been created – positive change has been brought about, which is the purpose of the exercise. It is very important that we always remember that each Part – the Warrior, Settler and Nomad, as well as any other parts that have surfaced and are still active in the final stages – must have equal consideration to their wishes and intentions. In other words, we must ensure that their integrity remains intact if we are not to lay the ground for further problems.

Now we will do just a little more work to ensure that Dave gets the very best possible result from his therapy – we will introduce him to his Inner Advisor, as shown in Lesson Five. For our purposes here, we will say that Dave has discovered his Inner Advisor to be a Fox. Wily and cunning, this is the just the sort of symbol that Dave would need to help him make up for lost time in the career stakes. So:

Therapist: *"A fox... that's good. Ask Fox if it will talk to you."*

Dave: *"It's a dog fox. He says I should listen carefully and take notice."*

Therapist: *"What do you think of that?"*

Dave: *"Yes, that seems ok..."*

Therapist: *"So what does Fox have to say?"*

Dave: *"Um... I think that's it. I should listen carefully and take notice."*

Therapist: *"And does that make a sort of sense to you?"*

Dave: *"It does, actually. They're asking some of us to take voluntary redundancy from the factory...I think I'll do it. You know, get a new start and everything."*

In this case, the phrase 'take notice' can be understood in two entirely different ways and this sort of subconscious 'pun' is not unusual. The Inner Advisor will often make some cryptic remark which only means anything to the client and we should always leave the client to sort it out, rather than interpret it ourselves. Sometimes, they will not make any sense of it at all during the session and the best advice we can give then is to 'wait and see'. At some point during the next few minutes, hours or days, understanding will dawn and they will be impressed by their own insight.

Here is a good way to end the session.

Therapist: *"All right, Dave, you've done some beautiful work here today... now, I want you to see, in your mind's eye, Warrior, Settler, Nomad and Bratty boy all sitting close together. Can you see that yet?"*

Wait for affirmation before continuing:

"Good, now just see them as if they're having a sort of group hug... then gradually merging into one... then find yourself with the sudden realisation that all of them were just facets of your own self, genuine facets of self that you can now understand more clearly... and bring to bear to help you find whatever success means to you. You can talk to any or all of them again whenever you want to, but for now, just be very aware of just you, in that chair... and when you are fully aware that there's just you, then allow your eyes to open. And be ready to feel good!"

Usually, it will be no more than a few seconds before your client opens his eyes, although you can prompt if you feel it necessary, just as you would at the end of a session of hypnosis.

That completes this overview of the basic handling of a session – but do remember that it is only an example; there are very many other ways that it could have been handled. The final lesson that follows is a collection of actual case histories that will give you some extra insight into how powerful this sort of changework can be.

CHAPTER TWELVE
A few genuine case histories in Archetypal Parts work

It is not the intention to show entire case studies here, merely the 'meat' of several, which will show you how the relevant part of this style of therapy works. Always remember that there will often be much 'beating around the bush' before you get to salient details, and often considerable pauses – not shown here – in client responses. Not every technique covered in the course is shown here, since the aim of this lesson is to show you how we interact with the client.

Since the hypothetical client shown in Chapter Eleven used only the WSN Parts, all those shown here use other symbols as well.

Agoraphobia
Client: Clare, single woman, age27
Symptom: Agoraphobia. **Duration:** 11 years
Background: Mother died when Clare was 13, lives now with two sisters and ageing father, whose health is deteriorating.

Clare had done a fair amount of self-help and had practiced meditation for a good few years before presenting for therapy. She was very spiritual in her beliefs and was immediately interested in the concept of Ancestral Parts Imagery as soon as it was mentioned, which was after we had done a few sessions of hypnoanalysis and grief-work. She had responded to this quite well, though her symptom seemed not to have changed much.

On her first session, she had no trouble in creating her Warrior, Settler and Nomad archetypes; the Warrior was a Native American Indian, the Settler a Druid, and the Nomad a mystical psychic/seer. They all agreed that they would bring their own individual resources to bear to help her overcome her problems in life.

These characters fitted very much with her somewhat spiritual view of the world. Her Inner advisor, too, appeared almost instantaneously – a very large Tiger, whom she had encountered many times in her mind before. She said she had always known that he was an important part of her but had never been able to identify quite why this should be so. With the merest encouragement, she accepted that this fearless Part was actually a *true* part of her own mind and expressed some pleasure at the realisation.

On her second session, she reported that she simply could not see the Warrior, Settler or Nomad, and though Tiger was there, he was completely uncommunicative.

Client: *"I feel as if I have to do something on my own."*
Therapist: *"Find a symbol that represents your symptom in some way – the very first thing you can think of."*

Using this alternative way of getting her started saved the time that might have been lost in seeking to get the major Parts talking. Had she not responded to this, then I could have pursued the WSN methodology, or even asked her to find a symbol that represented the reluctance of her subconscious to work at the symptom. However, she responded with:

Client: *"Huge steel doors... they're called 'Fred', for some reason..."*
Therapist: *"Do you want to talk to Fred doors?"*
Client: *"Yes...and he says he'll talk to me, too."*
Therapist: *"What are you going to ask Fred?"*
Client: *"Why he's there... what he wants from me..."*
Pause.
Therapist: *"What does he say?"*
Client: *"He's there because of what I fear outside. He's there to keep me safe."*
Therapist: *"Does that make sense to you?"*
Client: *"Yes...It does make a lot of sense, actually."*
Therapist: *"Will he open?"*
Client: *"Not for me..."*
Therapist: *"For who, then?"*
Client: *"I don't know. I can't be bothered to ask."*

It is usually best to go <u>with</u> resistance, where possible, so:

Therapist: *"What do the others think of this? Can they help?"*

Most clients will accept the implication that you are talking about the Warrior, Settler and Nomad, although you can be specific if there are already a lot of other parts being accessed. There was considerable discourse between Clare and each of the Parts – some of which she did not tell me – at the end of which she sighed and said:

Client: *"They all say I have to make the first move… Warrior is sure I can do it, Settler says I'm definitely worth it, and Nomad is looking forward to doing some travelling…"*
Therapist: *"So what move do you think you could make?"*
Client: *"I could ask Tiger to have a look outside. I think Fred will let Tiger through…"*

Although it is a little unusual for the Inner Advisor to be used in this way, we simply go along with whatever the client feels is right.

Therapist: *"What does Tiger think about that?"*
Client: *"He wants to. He wants to prove that it's safe for me out there."*

This is close to Inner Advisor's <u>true</u> role – guiding us. In this case, Clare's subconscious is apparently seeking to give Inner Advisor some credence by having him investigate that which Clare is afraid of.

Client: *"Oh! Fred suddenly opened just a tiny little bit and Tiger's slipped out through the gap. Fred's closed again now, though… I don't think I like this very much."*

Over the next few minutes, Clare became increasingly anxious but elected to consort with Warrior, who reassured her that all was well. Tiger would be back soon. She visibly relaxed and smiled, commenting that it felt as if Warrior was a real person and that he had special knowledge that Tiger would be completely safe. After some time and some fairly inconsequential secondary work concerning the way that her relationship with her family worked as a result of her illness, she announced that Tiger was back, and looking very pleased with himself as he told her that there was nothing out there, that she was frightened of nothing. Clare understood this instantly and agreed that she had always felt that she could easily be frightened of absolutely nothing at all. A moment later, she said:

Client: *"Fred's opened just a little bit... I'm going to have a look."*
Pause
Client: *"It's just a very long corridor...I don't like it much because for some reason I know it represents my life so that the end of it is when I die."*
Therapist: *"Can you see the end of it?"*
Client: *"No... it curves round somehow."* (Smile) *"Warrior's talking to me – he says he'll keep me vigilant and safe – oh, and Nomad's saying that we all have to get to the end of the corridor at some point and he'd like to have some fun on the journey. Settler says she'll look after me."*

At this point it, it was time to finish the session, which we did after thanking the parts and reintegrating them all. Clare professed herself very pleased and decided that she would have more conversation with them all on her own. When she came in the next week, she said that she had wanted to go through the doors into the corridor but had not quite managed it on her own. She had also realised that Tiger was more a sort of guardian than an Inner Advisor, but that she was very happy with this situation. Since it felt all right to her, I went along with it and we commenced the session, rapidly coming back to the place in front of the doors.

Client: *"I feel like I can go through...Fred is letting me through and Tiger's with me. I'm holding on to his fur – it keeps me feeling safer. Oh... it feels... sort of dark, even though it's light."* At this point, her hand went to her mouth and she drew her breath in sharply and held it before saying anxiously: *"There's this big black circle on the wall and it's moving with me, staying with me."*

Just occasionally, your client will give you a symbol instead of the emotion, even though the emotion may already be present. The rule remains the same, though – work with whatever the client gives you.

Therapist: *"Ask the circle what it's there for."*
Client: *"It's fear! The circle is my fear! It's horrid, like oblivion."*
Therapist: *"Ask circle what it wants."*
Client: (Frown) *"To protect me... aahhh... I understand... it's taken over from mum, in case I manage to get too far away..."*

Of course, there is some fine symbolism going on here, in that Clare's mother had been quite protective and may very well have worried about Clare going to far away from home. Clare had not seemed to recognise this and whilst I *could* have guided her to such a recognition, I decided to just 'go with the flow', which is usually the best approach with this style of therapy.

Therapist: *"What do the others think of circle?"*

Client: *"It's odd. I already asked Tiger but he can't see anything at all. He says it isn't there."* (Sigh) *"It's all in my mind, isn't it? It's not real at all. It's turned into a small triangle and it's just sitting there on the wall and not moving – I can actually get away from it if I want to."*

Therapist: *"Do you want to?"*

Client: *"Not yet. I think I need just a little bit of it, for the time being. Warrior will get rid of it when I want him to, I know that now. Do you know, there are doors all along the walls of this corridor and they are doors to different parts of life."*

Therapist: *"How does this all feel to you? Can you make sense of it how it fits into your life?"*

Client: *"Oh yes, definitely! I know I have to do this on my own ultimately. I think I've been kind of waiting for somebody to do it for me, but that's not going to happen, is it?"*

Clare was not yet ready to go through any of the doors but was pleased to have discovered that they were there. We ended the session with her returning through 'Fred doors' then re-integrated WS&N; Tiger wandered off, but this did not bother her, because she knew she could find him whenever she needed to. She reported that she felt more positive than she could ever remember.

We did two more sessions after that, both of which saw immense improvement in Clare's general well-being. Her

221

agoraphobia still persisted but she elected to finish therapy at that point, feeling that she now had a greater understanding of how she might work through the problem in her own time. There are many times when a client will need to process the work that has been carried out, before the symptom can abate. We do not necessarily achieve an instant 'cure'. Some 5 months after her last session, her father died and she attended the funeral without any more difficulty than would be expected on such an occasion.

Relationship Difficulties
Client: Alison, 31 Married for 11 years.
Symptom: Inability to remain faithful to her husband.
Duration: 3 years
Background: 'Nice' middle-class family, private school, married childhood sweetheart when they were both 19 years old. No problems for the first eight years, then had her first affair and experienced her first 'real' orgasm.

Alison was quietly spoken and apparently demure – but it soon transpired that this was *only* apparently! When she presented for therapy, she explained that she had left her husband for a while but he was so distraught that she felt she had to go back to him. She was now acutely uncomfortable if he made any attempt at sexual contact and found herself irritated by him most of the time. As is often the case, they had not fully discussed their difficulties; she had tried, half-heartedly, but he refused to listen, insisting that it was all just a passing phase and that everybody hit a 'bad patch' now and again. She had not persisted, for fear of causing him more pain.

Recently, she had 'had a fling' with a male at her place of work and had once again experienced enormously satisfying sexual activity. I asked her how important her sex life was to her, on a scale of one to ten, and she smiled as she said: "Twenty!" She went on to explain that she was feeling very restless and hankering after a more exciting sex life than she had ever had with her husband; she was trying to stay with him, respecting his kind and caring attitude, but needed excitement and passion in her life. There was a tendency to be drawn towards males who were exciting, though utterly unreliable.

When I asked her what she wanted therapy to achieve, she responded that she wanted to be able to make up her mind once and for all, whether to stay or leave, instead of continuing with the vacillation of recent months. I asked her which decision to make if she had to choose at this very moment. She became somewhat incommunicative at this, save to say that sex with her most recent lover was the best she had ever had and that she was better at it with him than she had ever been with her husband.

Initially, we had some difficulty with the development of the Nomad Part; her first 'version' was a courtesan who cared for nothing but the fact that she got money for being pleasured and could not contemplate giving any thought to somebody else's needs. Given Alison's apparently demure approach towards life and relationships, this was a *real* bit of alter-ego work! She was reluctant to let go of this Part, until she came upon the realisation of what others might think of such a female. She eventually settled upon a 'tart with a heart' type of character and seemed pleased with herself at that. She named this part 'Rebecca' and was amazed at how real she seemed and how different she was from what *she* had always thought she was 'supposed' to be.

The other two parts had presented no difficulty in developing; Warrior was a Gladiator, while Settler was a milkmaid called 'Sally'. We decided that it was a good time to talk to them and started with the 'meeting' method outlined in Lesson Four, using method 2, client dissociated. You'll notice that at no time do we discuss Alison's wishes directly, only those of the parts. This is always a good way to work, but is especially important where the client is dissociated. There are a couple of occasions when Alison perceives a Part as talking to another Part without her volition, which is not unusual.

Therapist: *"All they all there?"*
Client: *"Yes…Rebecca looks bored, though. She wants to leave."*
Therapist: *"Will she talk to you?"*
Client: *"Yes. She says: Just get on with it."*
Therapist: *"What does she want to happen?"*
Client: *"She doesn't care much, as long as we can have some fun and more sex."*

This is a fairly typical attitude for this type of Nomad Part and one which can be worth exploring. The problem is, though, that the Part can easily decide not to cooperate at all, if pushed. On this occasion, I decided to take a slightly different tack and one which is actually 'cleaner' anyway.

Therapist: *"What do Warrior and Sally think about that?"*

Client: *"Sally thinks it's disgusting. Warrior says it's up to me and he will help me find whatever strength I need."*
Therapist: *"Do you want to ask Sally what she thinks should happen?"*
Client: *"She thinks I should stay with Brian* (husband). *She says I should just get on with my life. Sex isn't everything."*
Therapist: *"And what do Warrior and Sally think about that?"*
Client (Grinning):*"They're both looking at Sally and kind of rolling their eyes at her... Rebecca is saying she simply <u>cannot</u> even think about staying."*
Therapist: *"And what about Warrior?"*
Client: *"He's going to help, whatever is decided. He'll help to make it happen."*
Therapist: *"So Sally and Rebecca have to find some sort of agreement, then?"*
Client: *"Yes... They're glaring at each other, though. They don't like each other. It's Sally that's got the problem, you know. She just thinks you have to be so... **nice** all the time...It drives me crackers, sometimes."*

Of course, what we are seeing here is the 'seat' of inner conflict. For our client's piece of mind, we always need to achieve harmony.

Therapist: *"Will they talk to each other, Sally and Rebecca?"*

This is where this style of therapy departs radically from more 'traditional' Parts work, since we seek to allow the elements of conflict to resolve their differences with as little mediation as possible.

Client: *"They will, actually...this is weird! Rebecca is saying: 'Look, it's no good being bored all the time. Life's just too short.'"*
Therapist: *"And Sally?"*
Client: *"She's saying that you should settle for what there is instead of constantly trying to find something better."*
Therapist: *"Ok. Will you ask both of them, and Warrior, if they'll wait where they are for a little while? Tell them you'll talk more later."*
Client: *"Warrior says he needs me to make a firm decision. He's concerned in case I try to please too many people at once."*
Therapist: *"Tell him you are going to do some more work right now, which will end in a firm decision. Ask him if that's ok."*
Client: *"He says that's all right. He seems a bit doubtful, though."*

We continued with the development of the Inner Advisor, which turned out to be a Dog – this was not surprising, since a Dog is 'man's best friend' and constantly faithful. You will remember reading that the client will often select an Inner Advisor which has the quality they believe themselves to be lacking. It took some time for Alison to fully embrace this Part as part of her own psyche because, at first, she read a completely different meaning into it! Eventually, though, she came to the recognition of faithfulness and accepted it instantly, saying that it actually *felt* right.

'Dog' advised that she had to be true to herself; Alison understood immediately that this meant that she <u>had</u> to get things sorted out once and for all, because it would be unfair to both her and her husband if she did not. She shed a few tears at this point and said that she could not make her mind up – it was just too horrible to think about, either way.

Therapist: *"Ok, that's fine. Now, I want you to find an image that in some way represents the way you feel right now... the first thing that comes to mind."*

Client: *"It's gates... great big wrought iron gates. I'm inside them and it's dark outside."*

Therapist: *"And what do those gates mean, to you."* There was a very long pause, with some quite pronounced grimacing, at this point, throughout which I remained silent. Eventually, she continued: *"They represent restriction. They're locked and I can't open them because I'm frightened."*

Therapist: *"Find an image which represents frightened."*

Client: *"A key. A great big key..."*

Therapist: *"What does key want? Will it talk to you?"*

Client: *"Key wants to unlock the gates – he says it's all right to do that."*

Therapist: *"Can you do that?"*

Client: *"I think so...yes..."* Again there was a pause and some grimacing for perhaps a minute or so before: *"I've unlocked them now. I'm outside and it feels really, really good! Freedom."*

Therapist: *"Now find something that represents freedom."*

227

Client: *"It's a car, a red Beetle – it's waiting to take me anywhere I want to go."*

Therapist: *"Are you going to get into the car?"*

Client: *"Not yet. Another time. It's not time yet."*

This was probably an allusion to the idea that there is work to be done before she can leave her husband. I could not know this, though, so kept quiet. And it turned out to be just as well, because a few moments later, we got:

Client: *"Dog's here. He says I have to talk to Brian before I make any decisions at all. I have to find a way to <u>make</u> him listen to me, because I'd know it wasn't fair otherwise."*

Therapist: *"What do you think about that?"*

Client: *"I know he's right...it's as if I've always known it. I have to do that, I know I do. I just can't live a boring life. It's not me."*

Therapist: *"Just for a minute I'd like you to think all the way back to when you were first with Brian. Just pretend that Warrior and Nomad had been allowed just a little bit more-"*

Client (interrupting): *"I know what you're saying. It wouldn't've turned out like this, would it? That's what Dog meant when he said I had to be true to myself. And he's told Sally, too. He's told her that you don't have to be nice **all** the time – sometimes you have to be cruel to be kind."*

Therapist: *"So how do you feel about that?"*

Sometimes, this sort of realisation is a 'double-edged sword'; on the one hand there is recognition of the possibility of a better life, on the other there can be guilt and regret which would need to be worked at. In this case, though, there was no problem.

Client: *"Well, it's better to be able to understand and start again now, than to have spent a lifetime of misery. I can see that I tried too hard to be what mum and dad wanted me to be, instead of being me."* She suddenly burst out laughing and said: *"I'm just a little harlot at heart! Well, no, that's not really it... but I do like sex and I do like having fun and I really can't see anything wrong with that. It's just me. I don't like boring and can't do it. I'm not the only person who's like that. It's been the trying to be nice all the time that got me into this, isn't it?"* She laughed again. *"It's all Sally's fault!"* she joked.

This was a satisfactory outcome to this section of the work, so I decided to see if we could move things on somewhat.

Therapist: *"Ok. Do you want to go back to talk to the others now?"*

This is a bit of guiding on my Part, because I could see that there was material here to keep all three Parts as happy as possible. (It was not <u>leading,</u> which would have been: *"Ok, now let's go and talk to the others."*) Had she said that she did not want to go back to talk to them yet, it would have been an indicator that there was more work to be done at the place where she was in her psyche, and, of course, there would be no option but to go along with that. In the event, though, she nodded and almost instantly told me that they were all happy at the idea that she would talk honestly with her husband before making a decision about what should ultimately happen. We then reintegrated the Parts before ending the session.

All this work had been carried out in one rather long session, after which Alison said that she now realised she HAD to talk to husband about her needs in the marriage and realised that unless he and she could find a way of creating change in the way that their relationship works, then there was no lasting future. She felt both the need and the resolve to fully address the issue – something that she had not experienced before.

She returned two weeks later, requesting to do some more work, though did not want to tell me why – she was concerned in case I influenced her in some way. Since I already knew the nature of her problem, I agreed to this.

Although there was some 'WSN' work involved, the session centred on the wrought iron gates, the key, and the car. This time, though, she got into the car which raced away so fast that she could not see the outside world at all but this did not concern her at all. She was more interested in what she would find when the car stopped than she was at what would happen along the journey – a wonderful piece of symbolism.

When the car finally stopped, it was in a meadow with butterflies, birds, sunshine, green grass and blue skies and a forest at the edge, almost perfect symbolism for an end to a successful therapy. Afterwards, she told me that she had now left her husband (although he was unhappy about this, he eventually understood that it was in both their interests) and had wanted the session just to give her confidence that she was doing the right thing for both of them.

She telephoned me a few weeks later to say that her life was 'working out'. She had done some Parts Work successfully on her own, all the Parts were in harmony with each other and she communicated with Dog when she felt the need. All in all, a successful therapy!

Now that you have an understanding of how we work, the remaining case studies will be shown in 'précis' form but will be no less educational. In the next case, it may seem that there is some leading from me, but on closer inspection you will notice that I am simply pursuing what the client presented. Also, don't forget that a fair amount of guiding, where necessary, is perfectly in order, as long as we allow the client to produce the imagery.

Weight problems

Client: Eric, Married, self-employed.

Age: 52 **Duration:** 20 years

Background: Family man, high earner, evident Nomad personality with a taste for the 'high life', with a very pronounced work ethic to support it. His work was as a fencing contractor.

Eric had presented with weight problems previously and we had employed Parts therapy. This had been successful for some considerable time, then came an inexplicable 'crash'. His Inner Advisor, 'Owl', was present throughout this session. The Part that wants to be 'taut' (not slim) is James Bond – James Bond says 'Image is everything'; The Part that wants to remain big is 'Belly', who wants to be big so that he'll be noticed. Belly has a black belt and shirt bursting open.

I could have worked at the fact that both Parts wanted the same objective, but, for some reason, didn't even notice this at the time of the session!

The session under way, I asked for the first image that came to mind. A huge tube, sloping down, big enough to get into. I suggested that Eric get into the tube and follow it. A long time later, the tube corkscrewed upwards and he came out into the sea – body temperature, since he could not feel anything. He said he didn't know where to go. I suggested he could move in any direction he chose and he started flying 'across islands, like a low flying plane'. He Landed. *"What can you see?"* Fingertips. *"Male or Female?"* Male. Right hand. No thumb visible. I was suddenly aware that his mind was working with puns.

Therapist: *"So you could put a finger on it, then?"*
    Client: *"Well, I nearly could but it's turned into a fist... no – a clam."*
Therapist: *"First you could see* (sea), *then you could put your finger on it and now it's clammed up?"*
    Client: *"Yes, that's about right."*
We got the clam to open and it was full of bubbling lava – probably symbolic for danger from the depths of his mind (though I obviously did not point this out)
Therapist: *"Let the lava cool."*
    Client: *"OK, it's really cool now."*
Therapist: *"How does that feel?"*
    Client: *"Yes – feels good."* Suddenly: *"This isn't a part – it's just me thinking a thought..."*
Therapist: *"Tell me."*
    Client: *"Belly is Dad's belly. I want to be like him."*

This was interesting, because there had previously been identification issues with his father, whom he had twice or three times described as 'a big man, in all sorts of ways.'

Therapist: *"What does Belly want?"*

Client: *"Belly wants me to find Dad. Now Owl's flying off somewhere. Never seen Owl fly before."*

Therapist: *"Follow him. See where he takes you."*

Client: *"I am. He's taking me to Dad... I can see him now, sitting in his chair."*

This regressive type of event is not unusual and we should just go with it.

Therapist: *"How does he look?"*

Client: *"Big, like he was at the end. Belly's gone to him, but it's not really Dad's belly."*

Therapist: *"Is that important?"*

Client (after a long pause): *"No. Dad can have it. I want to be like him though."*

Therapist: *"Can you have his way* (weigh), *but not his weight?"*

There was another long pause her, during which Eric smiled broadly.

Client: *"That's true. I see, yes... weigh not weight. I like that. Yes, I think so. Ah – Tube's back. Pointing straight at Dad's nose now."*

Therapist: *"Is that because Dad nose* (knows)*?"*

Client (Big grin): *"I think Dad knows we've fixed something. I don't feel sad – I usually do when I think of him."*

Therapist: *"OK – combine belly, Dad, James Bond, Clam all into one whole being all part of you. Can you do that? (in this context, 'Dad' was a part, hence the integration)"*

Client: *"Yes – feels good."*
Therapist: *"Now let yourself drift to some special place just for you. Tell me when you've found it."*
We had done 'special place' work in a previous session so he knew what this meant.
Client: *"It's an Island on top of a mountain... it's wonderful here. Feeling of lightness."*
Therapist: *"Is that lightness something you're going to find, do you think?"*
Client: *"Yes – I feel very confident right at this moment. I know that I'm going to reach my target weight. It feels absolutely certain. It all makes a lot of sense – I **knew** I was trying to be like my dad, somehow. I don't have to be heavy to be like him, though."*
We finished the session and arranged for another. But true to Nomad form, Eric did not arrive.

Marital problems
Client: Andrew, five times married.
Age: 60 **Duration:** 10 years
Background: Many failed relationships. Current wife has terrorised him for 10 out of 11 years together. Wants to leave, but 'something inside' stops him from saying so or doing it.
Andrew had a difficult childhood with an uncomfortable relationship with his step-father, whom his mother married when he was 8. His father had died in World War II. He manages to seem cheerful even when he is not and believes he should stay with his wife even though he is unhappy. He cannot say why he believes he should stay – *"It's just a feeling."* He insisted that he truly wants to leave, all the time,

234

but feels completely unable to do so. Seemingly of only average intelligence, if that, he had trouble focussing and at times seemed bored.

This was a long drawn out therapy, using an eclectic mix which included hypno-analysis, and only a particularly relevant section of the Parts Work is covered here.

Working with WSN quickly found a stalemate situation, with the three parts all denying responsibility or interest, and so I decided to work with the abstract Fantasy World concept instead. Searching for the source of resistance proved equally fruitless so I opted for something approaching free association.

Therapist: *"Find me a symbol that represents a part of your life – the first thing you can think of."*

Client: *"A huge white ball...it's a great big bouncy thing."*

Therapist: *"Will ball talk to you?"*

Client: *"Nah...it's only bouncy 'cos if you stay down you get kicked..."* There followed a long-ish period of not much communication at the end of which he suddenly announced: *"I always have this problem with saying 'No'"*

Therapist: *"Find a symbol that represents the problem with saying 'No' – the first thing that comes into your mind. The first thing you think of."*

Client: *"It's a little kid. About five or six. A nice little kid, he is."*

Therapist: *"Does he have a name?"*

Client: *"Dunno. He's wearing a pair of them great big glasses."*

Therapist: *"Does he want to talk to you?"*

Client: *"He says he can't see nothing. Poor little sod."*

There was some evidence of emotion here, but when I asked why the 'nice little kid' was a 'poor little sod', he shrugged his shoulders and denied that he felt anything at all, other than being bored with the whole process.

Therapist: *"Would you like to search for the part that wants to leave? Perhaps we can find what the problem is that way."*
Client: *"If you like."*

We struggled here for quite a while, with Andrew continually insisting that there was 'something there but I can't get hold of it.' It appeared to be a shadowy image, indistinct, probably male, which Andrew could apparently feel rather than see.

Eventually, he comes forward as if from a dark mist, covered in bandages, and crawling on all fours. He has been badly burned. Andrew said with some surprise that his three WSN characters had suddenly appeared as if out of nowhere. The Nomad, a Negro medicine seller, helps the newcomer to his feet and gives him some strength to stay upright. The Warrior stands respectfully – this is a commander, long gone and thought dead. He is taken away by the Settler and some 'handmaidens' (Andrew's term) to be healed – it will take a little while, because he has to gather strength. *"This is a part of me that was damaged and left a long time ago. Years ago, when I was just a child... I think my mother damaged him; she knew how, because she was stronger than he was, then. He needs to recover, so that he can stand up to women. He will, I know that for certain."*

236

Therapist: *"How does that feel to you?"*
Client: *"Good. I feel as if I'm beginning to gain strength for myself. I can actually feel it and I know it's right, too. Gotta get that Warrior working."*

As mentioned at the beginning, this is a tiny fragment of a case and it is included as an example of working with a naturally resistant client. I believed that Andrew's subconscious was buying him time here by finding the Part that was needed but ensuring that he did not have to make the necessary changes to his life just yet.

On his final session of therapy, a week or two later, we achieved a deep state of hypnosis within which I delivered suggestion work, both direct and indirect, based upon his recognition of emerging resources based around his Warrior self.

Always late, always drunk.
Client: Lionel, single, City worker.
Age: 29 Duration: 10 years
Background: Youngest of 3 brothers, Lionel had had a problem with punctuality and excessive alcohol consumption since he had left school. He had a tyrannical father and rather weak and submissive mother.

Lionel's mother had died of cancer some two years before he presented for therapy. His father, always a despotic tyrant who had ruled his household by fear, had gone into a decline after the death of his wife and was now in almost constant distress, for which he was taking medication which was proving ineffective. Lionel's problems had accelerated since his mother's death and he often found himself feeling panicky when he observed his father's anguish. "He just never realised what he had until he lost it," he said quietly, "And I'm frightened that I'll never quite realise what life is all about until it's too late."

Because of the fear element that was almost constantly present in his childhood, we conducted a few sessions of hypno-analysis before the Parts work, in order that we might address any 'unfinished business' from those years. We found a fair amount, including more than one severe beating with a walking stick when he had transgressed – the most common 'crime' being coming home late from school or from friends. Only the most salient section of the Parts therapy is shown here; much of what preceded this rambled around without really reaching any point.

Client: *"You'll like this...I can see a great big stick."*
Therapist: *"Does stick want to talk to you?"*
Client: *"Stick doesn't talk...it's just there. It was my Grandfather's. It's the stick my dad used to beat me with. I want to get rid of it."*
Therapist: *"Throw it away."*
Client: *"I can't. It just won't go."*
Therapist: *"Can Warrior, Settler or Nomad help you?"*
Client: *"Nomad's hiding somewhere – Warrior's gone to look after him.*
Therapist: *"What about Settler?"*
Client (frowning): *"She's taking the stick away – it's going with her, as good as gold...this is odd. She's burying it in the ground and sprinkling something on it. Water, I think."*
Therapist: *"And then what?*

Client: *"You know, I understand this. That stick represented old age... it was an old man's stick all gnarled and knobbly. It was my grandfather's, and he was very old and shaky. I can smell him."*

Therapist: *"What's happening now, where Settler buried that stick?"*

Client: *"She's pointing to the ground. I have to go and look..."* There was a pause here, during which he smiled slightly. *"There are a lot of green shoots. All fresh and young. Growing really quickly."*

Over the next few minutes, a new 'young stick' appeared, straight and strong, with an energy contained within it. On the shrub that grew around it were vibrant leaves and flowers, which Lionel recognised as containing a special seed which was the symbol for energy.

After this, therapy proceeded rapidly, centring on self-worth and confidence. In total, there were six Parts therapy sessions, mostly concerned with the recognition of outmoded reasons for behaviour patterns. Almost all of them centred on the Nomad part of personality which, it transpired, always sought to avoid being present when any issues of responsibility were about to be discussed. One of the most profound recognitions was: "It you're rat-arsed, it doesn't matter if you don't make any sense."

I saw him three more times over the following six months and it became apparent that as his confidence increased, so his alcohol consumption steadily reduced to 'normal' levels. On his final visit, he reported that his punctuality was better than he could ever remember it being.

Violent Outbursts
Client: Jane, single, homosexual.
Age: 41. **Duration:** 'Forever'
Background: Jane was a journalist on a magazine running to tight deadlines; she had a long history of violent rages when things weren't going her way and her latest 'episode' had all but cost her her job.

This small snippet is included as an illustration of how this sort of therapy sometimes works without the therapist having the vaguest idea why – or what has been resolved in the client's psyche. Jane was adept at creative work and quickly became absorbed in the WSN concept, developing very complete Warrior, Settler and Nomad archetypes. Work proceeded, with the Warrior and the Nomad agreeing that they both 'owned' the problem; Warrior was very reluctant to contemplate any sort of compromise. I decided to do some Inner Advisor work.

I outlined the idea, as shown in Lesson Five and asked Jane if she was happy to meet her own Inner Advisor. She said she was, and her 'special place' turned out to be an ancient ruined village with a golden-domed temple the only complete building still standing. It wasn't long before her Inner Advisor put in his appearance:

> **Client:** *"I can see something coming towards me…it's not a person, though…"*
> **Therapist:** *"Tell me what you find."*
> **Client:** *"It's a wolf. He's kind of loping towards me quite purposefully, but he's not fierce, I don't think… He's here in front of me now."*
> **Therapist:** *"Has wolf got anything to say to you?"*

240

Client: *"He says I have to follow him... he wants me to follow him into that temple."* At this point she frowned deeply. *"This isn't my Inner Advisor...my Inner Advisor's in the temple...I have to meet him in there. I don't like this very much, actually."*

The wolf was just a messenger, it would appear; it may not be clear to us why the subconscious has chosen to work this way but we should not argue with it. There was a long pause here, and I eventually said:

Therapist: *"Are you going into the temple?"*

Without making a suggestion to do so, this gave her the option to change tack if she wanted to.

Client: *"No, I don't think so...Oh, wait a minute, I think... Ah, I've gone in there now – and this suddenly makes so much sense! My God, I understand everything! I remember now... I **know** why I've always been so quick off the mark... and it just isn't necessary, is it?"*

For the next few minutes, Jane's conversation was almost completely one-sided and made little sense to the therapist! I was wondering about what she had remembered that brought about such a sudden understanding when she opened her eyes and grinned at me. *"If you think I'm telling you about that, you've got another think coming!"* she said with a laugh. Then: *"You get much better results if you use your head instead of your temper, you know..."*

Clearly, much more had gone on than Jane was about to divulge; she was delighted with the single session we had done and said that she didn't need to see me again, she knew the problem had been fixed. She took her leave, saying that she'd call me if she needed to but I heard nothing more from her.

Stutter
Client: Gary, single, few friends.
Age: 21
Background: Critical and impatient father who has always been almost impossible to please. Mother constantly reminded him that he didn't try hard enough to get things right. Manages a retail shop that belongs to his parents and confesses to great fear whenever his father is around. Embarrassment about his stutter means that he seldom socialises.

Because much of Gary's stress and fear levels appeared to be directly connected with childhood experiences concerning parental attitudes and events, I commenced therapy with hypnoanalysis. There were several small abreactive states and one major one which I was reasonably confident was associated with the ISE from which his stutter had originated. He understood this and also believed that the event had been of great importance, yet his stutter remained unabated.

I was certain that it was now nothing more than an Acquired Behaviour Complex – something that Parts therapy can often resolve quite quickly, once the underlying emotional difficulty, if there is one, has been cleared.

Although I introduced Gary to the WSN concept, as usual, I decided to take a different route on this occasion. Since the symptom was so physical and specific, I asked Gary to find the Part that can only communicate by stuttering. Sometimes, things do not proceed the way that you might imagine, though...

Client: *"I can see me... when I'm little. About five."*
Therapist: *"Is that the same you that you saw when we were doing analysis?"*
Client: *"No... this one doesn't have a stutter. This one doesn't talk at all."*
Therapist: *"Does he have a name?"*
Client: *"Yes... he's Boy Gary."*
Therapist: *"Will he talk to you?"*
Client: *"No. He won't talk to anybody. He's forgotten how to talk."*

We chased around the edges of this for quite some time and I was just beginning to look for a different approach, when:

Client: *"He has a friend who does the talking."*
Therapist: *"Can you see his friend?"*
Client: *"Yes... it's a cartoon character, a goblin. **He's** the one with the stutter."*

So here we were at last, in the company of the Part with the stutter. Only we were not done yet. Goblin, apparently, did not really have communication skills, which is why he could only speak with a stutter, because he had to keep on

243

checking that what he was going to say was correct. Another problem reared its head; Goblin simply refused to give up his speaking job and refused to leave when asked. Gary began to become visibly annoyed and it was apparent that there was a need for stronger intervention here!

Therapist: *"Look around you. You'll find something that will deal with Goblin."*
Client: *"I've already found it. It's like a sort of gun, only not with bullets."*
Therapist: *"What are you going to do with the gun?"*

We could have had a conversation with the gun, probably, but since Gary already seemed to know its purpose, this might have been counter-productive.

Client: *"I'm going to fire it at Goblin... Ha! A thread shot out of the end and there's a bag which has completely swallowed up Goblin!"*
Therapist: *"And what are you going to do with that?"*
Client: *"Nothing. The bag's changing something – I want to open it, but I can't."*

After a few minutes of fruitless searching for a way to open the bag, we decided that Warrior would probably find a way – and so he did, opening the bag with a touch of his hand.

Goblin had been transformed into another version of Gary – called 'Gary 2' – this time a fine and strong young man but one who was mute. We 'found' a crystal which conferred the power of speech... with a stutter! More intervention was needed from the therapist...

Therapist: *"Ok, Gary. Will this new Part **learn** to speak easily, if somebody teaches him properly?"*
Client: *"I don't know. He seems quite comfortable. Safe, somehow."*

This was not surprising. Gary's whole persona was based around the fact that he had a stutter; change would be either dramatic or not at all. Of course, this was the reason for the stutter continuing even after the release of the ISE that had promoted it.

Therapist: *"Find a symbol that means safe. The first thing that comes to mind."*
Client: *"A house...Gary 2 likes the house. He wants me to stay there."*
Therapist: *"He doesn't want you to go out?"*
Client: *"No. He wants me to stay indoors where it's safe."*

We did some 'timelining' work here, projecting forward in stages of two years, then five years, with Gary describing how life seemed. After moving forward in time to fifty years old, where everything had remained the same, he described his projected existence as a 'waste of a life'.

Therapist: *"What do you think about that?"*
Client: *"It's horrible. I don't want that – I want to be able to go out and have fin!"*

245

Therapist: *"What will you do when you can go out?"*

The significance of this question and the phrasing of it should be evident.

Client: *"Get a girlfriend maybe...I had one once."*
Therapist: *"And how was that?"*
Client: *"It was fantastic! I met her when she worked in the shop, but it all went wrong when she laughed at me stuttering one day. Don't think she meant it nastily, though."*
Therapist: *"So will Gary 2 learn to speak easily so that you can find that sort of fantastic again?"*
Client: *"He says yes, this time. He's willing to try."*
Therapist: *"Is there a Part who wants to help?"*
Client: *"Yes...I think so..."* There was a pause here, during which Gary remained motionless, save for a faint tapping of one finger on the arm of the chair. *"All of them... the Warrior will control the breathing, the Nomad will make the words come out, and the Settler will make it feel really good."*
Therapist: *"And are you happy for them all to do this?"*
Client: *"Yes. They're saying that it'll take a bit of time, but I'm very happy about it all."*

We finished therapy with the WSN parts in agreement to perform their task diligently and patiently (important, because of Gary's background) and the agreement from 'Gary 2' that he would be equally patient about gradually acquiring a whole new pattern of speech. Reintegration completed, Gary seemed somewhat bemused by the whole process, though agreed that he felt very hopeful that his stutter would eventually disappear.

I had a telephone call from him about three months after therapy, with little evidence of a stutter, to tell me he had a new girlfriend and that her influence had built his confidence up so that he hardly stuttered at all now.

Nothing to do with the therapy, of course...

The foregoing will have given you a good idea of how this sort of therapy may be applied and how it works. In common with all therapeutic strategies, though, there is nothing to compare with hands on experience. So rustle up a few friends who'd like to make changes in their lives and then practice, practice, practice! After a relatively short time, you'll be ready to unleash your new skill upon your clients.

PART THREE

Some Miscellaneous Ideas and Concepts

This third part of the book contains various scripts, routines, case histories and other material that is bound to help you in your therapeutic endeavours. There are entire chapters on Abreaction and Catharsis, Sexual Issues, and Emetophobia – an illness which is often greatly misunderstood and which can cause a sufferer to live in constant fear.

As with the rest of the book, all the material here is in use on a regular basis by the author and all of it has been tried and tested many hundreds of times with clients and students.

CHAPTER THIRTEEN
Handling abreaction and catharsis

The author has been using analytical techniques of hypnotherapy since 1989 and has handled literally thousands of abreactive states in that time. For those who fear repercussions, it is worth the recognition that no client has ever complained or protested about any part of the therapy.

Abreaction

Of all the phenomena encountered by the working hypnotherapist – or stage hypnotist, for that matter – the abreaction is probably the least understood, or perhaps the most *mis*understood. The first encounter the therapist has with this process of the mind is inclined to polarise him/her and from that moment on s/he will either seek to avoid it like the plague or search it out with a determination that is at least equal to the client's resistance.

It can be the type of training we receive that governs this response, along with our observation of the effect and affects it has upon our client; those who are trained as analysts are delighted by abreaction, live (in the therapeutic sense) for abreaction, and firmly believe that it provides the fastest and most profound relief from all manner of psychological symptoms. Others, trained in methods other than analysis, may be less certain of this, viewing the sudden intensely emotional state with alarm, fearing that lasting harm is being done to the client and as a result start frantically searching for ways to calm down what their administrations have 'caused'.

Not a response

In fact, the therapy that was being applied has little to do with it. The abreaction is not a response to therapy (though there are many who will say that it is) but is the revivification of an event long past. Notice the word 'Revivification' – this most emphatically not a 'reliving' of the event, that can cause damage of some sort to your client's psyche. In truth, although it can often *appear* to be harrowing enough that an untrained observer might imagine that the therapist should be locked away somewhere, it is nothing more dramatic than a vivid recall of the emotional responses to a repressed or forgotten event, usually of a profoundly traumatic nature and usually from our formative years. Handled well, it can do nothing but good; it cannot cause your client lasting harm and it cannot leave them worse off than before they came to you, no matter what you might read to the contrary.

This is such a contentious issue for some that it bears further discussion here.

From time to time there have been stories of individuals who went to a therapist for a minor therapy such as smoking cessation and ended up remembering childhood abuse or some other traumatic situation. Sometimes, it is pub/stage hypnotist who 'creates' this situation. Often, the claim is made of the individual's life being ruined by years of depression, induced psychosis, even death, following the incident and, predictably, there are demands that all hypnosis and hypnotherapy should be outlawed. Of course, many of

250

the stories are apocryphal and sensationalised beyond recognition by the media – which not infrequently fails to take the trouble to find out what truth there is in the claim that has been made. The story would almost always be found to be not worthy of publication were they to do so.

One of the most recent claimants won the cost of the case only (with no damages), because the stage hypnotist had breached the terms of the stage hypnosis act by inducing regression. She had recalled sexual abuse and had apparently suffered depression for some considerable time afterwards. In an interview after the case, she somewhat sheepishly said that the depression had been resolved by hypnosis! The case made the National Media; the fact that hypnosis had 'cured' her did not.

The Real Culprit
The thing to recognise is that if abreaction is the revivification of a traumatic event past, that event was stored in subconscious and having an effect upon the psyche long before the client ever met the therapist. There are many who believe that we do not need to 'rake over the past' and that we can safely let 'sleeping dogs lie'. There are therapists who will assert that all that is needed is to collapse an anchor or unlatch a behaviour/thought symptomatic process from the event that is causing it. This is actually true – provided the client truly *does* know what event it was that is causing their current problem. It is when that event is an *erroneous association* that any unlatching or anchor collapsing process will ultimately fail.

Erroneous Association
This is the situation wherein an individual is absolutely certain that he or she is aware of the traumatic event which is the cause of, say, Claustrophobia. If the client is correct and that event is worked at, then he or she will be released from the symptom pattern and will probably stay released.

Sometimes, though, it is as if the subconscious prefers to attach the symptom to something which is easier to tolerate than the originating cause or *Initial Sensitising Event* and that is where we can run into trouble. Working at that secondary event will still produce a release of symptoms and everything will be fine until/unless the client encounters a bit of life that retriggers the emotional response that caused the symptom in the first place. Only, this time, it is likely that an entirely new symptomatic behaviour will occur and to the client – and the unwary therapist – it will seem totally unconnected with the original symptom.

We are not saying here that analysis is the only way to work. We are saying that sometimes, it is the only way to find a lasting release from symptoms and the agent of that lasting release is the catharsis that is created by abreaction. This is particularly common where the problems, either causal or symptomatic, are of a sexual nature.

The Secret
Leaving aside the techniques of regression, free association, clean language, and other necessities associated with analytical working, the secret of a good analytical encounter is **Completion.** It is when the abreaction is left in an incomplete state that the client may well suffer all sorts of

uncomfortable states of mind – and that *is* the fault of the therapist.

There is only one way to complete an abreaction and that is to go all the way through the traumatic memory until it can be discussed without much in the way of emotional arousal on the client's part.

Dragging your client off to a 'safe place' somewhere in his mind may well quieten him down and allow the session to be completed on time; but it will leave in a highly sensitised state in which he may well be far more reactive to any stimuli that remind the subconscious of that event. These are the circumstances in which a client may well end up depressed, anxious, panicky, tearful, suffering migraines, or any other of a host of reactions.

Complications

Of course, there are complications possible here. Here are the three main possibilities:

1. The abreaction happens entirely spontaneously with an inexperienced or maybe even incompletely trained therapist.
2. The client 'sticks' or becomes frightened and does not manage to complete the abreaction.
3. The client goes through the trauma over and again but the emotional levels do not abate.

We will examine each situation separately.

1. The Spontaneous Abreaction

There is no need to panic when this happens – in fact it is enormously important not to. The client will pick up such a reaction instantly and this will create a trauma all on its own.

Remain calm. Take the client to a 'Safe Place' if you have created one (and you should have done so) and continue to work at relaxation until you have achieved stability. At the end of the session, assure your client that what he has just experienced is nothing more dramatic than evidence that there is a memory of some sort 'down there' that is the cause of his symptoms. The good news is that it is now accessible and he can be set free forever simply by visiting a therapist who specialises in such things – and then contact your trade association to tell of the event and ask them to recommend a suitably experienced worker as soon as possible.

Although this is safe way to work, it is not truly the best method (except where there are age-related issues – see later); the best way is to remain confident and urge your client to 'stay with it', to allow himself to feel whatever he is feeling, while reassuring him that no harm will come to him and that when you take him out of hypnosis he will feel absolutely fine – and he will. Get him to discuss the event enough times that he begins to become bored by it.

Before long, the emotion will subside; the whole thing will usually last no longer than five minutes or so – and that five minutes will have improved your client's life inestimably. It is not at all unusual for a client to exit a session with such a sense of euphoric well-being that he bursts out laughing on opening his eyes!

2. The Client 'sticks'
The situation where the client seems unable to complete the abreaction for whatever reason can cause us the most difficulty. There is usually a strong physical component which abruptly disappears, leaving both client and therapist

wondering what on earth had just been accessed. The problem here is that there has been a 'shut down' for any one of a number of reasons – fear, protecting somebody else's integrity and/or protecting integrity of self amongst them – and it is as if the subconscious has now been alerted to what has instantly become a 'no go' area.

The problem is that there is definitely something in the psyche that needs to be resolved but to which the 'access path' has just been closed. It serves no purpose to go over and over the events of the session that led to the abreaction; that door has now been closed. In the experience of the author, it is extremely unlikely that the block will be breached by the same therapist or therapeutic method. Fortunately, this seems to be a fairly rare occurrence.

3. Emotion Not Abating

Although in some ways the most worrying to the inexperienced therapist, this is actually the easiest situation to handle. If the emotion is sustained at the same level after voicing the details of the memory four times or more, then it is highly likely that you are working at a Secondary Sensitising Event (or erroneous association) rather than the origination cause of trauma. Even more importantly, the *Initial Sensitising Event* is available to consciousness, otherwise the emotion would subside; so all the therapist has to do is to urge the client to *"go further back now"* if using age regression, or *"let your mind jump somewhere else and tell the very next thing you think of"'* if using free association techniques. This will almost always result in a sudden access of that which is being sought.

Contra-indicators

The following contra-indicators need to be observed:

- **Severe Asthma**
- **Cardio-Vascular illness (stroke, heart attack, angina)**
- **Advanced Age**
- **Epilepsy**
- **Previous ECT (Electro Convulsive Therapy)**

All of the above are distinct contra-indicators for the use of any form of age-regression or analytical style of therapy, although conscious work may be carried out with caution.

In the case of **Severe Asthma**, the abreactive state can trigger an attack; it is probably advisable to avoid hypnoanalysis (not necessary when the illness is mild to moderate) and when working consciously, always be sure that the client has his inhaler immediately to hand. It is best to avoid any sort of investigative therapy where there is **Cardio-Vascular Illness**; an abreactive state can occur even with conscious analytical psychotherapy and can place a great strain on a weakened system, creating a potential risk of an 'event'.

In the case of the remaining three contra-indicators, it is not so much that harm may be done (although some insist that epilepsy and hypnosis do not mix very well) as that analytical work is likely to be ineffective. Where there is **Great Age,** early memories, the ones we want to work with, most of the time, will have had many years of development of coping/avoidance strategies and these have become so entrenched that it is unlikely that we will break through them.

With **Epilepsy**, there is often difficulty in achieving any state of hypnosis or, indeed, acute mental focus; also, stress can trigger an attack.

Finally, when **ECT** has been administered, there will have been destruction of brain cells making recall unclear (which is one of the reasons that it is used to treat depression) and unreliable. It is worth noting, too, that this is a barbaric (in the view of the author) treatment actually creates a convulsive seizure. It was arrived at as a result of the observation that few sufferers of Epilepsy suffered deep depressions, or, at least, not for very long; the reasoning was that if you create convulsions by an electrical charge into the brain, then it may cure depression. Sometimes it works, sometimes it does not, and although evidence of its effectiveness or otherwise is inconclusive it is still in use in some psychiatric units today.

Three Parts
There can be three separate, though intimately connected, memories involved with any form of repression:

- **The perception of the event (most often visual)**
- **The physical sensations**
- **The emotional response.**

They entirely separate memories and each may 'surface' together or individually. It is not unusual for a client to recall, in one session, a physical sensation of some sort so strongly that s/he can actually *feel* it, yet not discover the emotional response or the exact nature of the event until their next session or even the one after that. It is the emotional part of any abreaction (often unwarranted guilt, shame, or vulnerability) that is the most important and once this has been 'surfaced' and worked through to completion, it is likely that the client will display little or no interest in further investigation of that particular memory. For this reason, we need to be wary when ascribing a physical event to an emotion that was previously released, however well it seems to 'fit'. Once the emotion has been discharged, then any physical event recalled after that is likely to have its own, as yet not discovered, emotional associations that may need to be 'unearthed'.

It is not uncommon, in fact, for an emotion to be released without ever discovering what was the cause of it; this appears to matter little, for the emotionally cleansing of catharsis will still be effected and associated symptoms alleviated.

Vividly Realistic

This revivification can be so realistic, as far as the client is concerned, that his body may actually reproduce the physical changes that occurred at the time of the event; if there was an element of suffocation, for example, your client may suddenly find great difficulty breathing – or may even stop breathing for a few moments. If they were physically abused in some way, then they may well feel that same abuse – or the results of it – whilst in your chair, just as if it were happening to them right at that very moment. The author has seen finger marks appear where a slap on the face has been recalled.

There is no mystery here, for it is simply the autonomic system perceiving pain and reacting by increasing blood

258

supply to the area to effect any repair that is necessary. A client may scream, shout, sob, sweat, shake violently, curl up into a foetus, gag... it can be a truly unnerving experience for the inexperienced worker. All the therapist has to do, though, is make sure that he 'goes for it' whole-heartedly. Urge him on through it, though being careful, via the use of *'clean language'* only to guide and not lead. Sound confident and *be* confident. Tell him to 'just be there in your mind'. Urge him to 'stay with it – give it room in your body'.

Now, this is of enormous importance: do not touch him – unless you are determined either to become part of the trauma or to close the abreaction down and make it irretrievable. Although it is difficult for some to observe apparent anguish, for your client to receive a physical touch at that moment can seem like an electric shock. And what if you just happen to touch where he is already experiencing some abreactive memory? Not only that, it may distract him from the job in hand and he needs no comforting right at that moment, anyway. Something wonderful is happening; he is setting himself free from a prison of his mind's making and his life is going to change immeasurably for the better over the next few months.

It can be difficult, for the caring individual, to sit and watch this event that is so evidently full of pain unfolding in front of them, but once you have experienced the sense of lightness and relief that a client can manifest immediately after the abreaction has subsided, you will have no more problem with that. It is not fair to say that all their symptoms will disappear overnight, but from that cathartic moment onwards, your client will start to *feel* well and his symptomatic work will very soon start to fade. Usually, you and your client will have an understanding of why the event that has been remembered should have caused their symptoms. If not, it always possible that there is something else to be released but, this time, it is likely to be less intense.

An Important 'Recap'

There is something that is so important about abreaction and analytical styles of therapy that it is worth a brief 'recap': make *absolutely certain* that your client had accessed the emotional 'roots' of his psychological difficulty and got it all out. It is the **originating cause of trauma** (or ISE) that we are after and nothing else will do. It is actually quite easy to ascertain whether he has been to the right place or not... if the emotional response does not start to fade within a few minutes, or if it returns to its former strength each time the memory is accessed, then there is still work to do. Work backwards from that memory using either direct regression or free associative techniques to an earlier memory with the same or similar emotional qualities and work through that one in the way you have just been reading about. Keep going until the negative emotion has cleared and cannot be restored. The client is then well on the road to sound emotional health.

CHAPTER FOURTEEN

Working with sexual issues without embarrassment

Client Sexuality

It is a fact that your client will be affected by his/her sexuality in some way or another, even if it is not directly part of the presenting problem. This is certainly not to say that sex is always at the root of everything, merely that sexuality is inescapably part of your client's life and therefore, via the connectedness of everything, it can be having more of an effect than might be recognised.

What is certain is that if you are not at ease with the subject, you will inhibit your client and in the event that the presenting problem *is* bound up with their sexuality in some way, then you may not provide the best therapy you can.

It may be that some of you find yourself feeling uncomfortable with some aspects of the work given here; if so, it is nothing more than an indicator that you have a problem yourself which should be addressed if you are to become the best therapist you can be.

To work effectively, it is absolutely essential that you:

1. **Understand the total difference between the way that males and females function as far as**

**instinctive and 'natural' sexual behaviour is
concerned.**

2. **Are totally at ease discussing sexual behaviour in a
non-embarrassing and non-embarrassed manner.**

The remainder of this chapter is based around an article
and the notes for a talk that has been given many times in
seminars by **Terence Watts.**

"The title of this talk, 'Sex in the Office' certainly raises
a few eyebrows!

Originally, the sub-title was: *Confident working with
sexual issues of the opposite sex* and, to an extent, that
remains the main objective of this presentation But there is
an awful lot of misunderstanding generally about sexual
function and what is 'normal' and I hope that, after this, you
will be able to begin to work more comfortably and
knowledgeably in this area.

Some years ago, I asked a client a question which
brought about a very interesting, if somewhat brief,
conversation:

Me: *Tell me about your sex life. Is it ok?*
Client: *There are more important things in life than sex,
you know!*
Me: *I find that difficult to believe – without sex there
would not **be** any life...*
Client: *Ah...*

There followed a few moments of silence, after which he
(yes, it *was* a male!) smiled somewhat sheepishly and told
me that it was an uncomfortable area for him, because he was
not very good at it and his wife didn't like it anyway. I asked

him to tell me more about this and for the next hour, listened to a tale of marital disaster centred on poor communication and many sexual misunderstandings.

After a few sessions of therapy, he discovered two important things that changed his life. One was that he actually *was* good at it if he took enough time. The second was that his wife *did* like it, with exactly the same caveat – if he took enough time.

Sex and guilt...

Now, I have a total lack of inhibition about discussing every aspect of sex and sexuality, be it heterosexual, homosexual or bi, fetish, fantasy or whatever, so I have always been able to work effectively in this area. The effect upon the psyche of guilt that surrounds the masturbation complex, fetishes and fantasies and other assorted 'no go areas', even 'normal' sex, has always fascinated me and I was working effectively with these situations from very early on in my practice.

My interest started many years ago with the somewhat stilted media coverage of the Masters and Johnson research and the Kinsey reports; it is an interesting observation that Dr. Alfred Kinsey actually filled Wembley stadium when he gave a public talk on female sexuality. Much has been written about their work – it has been the source of some of my own research – and the best place to find out more is the Internet search engines. You will soon see what I mean when I say that I can really only just 'scratch the surface' in this presentation.

Both those pieces of research centred around the sexual behaviour and response patterns in both male and female, and were quite clinical; what interests me is the interaction and misunderstandings that occur between men and women *as a result* of those frequently gender-specific responses. What was secret in the days when those research projects were carried out *remains* a secret for many people.

Not a 'Q-tip'!

There were two events which led to me preparing this talk. The first was a wonderful moment on one of my classes when a young male observed that he could not understand why women 'made such a fuss about the smear test' – we were talking about gender-related issues at the time. A lively conversation between him and one of the lady members revealed that he truly believed that a smear was gathered by something like a cotton-wool bud or a 'Q-tip'; amid much snorting, another female member of the class, a midwife, announced that she would bring a speculum with her on the next lesson – which she did. All of the males winced at the instrument.

The second event was some research I carried out on sexuality and personality (though this was actually carried out before the event in the classroom); the results showed an enormous gulf of understanding between men and women about how each *truly* functioned as far as sexuality was concerned. Worse, when I spoke to one or two colleagues, I discovered many of the same misunderstandings, along with some unfounded judgementalism. *"Men always..."* and *"Women never..."* were common 'universal quantifier' phrases that I heard over and again, though linked to a variety of different concepts and attitudes.

So it was that I decided to give working with sexuality a higher profile on my classes; not because I believe it is an issue with every client but because I wanted my students to work effectively and without embarrassment when it *is*. Knowledge and understanding create confidence; confidence allays embarrassment.

Embarrassed and embarrassing

Here is something of enormous importance:

If you are embarrassed, you will be embarrassing.

An embarrassed client will find it difficult, if not impossible, to talk to you about such intimate matters as sexual intercourse, anal sex, masturbation, vaginismus, erectile failure, penetration fear, ejaculation, anorgasmia and the like. Male therapists need to understand female sexuality, including the mechanism of orgasm and the importance of the 'plateau phase', even if they are working with a male client – you may need to 'educate' him so that he and his partner can have a better life. If you are working with a female client, then you will very quickly lose client confidence if you display ignorance or false understandings.

Female therapists need to understand the emotional and psychological difficulties that surround male sexuality. You will be able to help your female clients to more readily understand their partner's sometimes rather excessive attitudes (which so often give rise to the *'men always'* type of statement); and you will create a wonderful working relationship with a male when he realises that you *truly* understand the way he functions. He will respond to therapy

265

from the part of his psyche that is associated with our most profound function – the perpetuation of the human species.

Male therapists need to understand that sex is usually not as immediately important to females as it is to males. This is not something that is a matter of choice, but of evolution; women do not need sexual arousal to complete the act of procreation, while men *do*. Men, like most male animals, constantly hunt for it. Females have therefore never had to. You will be able to help your male clients to recognise that they are *not* being rejected when their partner is simply 'not in the mood'. You will also help them to understand that a lot of the time, when their sex life is not working the way they want it to, they may have had more responsibility in the creation of this unsatisfactory state than they might otherwise have imagined. Females are capable of *seven times* the amount of sexual pleasure than is a man; the male who does not take enough time to help his partner find that pleasure will usually be missing out.

Females will respond extremely well to therapy with a male therapist who truly understands the way she functions; it is even likely that she will be more comfortable discussing, for instance, Vaginismus, than she would be with a female therapist who she believed functioned perfectly well.

All therapists can gain an understanding of the way that each sex functions and why, in order to help clients rebuild that area of their relationships.

Same sex therapist?

Some therapists believe that sexual issues should be dealt with by a therapist of the same sex.

When I have asked those 'same sex' pundits why they feel that way, I usually get told it is obvious that somebody would prefer to talk to their own sex about such matters, and anyway, it is a quick way in to litigation. But I have often felt that this is a rationalisation and that the real reason is lack of sound knowledge of how the opposite sex works. If so, then they are foregoing some wonderful opportunities to restore to their clients one of the fundamental pleasures of life and relationships.

I have had females discussing masturbation, for instance, quite comfortably with me; and my female students and graduates report that men find it easy to talk to them about erectile difficulties – something a male may very well *not* want to discuss with another male. By the time they have finished their training, most of my students are no more uncomfortable than I am talking about any sexual issue with either sex.

Discomfort on display

If you are uncomfortable when talking about sexuality, you will soon give the game away. You will say relevant words louder, softer, faster, or mispronounced; you will speed up or slow down your body language, shuffle your feet, or exhibit some sort of displacement activity every time you have to utter a 'forbidden' word or the conversation moves into a 'risqué' area. All of this will perhaps be almost imperceptible, but your client will notice, albeit at a subconscious level, and start to exhibit very similar behaviour patterns; so if you observe this, pay attention to your own comfort level whilst dealing with such matters. If you are *genuinely* at ease, then you will feel no different from when you are discussing any other serious subject; bulimia, say, anorexia, or perhaps emetophobia (fear of vomit or vomiting).

Here's an experiment in thought process:

1. Client A presents with emetophobia and becomes panicky talking about vomiting.
2. Client B presents with a vomit fetish and becomes sexually aroused when talking about it.

If your reaction to those two scenarios differs, then you may have a problem.

Of course, you could just give yourself some suggestion or reframe work to help you get past such difficulties; you could refuse to work with sexual issues with the opposite sex, or with sexual issues at all – easy enough, because you would simply refer such clients on to another therapist, with the advice that this is somebody who specialises in this sort of issue. Or you could deal with it the easy way; that is, by gaining knowledge and understanding. So, to that end, we'll now have a look at some of the differences, confusions, and oddities of human sexual behaviour, along with some possible reasons for those anomalies.

Eating pillows

One of the major differences between men and women is in sexual urgency. If sexual activity, including masturbation, is suspended for some reason, most women are able to get on reasonably comfortably with their life and will function fairly normally – more so with the passage of time. Not the male, though. After just a few days he's almost beginning to bite lumps out of doors and eat pillows! And after a few weeks, he will be looking at the backsides and/or breasts of females in whom he might not show a great deal of interest in the usual way. He has no choice in this matter; it is a function of the male psyche and he would be abnormal if he did *not* work that way. Women also have no choice in their adjustment to the situation and there are few who *actually need* regular sexual activity to remain psychologically comfortable, even if they may prefer it. The following paragraphs might throw some light on the reasons behind this...

Expectation v. hope

Many women get understandably irritated because it seems to them that men <u>expect</u> them to join in sexual activity at the drop of a hat; the reality is that men <u>hope,</u> rather than expect, that their lady will be amenable to the idea. They do not help their cause, though, by becoming bad-mannered and bad-tempered when it does not work out that way. But consider:

Biologically, a man is designed to father 365 children a year and he knows this at a subconscious level; biologically, women are designed to produce **one** *child a year. The window of opportunity to the female is quite wide and there is therefore sometimes little urgency associated with a single act of intercourse. But to the male subconscious, ONE missed chance equals one less progeny, one less procreative effort on behalf of the species. This is a threat to the survival of the species.*

<u>Obviously, it's not interpreted that way as far as the conscious mind is concerned and it's only a hypothesis, in any case.</u> But it accounts for the way that a perfectly

reasonable male suddenly transforms into a scowling, vehement individual, which serves to convince his partner that he was only interested in sex, anyway, and not in her. Not a surprise, then, that she might become irritated and unwilling when he wants to do it the next day... or compliant, but unenthusiastic.

Unfortunately, the male interprets this perfectly understandable response as if it means what it would if *he* were behaving the same way: *"She's punishing me."* Without communication, this situation can so easily self-cycle to the point where masturbation becomes more frequent than intercourse and ensuing guilt means an even greater block to sexual communications.

Always on or always on standby?

One of the difficulties of maleness is that the sex drive, in normal health, is permanently <u>on</u> and can only be turned off with difficulty. They have no choice in the matter. Women, on the other hand, have a sex drive which is permanently on standby but can be turned on relatively easily... if the circumstances are just right (though they actually have somewhat more choice in the process than the male has in his). The possibilities for misunderstanding here should be obvious and it is important to recognise that *neither male nor female has any choice in this basic method of functioning. Men do not **choose** to be constantly aware; women do not **choose** to be generally less speedy to arouse. Neither one is better or more responsible than the other, neither one deserves criticism for this inherited instinctive behaviour.*

270

A sign of the times

Men often suffer sexual insecurity – in our modern life they know they cannot necessarily follow those inherited instincts for frequent sexual activity and yet it is a psychologically essential part of male behaviour patterns. This psychological need, when not met adequately, can sometimes result in depression.

Women tend to be less prone to this sort of insecurity for two reasons: firstly, the instinctive need tends to be lower, for the reasons discussed in the hypothesis given earlier; secondly, in general it is far easier for a woman to get sexual activity when she wants to, especially within a relationship.

Sexual insecurity manifests itself in many ways, two of which are immensely irritating to women:

1. 'Pawing and grabbing' at every opportunity
2. The constant harangue/innuendo

Must that always happen?

A female client complained to me that her partner would always get an erection whenever he cuddled her. As far as she was concerned, this showed that 'that's all he thinks of'. She felt better about it when I explained that a man doesn't actually have a great deal of control over the wretched thing – cuddle a lady he loves, and up it comes! It is actually a compliment, for it would not happen if he did NOT find her attractive.

Whilst it is perfectly possible for a man to want sex with someone without loving that person, just as it is for a woman, if his psycho-sexual function is 'normal' he simply *cannot* love a woman without wanting to have intercourse with her;

and if she is clinically unable for some reason, it <u>will</u> create problems for him (though he may very well choose to discover a coping strategy to deal with those problems).

Women function differently here, in that it is far more likely that she could love an impotent man without suffering unbearable sexual frustration. I am not saying here that she always will, only that research suggests that women find it far easier to deal with this difficulty.

Something contentious

Now here is something that tends to be anathema to women – until they have thought about it: *What's wrong with a woman having sexual intercourse with her partner when she doesn't really want to?* A man simply *cannot*, if, for some reason, he's not 'in the mood'; but a woman can, albeit with the aid of some KY jelly or baby oil to avoid discomfort. So, <u>if she loves him</u>, what on earth is wrong with just doing it? No need to harbour resent – if it is done from choice and love rather than to 'shut him up'.

Yes, ladies, I *do* understand the 'it's my body' argument; but it's also your relationship and the needs of the partner you love.

But males don't escape here! What is wrong with a man encouraging and helping his partner to masturbate against his leg if she wants/needs sexual gratification when he does not? If he loves her, he will be pleased at the intimacy this produces. This is actually a wonderful aid to couples where the male suffers impotence – I refer to it jokingly as a 'leg shag' and it has helped many individuals to restore happiness and sometimes restored virility as a result of increased excitation and the removal of 'performance anxiety'.

272

The best evidence

Now, if you need a bit more convincing about the differences between male and female attitudes toward sexuality, try this: Tell a man something like: *"If you take her out for a meal in a romantic restaurant and court her, buy her champagne and a red rose, tell her she's beautiful, and be attentive to her every need, then you'll be very likely to have good sex later on…"* and he will more often than not decide that it's a good idea. Suggest to most women that they should behave in that manner toward a man in order to get good sex and most will make some disparaging remark… but then again, all women know that they do not have to do that – all they have to do is ask!

In a connected vein, offer a women the choice of a wonderful meal in a wonderful restaurant or three hours of sex and most of the time, she will choose the meal; offer the same thing to a man and… well, no contest!

You may feel that this article has carried a slight bias in favour of maleness. If so, consider:

- *It was written by a male and there may be a natural bias to write that way, even though I sought to avoid it.*
- *If you are female, there may be a natural bias to read it that way, even thought <u>you</u> may seek to avoid it.*
- *Traditionally, males have tended to receive more criticism about their attitude to sex and sexual activity, so there is necessarily more ground to cover in an article of this sort.*
- *That it seems so may well be an illustration of the problems that I have been writing about.*

Conclusion

In conclusion, I leave you with what I hope is a helpful thought or two: none of us, male or female, can help being turned on or not being turned on. We cannot help being sexual or non-sexual. We do not actually choose any of it and we cannot help finding the 'wrong' person attractive sometimes; it is a fact, though, that we do have free choice as to whether to act upon that attraction or not.

Therapists, more than anybody else, must understand this – man or woman, we do not *choose* our feelings and all feelings are valid, even if not rational.

"God gave man enough blood to power both his penis and his brain – but not at the same time!" Anon.

CHAPTER FIFTEEN
A fearful illness – obsessive Emetophobia

Obsession v. Phobia

One of the most important things a client should recognise about Emetophobia is that it is not always a phobia. Most of the time, it simply will not respond to **Barnett's** six step cure, NLP, EFT, TFT, dissociation, or any other 'quick fix' techniques.

Just occasionally, it *is* a 'normal' phobia or conditioned response, when some of the above might work. Indeed, under those circumstances, it is even possible that simply hypnotic suggestion can work – for a short while at least. But we are talking about something different here; we are looking at a 'version' of Obsessive Compulsive Disorder, complete with rituals and ritualistic thinking. We will look at the fine details of the illness later, but for the moment, here are the indicators of obsession, rather than phobia.

Phobia

Where the illness is a phobia, the client is able to function normally all the time she does not feel nauseous and/or has no reason to believe that she will vomit. Other people vomiting will create some anxiety which, although at a high level, will pass quite quickly. She will not unduly restrict her social life and will function well enough in relationships.

Obsession

When it is obsessive, the tone of the illness changes considerably. The client is *not* able to function normally most of the time. Upon waking in the morning, she will test to see if she 'feels ok'. If she has breakfast, she will again test for nausea after she has eaten. This testing will continue throughout the day at intervals of fifteen minutes or so or maybe even less.

It does not stop there. If she has to use public transport, she will constantly observe the other passengers, scanning to see if one of them looks as if she or he may vomit – and if she sees that will alight from the train/bus/coach and wait for the next one. Typically, she will only be able to eat food of a certain colour and will treat all 'shop prepared' food with suspicion. Foods that are typically avoided are chicken and shellfish.

If somebody has vomited on the pavement, she will be fixated by it and is likely to suffer a panic or anxiety attack which, in severe cases, will cause her to have eating difficulties for as long as *three days*.

This is only the 'tip of the iceberg', for there are many other difficulties associated with the problem, which we will consider later on; the rest of this chapter is concerned with the obsessive 'version' of the illness.

Promising a miracle

This is a situation in which the: *"I'll fix it in one session!"* brigade are doomed to failure and to distressing the client even further than she already is. There is nothing much worse than promising somebody a miracle (and that is exactly how it would seem to the sufferer from this illness) and then

276

having to confess that you have not a clue what to do after giving it your best shot. Nothing much worse, perhaps, unless it is where the 'therapist' continues to work for X number of sessions, then finally tells the client that she is resistant to therapy and that she should simply accept that at some deep level she *needs* the illness.

This will often have the effect of convincing the client that the therapist has seen something 'weird' about her and with which she or he is not prepared to work. Worse, she will begin to believe that the therapist has never actually seen this illness before, or at least at not such a severe level, and that she is most definitely an 'odd one out' who must now keep her secret even more closely guarded than it was before. Now, of course, she is worse off than ever, for she will believe that she is beyond help and therefore will always have this problem – but she *knows* that she will be sick again at some point in the future and will begin to obsess about how long she has got before this happens.

Diligence, Patience, Understanding

One client that presented to the author had received a full year's worth of therapy, and expensive therapy at that, before being told that there was nothing that could be done for her unless she changed her attitude. Fortunately, a considerable alleviation of symptoms was found after a good few sessions of psychotherapeutic work – it is seldom a quick therapy and diligence, patience and *understanding* are required if you are to work successfully:

- Diligence, because if you miss something, any release may not be permanent.

- Patience, because your client will often question why she is not better yet, and has not infrequently been told by friends and family that Paul McKenna or some other high profile hypnotist would have 'sorted it out by now'. Her obsessive drives will cause her to fear that they may be correct.
- *Understanding* because your client will have no confidence whatsoever in your abilities if you seem not to know the illness 'inside out'. **Do not forget that we are talking about obsession here.**

Now we will examine:

- A complete profile of the typical individual suffering from obsessive Emetophobia (do not refer to such a person as *'an emetophobe'*; the label can cause the illness to be even more difficult to resolve).
- Some *possible* origins of the illness
- A treatment method which usually gets results
- Two case histories

A profile
This profile is extremely lengthy but do not be tempted to skip over sections of it, for you will need to know this illness completely if you are to be of help to your client.

Guilt complex
Typically, your client will illustrate that she suffers *guilt* about her illness in her statement as to why she has presented to you. She will say something like: *"I'm a bit funny about being sick,"* and the word 'sick' will often be only mouthed,

with a great deal of evident discomfort, and often, a blush. There is often a general guilt complex.

Illness

Investigation will reveal that if she hears that somebody was sick, she will obsess about why and will need to know that it was something that had been eaten, or a non-contagious illness or condition. If it is thought that a 'stomach bug' is responsible, then she will fret for days in case she catches it.

Sensitive to gut movement

She will be extraordinarily aware of the tiny movements of the gut that is normal for the human animal. Most of us are completely unaware of this apart from the occasional 'stomach rumble' – and even this innocuous event will strike fear into the sufferer of emetophobia, especially if it is perceived that there is more movement than usual.

Holidays

Public houses are often 'no-go' areas, as are restaurants and dinner parties. For this reason, holidays are rare and holidays via aeroplane are even more so, since there is almost always a fear of somebody vomiting on the aeroplane – *which will often present as aerophobia.*

Confronted with a situation in which it is essential to be in a restaurant or dining situation, this individual becomes an expert at managing to *look* as if she is eating and will become adept at hiding one piece of food under another. She will also claim that she is on a diet or that she didn't feel too well earlier and is 'taking it easy' – although superstition may prohibit such a claim, in case she really *does* start to feel unwell.

Irrational

There can be an amazingly irrational attitude within this illness; the author knew of one individual who lived in fear of a third World War *"Because the Russians will drop an atom bomb on us and I'll get radiation sickness."*

Somebody else would judge an illness or condition around the likelihood of it causing vomiting; if there was no likelihood of this, even if there was a threat to life, then the illness was tolerable and 'not as bad is it might be'.

It is not at all unusual for pregnancy to be greatly feared because of the probability of morning sickness.

Words and sounds

Just the words 'vomit' or 'sick' will often be enough to produce a sensation of panic. If somebody coughs with their hand near their mouth, it can cause a surge of alarm; if somebody hurries to a lavatory it can cause an even great surge of alarm; if somebody is a 'long time' in a lavatory there will be worry; and if there is a sound remotely like somebody vomiting then there will be a profound 'flight reaction' which may even be accompanied by tears.

Seeing somebody vomiting on film can cause a reaction akin to Post Traumatic Shock Disorder. Desensitisation techniques that involve showing video film in stages, beginning with no sound and in black and white, and so on, can therefore actually have the effect of making the illness worse.

Anchors

If somebody has been sick at a particular place, it will take a great deal to get them to visit that place again. The same 'anchoring' effect can happen with clothes, unusual weather conditions, vehicles (*"I got travel sick on a coach once and I'll never go anywhere by coach again in my entire life..."*), having seen vomit on the floor in a particular building, television programmes – an obsessive anchor can attach to almost anything.

'Poophobia'

This, of course, is a *neologism* – a made up word. It is one that the author uses with emetophobic clients to introduce a somewhat delicate facet of the illness into conversation. This is not <u>always</u> present, though frequently is so.

It refers to the fact that the client often needs excessive privacy in the lavatory, often to the point where she simply cannot 'go' if she is anywhere other than at home – and sometimes she needs to be completely on her own in the house, even then. This is a little-known symptom and for the client who suffers it, it can be amazingly reassuring that the therapist knows about it. For the client who does *not* suffer it, it can be amazingly reassuring that some others are worse than she is.

A nice win-win situation.

One case that was presented to the Author was a fifty-year-old male, who would occasionally get up in the middle of the night and go to his office some twelve miles distant on the pretext that he thought he had left a heater, computer, photocopier or some other piece of machinery switched on.

Even when his wife accused him of having an affair and threatened divorce, he could not bring himself to tell her, so deep was his unwarranted shame.

Often, where this symptom *is* present, there is a degree of sensual enjoyment associated with defaecation; it is extremely unlikely that the client will volunteer this, though with good client/therapist rapport, it can be investigated. Where it is the case, then discharging the associated guilt (and it may be part of the source of the guilt that so often accompanies this problem) and reassurances of the 'non-freakiness' of this anal satisfaction can go a long way towards helping this client.

This 'poophobia' occasionally has two other facets:

- Coprophilia – a sexual fascination with faeces and/or defaecation. This is more common in males and is often known as a 'scat fetish'. Not everybody who is prone to the fetish suffers emetophobia, though.
- An anger/jealous reaction to the knowledge that a sexual partner is defaecating. This can be profound enough that it takes on the same qualities as sexual jealousy. This is quite rare.

Sexuality

The client's sexuality will in some way be affected by, and inextricably involved with, emetophobia. There is commonly a masturbation complex and a total denial of masturbatory activity is not unusual. Sometimes, there is a fear of sexual activity in case it causes vomiting in either the client or partner. It is as inevitable that there will be sexual issues involved as it is that we will need to work through them, if we are to get any useful and lasting resolution.

Possible Origins

It is important to recognise that the following is presented as a series of possibilities to help with an understanding of the problem.

When we are born, we know nothing of defaecation shame – we just do it. As we get older, we become aware that *sometimes* some other people seem to express disgust at this activity, holding their noses and making strange noises. Then comes the day when we are sitting on a potty doing what we know mum wants, when others again express distaste or disgust, whereupon mum carries us off into a different room... and at that point a thought process occurs, along the lines of: *"I do this disgusting thing that offends some people."*

Now, the point is, we have no way of knowing that everybody else does the same thing – we have just learnt that *we alone do this disgusting thing!*

This, or something like it, is, I believe, the origin of defaecation shame.

Chamber Pot

Now consider: When a child feels sick, a parent will sometimes hold a **chamber pot** in front of her. Post vomit, there may be an indication of some sort that this was even more unpleasant to others than defaecation.

When a child vomits, others in the vicinity may well react in the same or similar way that they did to defaecation. A parent on clean-up duty might exacerbate that situation. Also, much is made of the fact that you should get to the bathroom so that you can throw up into the lavatory bowl.

283

When others are sick and rush to the lavatory, the above is reinforced.

So the illness may well be the result of a familial conditioning – there is much that suggests this to be the case. Often, one or both parents has shown fear or anxiety associated with vomiting or the possibility of vomiting.

Other observations: Many people who suffer emetophobia have been severely bullied at school; many people who suffer emetophobia have grown up with parents who were emotionally aloof, unable to demonstrate affection and love. It is not clear, perhaps, why these situations would lead to such a response but they are offered here simply to increase knowledge and understanding of the problem.

One more thing: *"Don't eat too much of that! It'll make you sick!"* is a wonderful sensitising statement. Delivered as if the act of being sick is a punishment for excess, rather than a natural process of eliminating waste, it can inspire fear, self-recrimination, and feelings of guilt.

A Treatment Method

There is no assertion that what is written here is the <u>only</u> way to treat obsessive emetophobia, only that this is a treatment method which has proved effective for very many sufferers in the past.

It is important to recognise that a combination therapy is needed, including some sort of cognitive/understanding work and psychological destimulation, which is *not* the same thing as desensitisation. In this illness, there is a constant state of excitation (stress) caused by the constant checking of physical body and surroundings to ensure that the individual is 'safe'. Since we can only search for anything by activating a template (see Chapter Six) all relevant triggers are fired (stimulation) on a second-by-second basis.

A good start

The best start to therapy that the Author has found for this situation is to instantly create a humour response – it is difficult to be frightened of something that can make you laugh. This has to be done with great care, though, because being too blasé will convince your client that you really don't have the vaguest idea of how distressing the illness actually is; being too serious will convince the client that you are trying hard because it is such a serious and difficult problem to deal with. A considered casual approach is best throughout therapy, in fact.

In the UK, there is a soft drink called *'Vimto'* and it can be useful to point out, with a smile, that Vomit is an anagram of Vimto. More often than not, the client will smile at this sudden realisation and therapy is off to a flying start. It is possible, of course, that some individuals will not respond with humour but at least you have said the word 'vomit' without them feeling ill, this starting the process of destimulation. This is usually incorporated into the initial consultation and at the time of writing this book the Author has never had a 'no show' for therapy afterwards.

The rest of the initial consultation can be usefully taken up with:

- An assurance that the problem can be greatly helped

- Assurance that it is extremely unlikely that the illness is in any way related to an occasion when the client *was* sick.
- Information – given in an easy manner – that the problem is almost always related to a small guilt complex and can sometimes even have its origins in *"One of those little private secrets from our early years."*
- Find some way of including some reference to masturbation and ensure that the client 'takes on board' that, at least in your consulting, this a totally acceptable thing to talk about. Be careful not to overwork or overplay this; it needs to be kept almost casual.
- Mention that some people with this problem also have a 'bit of difficulty with a greater than usual need for privacy in the toilet'. Once again, you should be sure not to emphasise interest here.
- Give an outline of analytical therapy (you are unlikely to get a lasting result without it) with a repeated assurance that you are not searching for a time when the client was sick. It is highly beneficial to explain that this style of therapy simply releases all sorts of underlying stress and 'unfinished business' from the psyche and allows a more relaxed way of being. **Keep this light.**
- Give an assurance that although you cannot *promise* a release from the illness, you have done it before and you *can* promise that you will give the therapy your 'very best shot'.

The therapy proper

Begin with six or so sessions of hypnoanalysis, using a specific first session (the subconscious primer shown later in this book, and also in **Rapid Cognitive Therapy**, which also details analytical working) followed by five or six sessions of free association work, once again being certain to assure the client, albeit casually, that we are not searching for one time when they were sick. This reassurance is vital, because it allows the client to relax and explore the subconscious process of thought. Just occasionally, we find a sensitising event here, though it is likely to be only associative – that is, parent has 'freaked' at something 'shameful' and the child has felt sick with fear and associated the two.

It is a common occurrence that the client will recall an early masturbatory memory, usually with great shame and only able to speak of it with some difficulty unless you have carried out some preparatory work as described earlier. *It is the Author's opinion that this is frequently the 'root' of the illness, for without exception when this type of recall has been encountered and 'worked through', the therapy has been successful.*

You should generally do no more than six sessions of free association – not usually regression to cause, which seems far less effective – although there are occasions when it becomes evident that there is a need to continue with this process. This is when the pathogenic material that is being released is of a particularly intense and vivid/dramatic nature; in these circumstances, you will continue until this process naturally completes, when you will often discover that the client pronounces herself 'cured' and the work is done. You would then have no need to continue with what follows here,

287

but will simply discharge your client from your care and wish her a good life.

Conversational Therapy

We continue with some conversational therapy which seeks to destimulate the subconscious further by minimising the whole process of vomit in any way you can.

Humour is a great help; it comes as a surprise how easy it can be to make individuals with this problem laugh at some coarse joke or euphemism or two. If you can in some way mimic the excesses of comedian **Billy Connolly** (there is a superb and profoundly relevant and hysterically funny scene towards the end of a video recording called 'Billy and Albert') or any other 'observational humour' comedian – as long as it is relevant – then it is of enormous help.

You have to use as much charisma as you can muster for this, because the client has to be carried along on your own wave of fun – it gets them past the conscious critical faculty and the laughter acts as a suggestion that it is not really that bad. Usually, the client will begin to be able to talk about vomit and vomiting without anywhere near as much of a reaction as when she first presented – even when it has been 'impossible' for her to talk about it before. Much should be made of this, praising her for begin so at ease with something which was once so difficult.

Cognitive Work

We can follow this up with some cognitive work. This works well, as a rule: explain that 'Vomit' is a badly used Latin word. In fact, another word for stomach content is called 'Chyme' while it is in the stomach until it passes through into the small intestine. We can also explain that when they can hear their stomach rumbling, this is a good thing (many actually believe that it is a warning signal!) because it shows that everything is progressing normally.

Sometimes, it is useful to teach a client how she can make her stomach rumble by thinking about it and imagining it happening. This can have the positive benefits of putting her in control, as well as allowing her to think about her stomach in a positive, rather than fearful, way.

More Destimulation.

It can also be beneficial to explain very conversationally, almost as if talking about writing a letter or making a phone call, that the wealthier Romans of 2000 years or so ago used to have a Vomitarium in the part of their villa where they held their parties and banquets – this was so that whenever they were full, they would go and get rid of it, in order to be able to enjoy more food. It was like a long low bath/trough with water constantly running through it and there is actually an example of one in a villa in the ruins at Herculaneum, in Italy. Make the point that, to the Romans, this was a totally normal part of their life.

All of this leads to more destimulation and the client will often express great surprise that she can begin to talk about it without panic or fear, or nausea. When this happens, you are pretty much home and dry, though the client will not *necessarily* notice a huge amount of difference for a few weeks. In some ways, the hardest part of this style of therapy is to convince them of the truth of this delay in noticeable improvement; something that usually works well is to point out that, by now, you and your premises are reminding them of the problem they used to have and when they stop coming to see you for a while, they will leave the problem behind with you.

There may well be other therapies than this which are effective; the Author heard from an acupuncturist who reported some success by teaching the relaxation response, and EFT practitioners have reported noticeable reduction in severity of symptoms.

Two Case Histories

The case histories illustrated here are outlines detailing salient points, rather than completely detailed discourses.

The first was a lady of forty-one years who had experienced the illness for as long as she could remember. She was married with two children; if the children were sick at any time, she was totally unable to deal with the problem (as is often the case) and had to escape, either by leaving the house or locking herself into another room, leaving her husband to manage the sick child. This gave her a sense of profound low self worth. Therapy proceeded as outlined here and it was not long before she alighted upon the first guilt memory – of stealing from shops when she was young and selling the items to her friends.

There followed a series of recalls concerned with sexuality; her obsessive sexual fascination for a school teacher of the same sex, some promiscuity at around age 13 and several early masturbatory memories going back to being seven years old and discovering that her 'parts' felt nice when she sat on the arm of her father's favourite armchair – but only if her father was sitting there as well. She commented at this point, completely 'out of the blue' that if she had ever thought about her parent's sexuality, it made her feel sick.

Anorgasmic

During the initial consultation, she had insisted that she never masturbated and never had felt the need, thanks to a low sex drive; now she 'owned up' that, in reality, she did it frequently but was actually anorgasmic. She confessed that she seldom had sexual intercourse with her husband in case it made her feel sick – and instantly realised that there was a link between that and the memory of sitting on the arm of her father's chair. It was very shortly after that that she commented that talking about sexuality and stealing things seemed to be 'not such a big deal any more...'

Guilt complexes now abated, she began to respond astoundingly well to the conversational therapy and cognitive work, becoming intrigued at the story about the Vomitarium. The references to Billy Connolly amused her greatly and she began to be completely at ease with the conversational work, even laughing, albeit with a grimace, when the therapist spoke of 'pavement pizzas' and 'the technicoloured yawn'

It is important to recognise that all of this work needs great care and a degree of exuberance on the part of the therapist. The therapist with a conservative personality may well need to avoid some of the slang references and work only with what she/he is comfortable.

On her final visit to the therapist, she proudly announced that one of her children had felt ill, yet she had not felt the need to escape and had instead tucked the child up in bed with the reassurance that he would feel better in the morning.

She was both impressed and amazed that she could now say the word 'Vomit' without feeling ill and had not felt unduly uncomfortable even when she encountered where somebody had sick on the pavement.

It was almost as an afterthought, as she was leaving, that she said: *"Oh, by the way, my husband says thanks – and if you can't guess what for, I'm not going to tell you!"*

The entire therapy had lasted for around fifteen sessions.

Startlingly Fast

The second case is one that surprised even the Author with the speed of resolution; the entire therapy lasted for only five sessions and entailed no analytical hypnotherapy work of any description. Resolution was complete, even though there had been food obsessions and behavioural processes based on anchors and triggers.

The client was a young woman of barely twenty-one years, who was scarcely able to function at what most people would consider to be a 'normal' manner, exhibiting the vast majority of the symptoms detailed earlier. She lived abroad and the first contact was an email asking the Author if he knew anybody who could help. It was immediately evident that she was suffering and obsessive illness, a fact with which she agreed.

A series of detailed email exchanges followed, about which the client commented: *"It's as if you've been inside my mind and seen everything that's in there!"* It was this evident knowledge that eventually decided the young woman to attend therapy with the Author, even though it entailed a lengthy journey which was, itself, somewhat traumatic for her.

It is certainly worth recognising that the more you can illustrate that you have a professional knowledge of your subject, the higher the client's belief and expectation will be. In this case, it led to the client making a huge commitment and investment in therapy, which was probably instrumental in her extraordinarily rapid and complete recovery.

During the initial consultation, the Author touched casually upon the fact that there is occasionally a guilt complex at the root of the illness, often something that the individual has always felt they could never tell another living soul. The client drew an almost imperceptible breath and a wonderful few moments followed:

Therapist: *"What was that you were going to say?"*
Client: *"Er... nothing. No, nothing at all."*
Therapist: *"Oh... ok..."*

------ HIATUS -----

Client: *"Erm..."*
Therapist: *"Erm...?"*
Client: *"Actually, I'm remembering something that I can't tell you..."*
Therapist: *"Will tell you me what that is?"*

As unlikely as it sounds, the client frequently responds to that technique and tells the therapist the 'forbidden' secret. And so it was in this case; the memory was of a masturbatory event which involved the client putting a favourite toy inside her knickers and savouring the sensations it produced as she walked around. The client's embarrassment levels, high at first, fell dramatically as she recounted the tale; there followed much conversation about the nature of sexuality, the normality of masturbation, and the early age at which female children frequently discover it.

Over the next four sessions, the work was of an entirely conversational nature, covering much about the way that instinctive drives often have to be suppressed as a result of the need to live in a civilised society. She was both fascinated and amused by the description of how we learn that something we do is offensive to others (as shown earlier) and readily agreed that her parents tended towards respectability so that more earthy subjects were not easily discussed, if at all.

There was a further guilt memory, in which her perception was that she had shown herself up so badly that nobody could possibly love her afterwards. This gave way to a reframe within which she was asked to view it from a dissociated position, then 'reach back through time as a grown-up' to comfort the distressed child. This produced a visible relaxation.

On her penultimate session, she bounced into the therapist's office and gleefully recounted how she had watched somebody 'throwing up' on a television programme and had bee so impressed that it had not disturbed her, she had watched it several times. Ordinarily, something of this sort would have produced tears and extreme fear. Her joy was a delight to behold, and this positive emotional response was compounded by praise from the Author, along with: *"Mind you, I suppose we shouldn't be surprised – you've done so well right from the beginning that you were always going to be a star client!"*

Her last session was uneventful; we checked for any remnants of guilt complex, completed the 'central core' routine as shown in Chapter Five, and discussed how her life might become that she was free. There was one other thing that happened that illustrated good emotional health and confidence; with a sparkle in her eye she told me that she had bought a sex toy which 'does exactly what it says on the box'.

Desensitisation Warning

Many therapists attempt to use desensitisation or 'exposure therapy' via the use of video scenes of people vomiting. The idea of this is that you show them fast forward at first, then in black and white, then in colour and eventually in full colour at normal speed with sound.

It cannot be stressed strongly enough that this is an extremely risky, if not downright dangerous, method to attempt with the individual who is obsessively emetophobic. Not only is it unlikely to produce an alleviation of symptoms, it is entirely possible that the client's anxiety levels will become intolerably high, creating the situation in which there is a retreat from reality – apparent psychosis or what some might call a 'nervous breakdown'.

It is to be hoped that this chapter has given you a new 'slant' on an illness which can be nothing short of total misery for the sufferer.

CHAPTER SIXTEEN
Dramatic emotion & withheld emotion

The Dramatically Emotional Client

Every so often, you find a client who is determined to have the worst out of life. His illnesses are more profound, fooling the experts into wrong diagnoses. This, of course, means that cures do not work very well, if at all, so he has to be submitted to new and/or experimental medication. His relationships are awful, his family even more so, he can scarcely function any more and, in fact, it often feels as the entire universe is ganging up against him. Almost everything he does tends to go wrong. He has been everywhere for help and you are most definitely his last hope...

There is actually not a lot more exaggeration here than you will often find from such a client. He is usually the proud possessor of too much emotion (usually negative) and almost without exception will have a hidden agenda to ensure that they get nurturing attention or sympathy from others.

He might well glory in his failures and 'differentness', maybe even grinning (though he may weep instead) as he tells you of his latest disaster or about how some part of his body is the wrong shape or does not function as it is supposed to.

Right Brain Active

This individual is right-brain active (the right half of the brain deals with, among other things, *creativity, mental imagery, awareness of self, emotional responses and dreams*) and it is certainly no good appealing to or seeking to work with his 'logical self'. For him more than most others, in any contest between imagination and logic, imagination will always be the winner.

This is actually a very useful state of affairs for the therapist, for if we manage to entrain his imagination into a more positive mode, the work is unlikely to be questioned by his conscious mind and is therefore more likely to be successful. Before we do that, though, we need to be sure that we have uncovered any hidden agenda. We are not going deeply into that process in this article; there are many methods that can be used and it is up to the individual therapist to use whatever s/he feels comfortable with.

Always remember, this client wants to be noticed – he is almost certainly a closet extrovert. The only reason he behaves in a negative mode is because his sense of self worth has not allowed him to believe that he can achieve anything worth boasting about.

Once the secret agenda has been laid bare by whatever methodology you favour (the first section of this book contains many suitable tools), we need to boost his fundamental belief system about self by using deep trance states and vivid imagery and suggestion.

Basic Area of Work

This client is suitable for either suggestion work or analytical styles of hypnotherapy; PARTS work can be profoundly effective as can anything which truly entrains the imagination.

There is no actual script given here, for you will need to ensure that whatever you use matches perfectly to the information that you have gathered in the earlier sessions. The basic area in which to work is the concept that being viewed as *positively* different is far better than being seen as *negatively* different, or inadequate and needy. Being an optimist gets more accolades than seeming like a pessimist; being cheerful/amusing <u>guarantees</u> attention from others; becoming successful in the face of adversity <u>always</u> garners admiration. People who are different because they are successful are admired and applauded – those who are different because they always fail are often dismissed as being of little consequence by all but those who get their kicks from nurturing 'lame ducks'…

Self Obsessed

As far as inducing hypnosis is concerned, this personality is easy to work with as long as you remember that he is self-obsessed. If you use the personality test shown elsewhere in the book, you will almost certainly discover that this individual is driven by Charismatic Evidential traits.

Progressive relaxation can work, but exploring body feelings is far better, especially if we can incorporate imaginative work. Getting him to imagine breathing in through his fingers and out through his feet, that he can feel a gentle, unidirectional current of air bringing in calmness and breathing out tensions is good; so is asking him to vividly imagine himself drifting gently downwards from a richly painted ceiling, so that he can gradually see more and more detail of the painting and in so doing realise that the painting is all about him and how his life is now going to be.

He will usually enter a deep trance state very quickly and then you can, and should, use any image-filled deepener before delivering your suggestions, which must *always* be written for that specific client if you are to be successful.

The Excessively Analytical client

This individual is more or less the exact opposite of the Dramatically Emotional Client. It is easy to believe that he is being 'resistant' but when this seems to be the case, it is actually far more likely that you are not approaching him in a way that truly works for him.

Quite frequently, he is hypervigilant – that is, he is on permanent alert, even though he may not realise it, and will be constantly checking self and surroundings. If you were to conduct a personality test, you would almost certainly discover the Resolute Organisational, or Warrior, personality. This personality can be retentive and often shares much with the Freudian **Anal Retentive Personality Type,** especially when presenting in negative mode.

Take a moment to reflect upon the fact that he has inherited genetics that are all about being in control, knowing what is going on, never being seen to be wrong (because that situation represents life-threatening vulnerability), and you will begin to see that you need a specific way or working.

This client is usually quick in thought, observant, and always on the lookout for any form of threat to integrity/security. Sometimes this is just a facet of their personality, though it may well be because of repression, or a learned response pattern. Whatever the reason, it makes no difference as far as working successfully with him is concerned – what he has brought in with him is what you have to work with.

Problems for the Unwary Therapist

This client can present several problems to the unwary therapist and although the following may *not necessarily* be exhibited, they are by no means unusual:

- Is too analytical for hypnoanalysis to work effectively
- Has a habit of being uncommunicative in or out of hypnosis
- Constantly seeks to be in control
- Has a tendency to reject 'colourful' or emotion-based suggestions
- Has a tendency to withhold salient information
- Has a tendency to be 'auto-contrary' or instinctively non-compliant
- Will determinedly resist convincers such as arm levitation, etc.

In many ways, you are better working with the conscious work shown in Section One of this book; PARTS work, as shown in Section Two can be effective, too, though you might run into problems with feelings of awkwardness on the client's part here, since this personality type is often somewhat reserved. If you want to work a one or two session therapy for any reason, you will need to use hypnosis.

Inducing a Good State of Trance

Inducing a good state of trance can be difficult and getting suggestions to 'take' even more so, since this client will instinctively defend any attempt that he observes to bypass his conscious critical faculty. He will tend to question everything you do unless it seems completely commonplace or 'normal', and he will not infrequently insist that other people have tried to hypnotise him and have always been unsuccessful. It is possible that, instead, he will tell you that his mind is so strong, he cannot possibly be hypnotised – and he has been told this by another therapist.

It is important that you do not accept that particular challenge. Anything remotely like: *"Oh, don't worry, I'm sure I'll be able to hypnotise you,"* or: *"Well, I don't work in the same way as others do,"* even: *"Well, that actually makes it easier to get into hypnosis,"* almost guarantees that you will 'fail', for it is just too easy to resist hypnosis, and your assertion that you can beat him (because that is often what it is about) will determine him to do just that. It is actually far better to go with it…

Getting the Client on Your Side

Something like this works well for most individuals of this type: *"Ok, thank you for telling me that, it's saved us some time. Instead of standard hypnosis, then, we'll actually use that strength of mind to produce a super state of enhanced subconscious awareness and concentration. It's something that most people just can't do, but you'll probably find it easy. Is that all right with you?"* This statement actually works very well, because he cannot tell you later that

301

he did not 'go under' without admitting that his mind is not as strong as he claimed it was.

We will assume that you have now got the client on your side and are about to start the induction procedure. It is a good idea, if you can, to position yourself on the right-hand side of this client; he is likely to be left-brain active (the left half of the brain deals with *language, logic, time-orientated matters, mathematics, etc.*) and speaking to his right ear affords a more direct communication – the left brain controls the right side of vision and hearing.

You can use one of the rapid induction methods, which rely on surprise, shock, or an overload to the central nervous system; or alternatively (better, in the opinion of the Author) make sure you use appropriate language patterns that will entrain the thought processes. Progressive relaxation will probably not work but getting him to focus on bodily sensations, how the tip of each finger feels, the sensations on the soles of his feet, testing to see if he can use the power of his mind to change his heartbeat rate, etc. will usually do the job effectively. So will asking him to concentrate on some mental task like counting the number of breaths they take whilst listening carefully to the sound of your voice. Confusional techniques of all types can work quite well here, too. Use anything which appeals to the tendency to analyse, observe and bring logical understanding to bear, especially if there is actually *no* real logic at all.

Milton H. Erickson was a master of this technique, using wonderfully confusing language patterns similar to: *"And you can wonder what you are here for…because four is twice two and we already know, too, what brought you too this place… even though this is only one time you were here…*

but you will get to two times next time and then you might know what you are here for... and I might know too, for what you are here..."

The Client's Actual Words

To get the best work out of post-hypnotic suggestion work with this client, you should make a note of the actual words he uses when he tells you what he wants from his therapy – paraphrasing him may cause irritation and may even carry a somewhat different meaning. With this one, above all others, accuracy is of paramount importance.

Often, you will be given the merest outline of what this individual wants you to do and you will need to persuasively gather as much else as you can. If you are told, for example: *"I want to pass the driving test,"* you need to discover a few other details:

- Why he wants to pass the driving test
- Why he thinks he needs your help to do so
- What will be the best thing about his life when he has done so
- How he rates his chances at the moment, on a scale of 1 - 10
- How he actually feels about taking the test
- What does he think of his driving himself

Your script should obviously be built around the answers here and here is something of immense importance: *Never attempt to use a 'made to measure' script with this personality.* They are not good at the best of times; consider: somebody writes a script for another person that he has never met, without discovering why the goal exists knowing the resources of the client. The script will be 'cold', based only on the ideas, fears, aspirations and conceptual thoughts of the writer of the script *which may be not remotely similar to those of the client.*

You should be able to see that this is essentially an undesirable situation, even though there are many 'therapists' who do nothing other than hypnotise, read, charge, discharge. There are many 'therapists' – and the quotes are well founded – who are taught by their 'school' to do just that, that this is the way to function; they may even have been given a handful of scripts for all ailments with the advice that it is all they will ever need.

With the Excessively Analytical client, the problems that this situation creates are exacerbated, for unless you get incredibly lucky, it will take him only a few moments to recognise that what is being said does not 'fit' with what he wants or what he has asked you to do. It is ineffective, and more importantly, in the mind of this Author at least, **it is totally disrespectful to the client.**

This type of client is driven by logic and cynicism rather than emotion; if he recognises that you are reading a prepared script, and one which does not cover his particular problem at that, that cynicism will ensure a total lack of compliance or involvement with what you are doing. The session will fail and the **rule of seven** will come into play.

The Rule of Seven

For those readers who have never heard of the 'rule of seven' it is a very simple, incredibly important, rule to understand:

- If you do something well, your client will talk of your skills to all those who are interested.
- If you do it badly, he will tell *seven times as many* about your incompetence, whether they are interested or not

You will see that this is not conducive to building your practice. If you doubt this fact, perform this simple test. Imagine that you have been on holiday abroad. The hotel was complete and perfectly adequate, the food was at least acceptable, the room was clean and airy, the staff were courteous and polite, and everything you needed was available. You get home and tell anybody who asks that you had a wonderful holiday.

Now imagine that the hotel was not fully built and that you had workmen immediately outside your window first thing in the morning. The food was sometimes inedible and the staff seemed not to care, the plumbing was inefficient and there were insects on the bathroom floor. Now, do you think you might tell only those people who asked about the holiday, or might you make sure that as many people as possible knew about it?

Of course, there are many shades of grey between those two extremes; but the professional therapist is not (or should not be) interested in shades of grey, only in giving the client the best attention he can.

Fortunately, perhaps, most clients will not be at either of the extremes shown in this chapter but it is worth remembering that each will tend to have a bias towards one or the other.

CHAPTER SEVENTEEN
Common difficulties in analysis (1)

This chapter, and the next, are both concerned predominantly with the difficulties that can arise during 'standard' hypnoanalysis.

Client Handling

Many of the problems in the hypnoanalyst's office stem from the way the therapist handles the client generally. You must always be 'invisible', yet charismatic, positive and with a manner engendering empathy. If you discover that your client shares one of your interests – *Keep Quiet.* If you discover that they like to go to places you do – *Keep Quiet.* If you discover that the client has anything in common with you at all – *Keep Quiet.* The reason for all this is simple but two-fold:

- For transference to develop properly (important in all analytical styles of therapy), the client needs to build up an image of you *as he or she actually wants you to be*, which may be nothing like the way you are.
- If that client gains the idea that we share part of their adult life of **now**, their subconscious may begin to believe that we are no different in any way from them.

To use an analogy, how confident would you feel in going to a dentist who had only your own level of skill at dentistry (assuming you have not been a dentist at any time)?

Thoroughly Professional

We must always maintain a thoroughly professional image; and professional for us means: Empathetic, understanding, non-judgmental, responsive and gentle, yet with a firmness and apparent confidence that imparts the belief that we know well what we are talking about and always know what to do. We simply cannot afford to appear 'ordinary' to our clients if we want the 'magic' to work.

A good rule to follow is to keep every personal detail about yourself secret, and to guard those secrets as if you were ashamed of them. Three points which may have been made during your training but which are important enough to make again here are:

- Never socialise in any way with a client.
- Do not talk for more than a few at the beginning of a session – and then not about the session itself or anything connected with it.
- *Never* discuss how the session went after it is over.

If you find any of these rules difficult to implement on a regular basis, *you are seeking something from your clients and you are suffering from a neurosis* – get it sorted out before you burn out. If you have not had some form of therapy (preferably analytical) as part of your training, then you are putting yourself and your clients at psychological risk. Whatever excuses you may make to avoid it, the facts remain the same: you simply *cannot* get anybody through a successful analysis if you have not been through it yourself. It would be like trying to teach someone to drive when you had absolutely no idea of how to handle a vehicle yourself. To put it more into perspective, how would you feel if you were to discover that those people who trained you had not actually been through that self-same process?

Jumping To Conclusions

Always wait to see your client's emotional reaction to her recalls before you make any decisions about whether to investigate further. Someone may recall something you think is dreadful – and then you see that they are grinning broadly at the thought!

It has as much to do with environment as with predisposition; a child growing up as one of a family of ten in a tough inner-city area is going to be less reactive to guilt about, say, stealing money, than would a single child of middle-class, 'respectable' parents living on an executive estate. Trying to release the guilt in the former will cause confusion because it never was experienced; ignoring it in the latter will probably stop therapy progressing. If in doubt about an emotional response, ask your client how he or she feels about their recall. If she says: *"How would you feel?"* or something similar, then just say: *"Oh, I know how I'd feel, but now I want to know how you feel."*

Another 'wait and see' situation: Never assume that you know what your client is talking about if they have not spelt it out for you. On one occasion, a young lady told the author she was remembering 'playing rude games with my friend.'

There was ample time to pass comment which would have been at best, superfluous, at worst, downright embarrassing; fortunately, the author remained silent. After a pause she continued: *"We used to run up and down the street, poking our tongues out at the neighbours, and calling them rude names, like Fatty Bum-Bum."*

A good response to that initial recall would have been: *"Tell me about those rude games you played with your friend,"* delivered in a style which echoed hers as closely as possibly.

Keeping it Clean

Much has been written about the need for keeping all our communication with our clients 'clean' in order not to lead them to where *we* think they should go, rather than to their own particular truth. Put simply, if you ensure that you avoiding asking direct leading questions like: *"How often did Mum hit you?"* or the suggestive types like: *"Did Dad ever come into your bedroom at night?"* you will do no harm. Remember that *tones* can be every bit as suggestive, if not more so, than words. An indiscreet *"Aha!"* a sudden intake of breath, or a thoughtful: *"Hmm..."* can make all sorts of implications, depending on circumstances. Even an *"Uh-huh..."* meant to indicate to your client that you are listening can be interpreted as showing particular interest to that which has just been said.

In general, when talking to clients in an analytical situation, in or out of hypnosis, we should seek to mirror their own tones as closely as possible, so that we can reflect back what they have said, with a question on the end: *"You are in your bedroom... and what happened then?"* Most of the time in analytical therapy, it is better if we say nothing, just waiting for them to continue. When we do have to speak, a bit of thought makes it easy to 'keep it clean':

- *And what happened then?*
- *Were you on your own?* (Not <u>all</u> on your own – it is too evocative)
- *And where are you when .... is happening?*
- *How old are you in that memory?*
- *What sort of clothes were you wearing?*
- *Tell me more about that.*

By now, you should have a reasonable understanding of what 'keeping it clean' is all about; if you are still in doubt, though, there are many books which cover the subject in some depth. A good one is **Rapid Cognitive Therapy,** by Georges Phillips and Terence Watts which covers a great deal more about analytical and regression therapy besides.

Commonly Presented Problems

Very few clients go through analysis without presenting their therapist with one or two problems along the way, so here are a few guidelines to inspire thought. The following pages will allow you to either bypass or deal with some of those most frequently presented.

The 'Blank'

"I can't remember anything..."
"My mind's just a blank..."
"There's nothing... I can't see anything...."

This is probably the most common – and sometimes most difficult – problem that the analytical therapist has to deal with. When it occurs during a period of emotional release, especially if recalls have been plentiful until that moment, it is a form of subconscious resistance which will often respond to a simple 'urging' response: *"Yes you can! Go on, it's safe to remember... just tell me what's in your mind,"* or similar.

Where this does not produce a result, you can sometimes trigger a suggestible client by saying: *"I'm going to count to three and then I'm going to snap my fingers... when I snap my fingers, at that very moment, **at that very moment,** your subconscious is going to jump **directly** to a memory... and you'll find an urge, a compulsion inside you to tell me what you find there... one... two... and – three,"* then snap your thumb and finger as loudly as you can (if you have trouble with this, you could, perhaps, try clapping your hands). This is a kind of very watered-down version of the **Watkins Affect Bridge** and the key factors are:

- your client must have been shedding emotion
- you must instil urgency by your tone of voice
- you must sound as if you believe it will work.

Very rarely does it fail; if it does, simply reassure your client: *"All right, that's OK, it's just not quite the right time yet... when the time's right, it'll just pop into your mind without you even trying. Just let your mind drift, now..."*

Another, similar, method that can sometimes be useful is to lift your client's wrist – after first asking permission, of course – and 'gently shake some relaxation into your arm and body'. <u>Gently</u> shake the wrist for a moment or two until you can feel that you have the whole weight of her arm; tell her to let you have the weight of her arm if she is tense – and keep on about it until she does. Tell her that in a moment or two you are going to drop her hand onto her lap and at the moment it lands, a memory will just suddenly be there in her mind. This can work well when there is unadmitted or repressed masturbatory guilt and it should take too great a leap of imagination to see why this should be so.

When the 'blank' occurs during a session, but not after or during any particular relevant emotional recall/release, the important thing is to maintain relaxation in your client. A good way to deal with it is to reassure them that: *"That's OK, everybody gets blanks from time to time... sometimes it's because the subconscious has actually finished with one train of thought and is resting for a moment... sometimes it's as if the subconscious wants to get its facts right before bringing them to conscious awareness. Just wait in that blankness and you'll find thoughts just drift easily into your mind without you even trying...In fact, it'd probably be just impossible for you to keep your mind blank for very long..."* Of course, if your client starts talking before you've finished that little discourse... shut up!

Some Other Methods:

There are some other useful methods of dealing with the problem:

"Some people find they can imagine dipping their hand into a large black sack, like a lucky dip, and drawing out a memory... I wonder if you are able to do that?"

"Sometimes, if you imagine yourself watching a film of your early years, you can be surprised at what suddenly comes to light..."

*"I had a client last year with an **enormous** blank that lasted for most of a session... then he imagined himself looking through a photograph album of his life and was astonished to see how much he found there... Uncles, Aunts, pets and toys, favourite teachers, Christmas times, Birthday parties, best friends and worst enemies..."* Of course, you can extend the list, or even be covertly more specific if you want your client to investigate a specific area of their life.

A method that can be useful is the **Body Exploration.** Starting at the tips of their toes, go through their whole body up to the top of their head, asking them to tell you whether that part feels relaxed or otherwise. Work in 'bands' across the body – feet and ankles, calves and knees, thighs to waist, torso, chest and shoulders, arms, head and neck. *Be sure to give no extra emphasis on any part.* Often, on the 'thighs to waist' area, they will say something like: *"Erm... my parts feel a bit funny actually"'* and suddenly, the blank mode disappears. This technique can sometimes trigger abreactive states.

Some therapists find success at overcoming the blank with a version of the **'Miracle Box'** routine shown in Chapter Four. In this method, have your client visualise a filing cabinet, box, safe, etc. inside which is a piece of paper; on the paper is written something of great importance... and the important thing is that she must tell you the first thought that comes to mind. On very rare occasions, this method will release a repression, but it has a problem in that it is possible to completely miss associated emotional trauma that would be released during a more gradual approach in 'normal' analysis.

In all of this work, there should be as little intervention from the therapist as there can possibly be – as mentioned earlier we should try to remain 'invisible' and let the client get on with the job in hand; the devices listed here are best thought of as 'emergency restart' procedures and should always be used sparingly.

The Word Association test.

When the blank resists all efforts to shift it, and especially when it has been present from the very beginning of analysis and we are on session 3 or 4, a word association test can provide a valuable 'kick start' as well as clues as to where to gently guide your client – there is a list of words later. When you study them, you will see that the order in which they are given (when read from left to right, rather than in columns) is often such that they are likely to trigger response. The use of a bio-feedback device is highly recommended here, because it will instantly show any particularly reactive states. To use the test effectively, here is a good work method:

Tell your client you are going to read out some words and you want them to give you the first response that comes into their mind. Give an example, explaining that if you say 'CAT', you would expect them to respond with, perhaps, DOG, rather than the name of their cat or someone else's cat. Is amazing how many people misunderstand word association if you don't explain it properly. What you are looking for here is:

- Any association that you cannot make sense of.
- A long gap before replying – more than two seconds.
- A surge on the bio-feedback meter.
- Sudden 'busy' body language, especially fidgeting, wiggling or 'paddling' feet.
- Turning away of the head.
- Change in breathing rate.
- Change in intensity of the hypnotic flush.
- Sudden appearance of any emotion, especially anger.
- Any other reactive signs.

In any of the above circumstances, mark the word and move on, *reading in a deliberately toneless voice*. <u>Do not give reassurance when she struggles for an answer</u> but just mark the word and move on to the next. It is also important to avoid waiting for her to answer, just reading the words at approximately two second intervals. This will sometimes put psychological pressure on your client and that is exactly what we want here – politeness has no place in this particular method!

When you have finished, go back to the ones you have marked; say you are going to do this first, but do not say why. If there is a reaction, unusual association, or both, then underline the word and continue. For the purposes of dealing with the blank, ignore any where there is no reply *or* reaction (though they may very well indicate areas of resistance and could possibly be used at another time). At the end of the session you will have a list of words that trigger thought processes in your clients 'blank' mind.

Use them wisely as devices to start the recall process, not just on that session but whenever your client goes blank, because it may be that they are 'hitting a button' somewhere. You can sometimes do this directly, as in: *"What do you think or feel when you hear the word ....? Concentrate on that feeling/thought for a moment or two... see where it takes you or what else it makes you think of..."* and sometimes indirectly: *"I want you for a moment to imagine yourself going into a CHURCH..."* or: *"You haven't said very much about your FATHER..."* You get the idea. The purist might feel that this is leading the client, but consider:

- Your client has illustrated that those words are connected to problem areas
- Your client is suffering a 'blank' and needs some kind of trigger
- You did not choose the words where your client stuck

Most therapists would actually recognise this sort of work as a 'permissive lead'. A 'last ditch' method to trigger the recall process is to explain to your client that this particular form of therapy needs her to tell you her thoughts and feelings if you are to be successful and that if she is not able to get that process working then you will have to discharge her. ***It is important that you mean it, because your body language will give the game away if you do not.*** Even if your client is totally unskilled as far as conscious 'body-reading' is concerned, you may rest assured that her *subconscious* will know and your threat will carry about as much weight as a parent saying: *"I'll kill you in a minute!"* If they are still silent for very long after that, you will need to do what you promised – discharge her from therapy, so that

she can seek an alternative method of dealing with whatever
ails her.

Here are the words for the Word Association Test – it is a
good idea to type them onto an A4 sheet which you can
photocopy as many times as you need it:

Word Association Test Words

Home	Uncle	Sister	Mother	Failure
Trousers	Night	River	Evening	Car
School	Thumb	Bed	Impotent	Exams
Brother	Holidays	Aunt	Dreams	Gamble
Chocolate	Food	Fire	Alcohol	Dog
Happy	Sleep	Field	Cat	Baby
Sex	Ideal	Birth	Drink	Tree
Chair	Memory	Father	Road	Pain
Shop	Church	Mouth	Penis	Mad
Water	Whole	Husband	Bright	Sick
Hate	Shame	Day	Lost	Parents
Love	Wife	Pants	Success	Family
Morning	Death	Cloud	Breast	Son
Desire	Sad	Control	Table	Grief
Head	Urge	Body	Crisis	Shock
Marriage	Child	Toilet	Jealous	Touch
Tail	Break	Virgin	Guilt	Adolescence
Talk	Real	Violence	Daughter	Embarrassed
Ill	Wedding	Hidden	Clean	Pain
Private	Dull	Heaven	Past	Fertile

CHAPTER EIGHTEEN
Common difficulties in analysis (2)

Total Silence

This is different from **The Blank** discussed in the last Chapter, in that your client is not saying *anything;* at least in blank mode he is speaking to you, if only to tell you that he has nothing to say.

Sometimes, if you ask the Silent Client *"What are you thinking now?"* you will get an answer. When this happens, your response has to be to remind them to tell you each thought as it goes through their mind, rather than waiting until it is a complete story. When you encounter this, you could do a lot worse than use the word association test shown previously, since it puts pressure on to the client to either speak up or be intolerably rude.

When a client insists on remaining totally silent in spite of your best efforts, then you have two choices:

- Switch to a style of therapy that does not need your client to talk
- Discharge him from your care, after politely explaining why

No Emotion Showing

This client has possibly been severely hurt at some time (not necessarily intentionally) and may be determined to *not ever* feel that way again. It can just easily be that he is determined not to let anybody *see* the pain. Because he is not

318

showing it does not mean he is not feeling it and a bio-feedback meter reveals the truth here, most of the time.

If the meter indicates that there *is* a reaction, you can badger, cajole, coax, or do whatever you think will produce the visible (and often audible) release that is obviously necessary to get him well. It does not 'work' if he is feeling it but not showing it, at least not very well and not for very long. The emotion **must** be expressed.

Where nothing is being felt or displayed when it seems reasonably evident that there should be, the following can be effective:

- Ask him to imagine what it would feel like if there *was* some emotion present
- Ask him to tell you where he would feel it in his body
- Ask him to remember when he felt that emotion one time

Now, this is important: *do not accept the excuse that he 'cannot remember', because how would he be able to imagine it and to know where it would be felt, if that were the case?* If he still insists, then tell him to imagine that he can feel that feeling right now, right this minute, and make it vivid in his mind...

Narrative Recall

The narrative recall sounds like this:

"Now I'm going down the road to my friend's house... I'm knocking at the door... they've let me in now... now we're playing in her front room... it's after tea, now... we're watching telly... don't know what's on..."

Unless you intervene, you will wait forever for this type of client to arrive at any sort of conclusion or point in his ramblings. It is possible that you will have to teach him how to free-associate – you should do this as a matter of course, anyway, at the beginning of the first free-association session, but sometimes it is necessary to re-teach it or emphasis its importance.

It can be effective to suggest that it is rather like a joke-telling session, where one person's joke reminds another of a different one and so on. You can also liken it to a chat over coffee, 'a bit of a gossip, really' where what one person says reminds another of something he or she heard or remembers. This problem is more prevalent with the male client; women are better than men at letting their minds roam free, one subject naturally leading on to another in social conversation. Men tend to frown on the idea of drifting from the point of a conversation.

Some analytical individuals tend to reject all efforts to help them with the problem and it is probably next to impossible to teach him to successfully free-associate if he does not do it naturally. This may be because of a wish to manipulate the sessions with the therapist, instead of allowing subconscious thought processes to reveal his true self.

The No-Go Area

This is typically characterised by the client suddenly stopping talking, turning the head away, sudden fidgeting, surges on the bio-feedback meter if it is being used, and other signs of discomfort.

Sometimes he will tell you there is something that he simply cannot bring himself to say and if coaxing, reassuring, cajoling, persuading, etc., does not work within a few minutes, you could be in for a long haul. A novel way of dealing with it is to say resignedly: *"Well, I'll just have to write down the worst thing I can think of, then."* Then pause for a moment or two while you write on your pad, then turn the page just loudly enough for them to hear, or even tear a page out (this can be effective because of its apparent finality) before saying: *"OK, just let your mind drift, now. And tell me what you find yourself thinking..."*

You may have to wait for a minute or two, but this will almost always have the result of the client asking what you have actually written and you, of course, will say: *"Hey, play fair! You wouldn't tell me what you **were** thinking..."* This will usually produce a result and if they then ask what you wrote, tell them you will show them at the end of the session. At session end, then you show them... and what you have actually written is: ***'The Worst Thing I Can Think Of'*** Use humour at this point and 'confess' that you really did not know what to write because it is not actually in your nature to be judgmental...

This method can work much better than the tried and tested: *"If you don't tell me, it's just going to fill your thoughts to the point where you simply cannot think of anything else... in fact the harder you try..."*

Fantasy Tales

At some point, you are bound to have a client telling you something which is quite obviously a fabrication. Most of the time this does not matter; fantasy can produce psychological illness just as certainly as reality, and fantasy can cure it, *as long as the relevant emotion is being expressed.*

As long as there seems to be some element of reality, or, at least, plausibility, present and as long as the all-important emotional release is occurring, then let him get on with it. Almost always, the real truth surfaces when sufficient emotion has been 'bled' by fantasy to make this bearable. There is nothing wrong with the occasional reminder to keep on *remembering things that happened one time,* but outright insistence on your client telling only what he knows to be the truth is actually not a good idea:

- You almost certainly guarantee that any repressions will not be released, because they tend not to feel like truth or reality at first
- You could be the instigator of resistance on such a level that your client simply does not come back next week.

If the fantasies are of a very profound nature and/or include violence either by your client or carried out against him – or both – and if it seems to involve some form of persecution or victimisation, then you might possibly be dealing with one of the forms of schizophrenia. If you suspect that this is the case, then contact your membership association's headquarters promptly with full details and ask for advice. **You cannot cure schizophrenia with analysis and may even make the condition worse.**

The Too Painful Memory

Occasionally, a client is just not able to face looking at something that needs investigation and release. We can use dissociation to make it more bearable and there are several ways of doing this.

- Make a film of it. Have your client, in his mind's eye, viewing the event from a safe distance on black and white film and knowing that he can 'freeze frame' the film with his mind at any time it becomes too uncomfortable; an imaginary 'stop' button can be quite useful here. When he can look at it in black and white then change it to colour. Each time you repeat this action it becomes less traumatic to the client and you will soon be able to suggest that he/she actually floats into the image on the screen, though still with the imaginary 'stop' button operative. Soon, they will be able to dispense with the film imagery altogether. This is tried and tested method of working with dissociation and is usually completely effective.
- Have him make the film first, within the safety of a camera crew.
- Double dissociation. Here, you ask your client to imagine being in the projectionist's box, looking down at himself watching the film, still with that 'stop' button.
- Triple dissociation. For truly horrendous cases. Your client imagines standing with his back to the screen, looking up at the projectionist's box, watching himself looking down at himself watching the film...

- Ask him to pretend it was someone he heard about... a friend of a friend, maybe, and relaying the tale to you as it was told to him – he can even visualise someone else playing his part in the event. After he has told you the story once or twice it will begin to feel less threatening and less painful.
- Get him to tell you the last part of the event/memory, the part just as he begins to realise he is safe/comfortable; then ask him about the very first part, just before he realised that anything was not as it should be. Gradually extend the recall in both directions until he can go through the entire scene.

There are several other methods of dissociation, but those outlined above work well. It is essential in each method that the client is able to talk about the event from an **associated** position – that is, remembering it as it happened and telling you about it as he thinks of it.

Same Recalls Every Session

There can be several reasons for this:

- These memories are safe, so your client sticks with them
- There is something of importance connected to one or more of the memories
- The client is simply remembering what he/she told you last week
- The client is being lazy; he just wants to enjoy hypnosis
- The client is seeking a certain reaction from the therapist, and not getting it

Whatever you believe to be the reason, deal with this problem in the same way. Interrupt the flow, even in the middle of a recall, and say: *"What else is there about that memory?"* If that does not produce anything, ask your client something that he *hasn't* told you; if anybody else was there, how old he was, how did he *feel*, was it day-time or night-time, was time of the year was it, was it indoors or outdoors... etc.

As a last ditch resort, ask him to imagine a different ending or a different beginning. This can actually produce quite startling results, because if anybody ever tries to imagine something <u>it will always be based on his life experience.</u> The 'down-side' of that, of course, is that his life experience also includes films, books, other people's stories... His own life is more important, though, and it is most likely that he will draw imaginative inspiration from that source. Whatever transpires will at least give you some leverage as you explore it.

Seeing Photographs

All clients will occasionally report that they are looking at a photograph. It becomes important if that is *all* he does, or if there is a particular photograph(s) he keeps on returning to. Then, it may be a form of dissociation, designed to protect emotional integrity. Get him to think about the time/age when the photograph was taken; who took it; where it was taken, etc. If he is in the photograph, ask him how he looks – then get him to imagine how that must have *felt*, even if he says something like 'just normal' or 'just ordinary'.

If he is not in the photograph himself, then get him to investigate everybody who is; how do they look, how does he feel about that, and so on. If there are no people in the photograph, then ask him to imagine what it would be like to be in that place shown in the photograph; ask them about the colours, the temperature of the air, what he can hear in his mind's ear, and so on. It is absolutely certain that the photographs are being recalled for a reason and any one of these methods could bring it to light.

Apparent 'Posing'

A clients will sometimes 'act the part' of what he believes a client in hypnosis should be. This can include using a pseudo 'child's voice' and mannerisms; talking in a strange manner; talking as if he is almost asleep, saying things like: *"I'm there - I'm really there,"* telling unlikely stories, and any one of a number of perceived 'symptoms of hypnosis'. These can be as diverse as feeling as if in a dream, to feeling as if he is looking through his eyelids and seeing everything in cartoon colours.

The difficulty is that most of these things can be genuine sometimes, but when the client is 'posing' it will tend to become theatrical, prolonged, and 'over-the-top'. Although many therapists (the Author included) tent to distrust the child's voice that the occasional client will produce (particularly if he insists afterwards that he did not realise or does not remember), a client using a child's vocabulary is not that unusual. It tends to be delivered in an adult voice, though, with perhaps one or two childish inflexions, and occasional pronunciation difficulties. It may still be the case that the recalls are in some way distorted to fit the client's perception of what is required as a 'subject'.

Acting like this tends to be the domain of the CE/Nomad personality and can be difficult to deal with. The only really successful method is total bluntness: *"Now that was a very interesting session, Mr. Client, but the problem is that we need **totally real** recollection if we're to get you better. Now you might feel that that was what you were getting, but I know it wasn't. I'm not going to tell you how I know, but there were several signs that it wasn't. Probably your subconscious having a game with you. Let's see how you do next time."* Of course, there is a risk that the client will 'bail out' – but the insistence on posing mean he was probably not going to get better anyway.

There is another type of 'poser' – the **Narcissus.** Technically, this client is suffering from **Narcissistic Personality Disorder.** The symptoms of Narcissism are:

- An over-valuation of personal achievements.
- Reacting badly to constructive criticism.
- Distorted impression of self-worth.
- The belief that others are not able to see them to be as good as they know they are.
- An inability to form emotional bonds, *__including transference.__*

The last one on that list makes it impossible for analysis to work properly; fortunately, the completely Narcissistic personality is rare and by the very nature of the fact, as a group, they believe themselves to be near-perfect, they do not often present themselves for therapy. When you suspect you are talking to one on your initial consultation you should ask a few carefully worded questions based on those guidelines

327

above. If this seems to confirm your suspicions, you would be well advised not to take this individual into any style of therapy.

Abstract Imagery/Colours

This is sometimes hypnotic phenomena, sometimes a form of subconscious resistance. The client will often become quite fascinated with the variety of shapes and colours that he can see, to the point where he simply forgets what he is supposed to be doing. On occasions he will report a whole series of abstract images which can be absolutely anything – usually some object or other which he will readily confess he has never knowingly seen before.

You can tell him it is the subconscious playing tricks on him and therefore he should get back to the business in hand; you can suggest that he looks through the images, like looking through a net curtain; or you can tell him that it is an excellent sign of 'the best quality hypnosis' and that being the case, you are going to count from one to three, and when you get to three the images/colour will stop and he will find himself with a memory or a thought.

Strange Bodily Sensations

"I feel like I'm whirling round and round..."

"I feel really giddy..."

"It feels like I've got my feet against your wall and my head near the ceiling..."

"I feel like I've got a huge head and tiny, tiny little hands..."

This is really an extension of the **Abstract Imagery** response, above, and you can deal with it in much the same manner.

Scenic Recalls

"I'm just standing in the playground... just looking around me."

"I'm just sitting in the lounge... just looking around."

"It's like I'm just looking through all the rooms in the house..."

This is one of the forms of dissociation, another type of subconscious resistance. One of the ways to deal with the constantly repeated scenic recall (if it keeps being repeated, it *means* something) is to ask your client: *"And what happened in that playground (or lounge/house)?"* If he says: *"Nothing."* you can respond with: *"But things **always** happen in playgrounds... what happened in **that** playground?"* Nine times out of ten a recall will be forthcoming.

The Rote Recall

The rote recall (from *learning by rote* – repeating something over and again until it is established in memory) consists of such statements as: *"There was this sweet shop I used to go into on the way to school each day..."* or: *"Every weekend we used to go to my Nan's house..."*

Probably the most effective way to deal with it is to ask: *"What about one time when something was different in that sweet shop?"* or: *"Tell me what happened in Nan's house one time..."*

It is important that you do not simply just sit and let the client continue with this type of recall pattern, for it will lead only one direction – <u>away</u> from that which you and he are seeking.

The Composite Memory

This becomes obvious to the therapist after a while, yet can still remain transparent to the client because of the reduced critical faculties during hypnosis.

Good examples are:

- A house that has two staircases in the hall
- An Uncle who was bald with wavy red hair
- The huge pet dog that used to sit in the little doll's pram to be wheeled about.
- The tiny little bedroom that had three beds in it.

You have to be careful here, because the composite memory is a form of screen memory but we have no way of knowing whether it is the uncle with the wavy red hair or the uncle who is bald that is the one we should be looking at. You can often sort it out with something along the lines of: *"When you imagine your uncle with the wavy red hair, is he smiling?"* Whatever the response, your next question would be: *"and what about your uncle who was bald... how does he look?"* The client will often, again because of reduced critical faculties, carry on to talk about both uncles separately without even realising that he had combined the two in the first place. And, of course, if one of those uncles is particularly important for any reason that will soon become apparent.

The Supposition Mode

The client in 'supposition mode' typically covers no actual event but says things like: *"I'm in the garden... just playing... think I was waiting for Dad to come home... I'm just sitting on the swing, waiting..."* etc.

These are not memories but reflections and suppositions that approximate how he believes his life was during childhood. The use of the word 'think' tends to suggest that the state of hypnosis is not very deep, if it exists at all; hypnotic recall tends to be specific even when it is inaccurate, because your client should be reporting thoughts and images, not evaluations of those thoughts and images. Probably the easiest way to deal with this is to ask some specific question, like: *"And how old are you in this memory?"* or: *"And how do you feel in this memory?"* Usually, the client will be reminded that you want actual memories and obligingly switch off the reflective state of mind. When he simply expands on the supposition instead, ask him to drift away from there and let his mind focus on 'actual things that happened one time.'

No Abreactions
- Not all clients will abreact.
- Not all clients who do abreact will do so in a way that you are able to observe.
- Not all clients who abreact will do so while they are with you.
- Not all clients who abreact will do it while they are awake.
- Not all clients realise that they are having an abreaction.

331

- Not all clients who abreact will tell you.
- Not all therapists recognise all abreactions.

Abreactions are not always huge and noisy; they can be tiny and last only a few seconds. Crying is often an abreaction, though sometimes it is not. It is an interesting fact that many clients will get better without apparent abreactive states occurring, especially if they have released a reasonable amount of emotion. It is also interesting that the longer a therapist is in practice, the faster his or her clients find a resolution of their problems.

Disappearance of Symptoms Without Warning
See 'No Abreactions', above.

Symptoms Remaining After Abreaction
There are three possible reasons for this:

- You have not yet 'hit' the Initial Sensitising Event
- The Freudian concept transference neurosis exists, in which case your client is not going to get better until you get them out of therapy and they can disavow that you have done them any good at all
- The symptom is simply an acquired behaviour pattern

Where you suspect that the first situation is the case, regress them from the *apparent* event to a different time and event in their formative years; this is usually earlier, though there are circumstances where it will be later. When this is the case, it is usually when a later understanding of an earlier event has taken place; for instance, at 13 years old, an individual suddenly realises what was going on in a certain event/circumstance when he was only 5 years old. That moment of realisation will be responsible for at least part of their neurosis and until it is accessed, their symptoms are likely to remain.

It can be difficult to tell the difference between the second and third scenarios, above, but in either case the answer is suggestion, making it as indirect as possible. Giving your client two of these sessions then discharging them from your care should resolve anything that remains after a proper abreaction has occurred.

During these two sessions, you should place frequent emphasis on suggestion along the lines of: *"From this day onwards, you realise that you are your own master... the equal of any other... nobody controls you.... So you can make up your mind to do anything you want to do in life... you can make up your mind to be happy, to be calm and more relaxed... you can make up your mind to be more self-assured and confident... so that all the things that could previously upset you..."* etc.

Adult Recalls

Most clients will produce a recall now and again that belongs to adult life rather than formative years. When this happens, you should look hard at his most recent 'young' memory, because since it is that which has triggered him back to 'now', it is likely that it has more than a little to do with the presenting problem, especially if the adult recall concerns the symptom pattern.

Obviously, there are many other difficulties that the analytical therapist may encounter but those listed here are

the most likely. In any event, the information given here may
help in other situations.

CHAPTER NINETEEN
The Virtual World – a Powerful Force for Suggestion

Working inside the mind

There are many times when you can use the work presented here but be warned – it takes practice! You need to be able to deliver a constant flow of narrative at a speed slightly above that of 'normal' speech. Something in the order of 210-230 words per minute would work well.

The reason for this is that we do not want the client pondering too greatly on any one thing that we say, in case he gets the chance to bring logic to bear and starts to reject that which we are offering. Keeping the speed up in this way minimises this possibility and therefore allows us to slip neatly beneath the Conscious Critical Faculty with our suggestion work. We are literally, 'working inside the mind'.

There are certain requirements:

- A high speech rate of at least 210 wpm
- A steady delivery without pauses or breaks
- There must be at least as many indirect suggestions as direct ones
- There must be minimal emphasis associated with indirect suggestions
- A strong focus on 'you' statements
- Unfailing positivity

- It should feel to the client as if you are simply telling a story
- It should have a chronology to it, with a logical beginning and end

This style of working really comes into its own when working with simple fear situations where some sort of activity is involved such as flying, eating in public, driving or driving test, horse riding, dancing, social phobia... anything, in fact, where there is a fear of doing something that is ordinarily (by most people) perceived as non-problematic and where the activity will normally involve other people doing the same thing.

It is not designed to deal with the true phobic response, though the high degree of desensitisation work that is possible may well alleviate anxiety to some extent.

The two examples given here illustrate how to do the work but it is advised that, rather than seeking to remember them or reading them to your client, you learn the *concept* and practice until you are able to deliver a confident 'performance' without recourse to any notes at all.

Fear of Flying

This has helped huge numbers of people to let go of their flying fear; it allows the use of some logical work as well as much covert suggestion. The whole thing is couched positively and allows many opportunities to show your client that aeroplanes fly thousands of hours without event and that many people fly on a regular basis and not only survive but find it so normal as to be boring. It is best carried out in a reasonably deep hypnotic state, though the author has used it to good effect in total wakefulness. You would use at least a brief settling routine before continuing with:

"...And I wonder if you can imagine yourself setting out for the airport being cheerfully surprised that you're not feeling nervous but accepting it just the same. In fact, when you notice something that you first think is the beginning of anxiety, you recognise that it is actually a healthy combination of excitement and anticipation, and realise that you are, in fact, actually looking forward to the flight. You have time to marvel at this strange notion that you are looking forward to flying, and are still enjoying the sensation when you find yourself within the airport buildings, with all the hustle and bustle that goes on in such places.

You look around you and you can see all sorts of fascinating people and scenes, small cameos being enacted so unselfconsciously as each person is involved in their own particular world, their own particular scenario, some of them clearly excited, some less so and some looking downright bored – those are the ones who travel this way on weekly or even daily basis, so that the journey becomes nothing more than a time-consuming inconvenience, a boring part of their weekly routines.

Bing Bong!

'Will all passengers for flight CE 987 please proceed to...' but you don't hear the rest of the message because it's not your flight that's being called. You wander lazily around the duty-free shop, wondering whether to buy any of the bargains you find there or whether to see if they are cheaper at your destination. Perhaps you will simply get a magazine, newspaper or book and while away the time with a cup

coffee and some relaxation while you wait for your flight to be called.

Bing Bong!

'Flight WY 654 for...' but you're only listening with half an ear because you know you've got ages to wait yet. Have another cup of coffee, read some more of the newspaper, stare absently at a couple who are clearly having a fight, and then at another couple, younger, who by the looks of it, would like to be in a far less public place for what they clearly want to do. You notice their hand luggage, emblazoned with labels from around the globe and wonder at the fact that such young people should have flown to so many of the World's tourist spots.

Bing Bong!

You listen to the flight being called and realise it's yours. At last! You gather up your things and make your way to the departure lounge, then groan inwardly as you realise that every seat is already taken and the boarding gate isn't open yet. It's a damn' nuisance, you think, that so many people seem to want to fly at the same time that you do.

It's not too long, though, before you're all making your way in a queue along the boarding corridor and then onto the aeroplane. You find your seat number straight away, stow your hand luggage in the overhead locker, and settle down into your seat, amazed at how comfortable it is. Amazed, too, at how comfortable *you* are, as you watch all the other passengers finding their seats and settling themselves down for the journey, some of them chattering excitedly, others producing newspapers, magazines, books or work materials.

After a while, the doors are closed and the cabin crew begin the usual safety routines; you notice how they know

338

these routines off by heart and you wonder how many thousands of times they've performed this same ritual, how many times they've stood in the walkway like that, going through the same mime over and over again until it becomes as common place as tying a shoe lace or drinking a cup of tea. No wonder they look bored some of the time, you think to yourself.

You realise that the plane is moving and have just enough time to believe that you're on your way at last, when the captain announces that you are held in a queue and there will be a delay. Through the window, you can see planes gliding in to land, others soaring aloft and you vaguely remember hearing somewhere that a plane is held up by a vacuum created by air flowing over shape of the wings.

You're still pondering on this thought when you realise that the plane really is taking off this time and you revel in the thrust of smoothly controlled power that lifts the plane so surely from the ground.

Somehow, it seems to you that hardly any time passes before you are seemingly just floating gently through the air; the engines hum steadily and you hear a faint hum of conversation throughout the plane, coupled with the sounds of people ordering drinks and duty free goods from the trolleys that are manned by the cabin crew.

You read for a while, look out of the window for a while, then read some more when you realise that everything outside seems to be moving so slowly that there really isn't very much of interest to see. You doze for a little while as the flight goes on and on, and on and on, with the occasional slight change of direction and accompanying alteration in the sound of the engines... until you feel a gentle increase in pressure in your ears that tell you you'll be landing soon. This thought is confirmed as you hear the engines just changing note slightly and then another sound that you hear somebody say is *'the landing gear'*.

The plane glides downwards steadily whispering onto the runway; you have time to realise that it was going faster than you had realised and then you feel the same reassuring power as you did on take-off, this time bringing the machine to a gentle halt. And this is the amazing thing. After a journey of hundreds, maybe thousands, of miles, the pilot brings the aeroplane to rest at precisely the right place for the disembarkation tunnel to be attached... a journey of hundreds of miles finishing with inch-precision perfection and you wonder at the skills of the captain and co-pilot.

The door is opened and you all file of the aeroplane, making your way to the baggage collection points. It's just another airport. More 'Bing Bongs'. More travellers coming and going... you realise that this coming and going continues incessantly, maybe abating a little during the middle of the night but never stopping completely. More people travelling thousands upon thousand of miles, thousands upon thousands of hours.

Finally, your baggage arrives and you tug it off the carousel and place it on a trolley, smiling to yourself as you leave the airport and really looking forward to your holiday."

The Boredom Response

Read at about the right speed, the above would take about five minutes to deliver; this would normally be enough but there are many places within the routine where it could be extended. It should not take too much of a stretch of the imagination for you to find them, though it is always best to keep the actual flight part of it reasonably brief, as shown here. The object of the exercise is to create a boredom response which, coupled with the high speech rate, will tend to encourage the client to 'switch off' the conscious mind, allowing the myriad suggestions that are being given to 'take root'.

There are very many hidden suggestions within the routine and it should be possible for you to observe them easily. If not, read and re-read the script, thinking about every phrase, until you find them, for this level of understanding is necessary if you are to be able to create new routines for your own therapist's office use.

Driving

This time, we will examine a virtual routine suitable for alleviating most, if not all, of the most common reasons for fear of driving by a process of normalisation. It is not designed for *driving test* fears, though it could serve as a useful basis for such a routine. Once again, we are seeking to create a boredom response, which will achieve two objectives:

- Our client will consciously 'switch off', allowing access to subconscious thought processes so that suggestion will be more likely to be absorbed.
- Our client will associate boredom with the feared behaviour; a beneficial response, since it is nearly impossible to be frightened of something which is perceived as boring.

Since this activity requires the client to be able to actually perform a learned skill (unlike flying in an aeroplane) a deep state of hypnosis is more desirable this time.

Once achieved, continue with something like:

"… And I wonder if you can just imagine, for the moment, a time when you will be driving your car, every bit as relaxed as you are at this very moment. You haven't go to do it today, nor tomorrow or the next day, so it's fine to just imagine it as vividly as you can, just imagining what it would be like if you *were* driving and being every bit as relaxed as you are right now.

Perhaps it's as if you can see yourself or maybe it's like looking out through your eyes and either way is absolutely fine for you to imagine because you don't have to do it today, or tomorrow, or the day after that… in fact you don't have to do this at all unless you want to do this at some point and then you'll find yourself to be every bit as relaxed as you are at this very moment.

So, just imagining yourself right now, driving your car away from your house just to go into the town and back, just for a drive, and seeing that thought in any way that seems right to you, just driving your car and the car doing exactly what you instruct it to do, moving faster or slower, stopping or going, turning to the right or the left. And you realise that there's nothing so very remarkable about this, because that what the car is designed to do and you know exactly how to make it do what it's designed to do and doing it so perfectly. And before long, you're into the town and driving so easily because you're in a line of other vehicles and they're all moving slowly and steadily and you go along with them. There's a bus and a lorry and a bike and a car and a van and a car and another lorry and another car... and you... and a bike and a van and a taxi and another bus and a lorry. And they're all moving along at exactly the same speed and then there are traffic lights turning red. So the bus and the lorry and a bike and a car and a van and a car and another lorry all slow down and your foot goes on the brake and you slow down, and then the bike and the van and a taxi and another bus and a lorry all slow down and all stop, waiting for the lights to change.

And the lights go green and you all move off and the bus turns right and the lorry turns left and there's a bike and a car and a van and a car and another lorry and another car... and you... and a bike and a van and a taxi and another bus and a lorry all moving off together, all moving at the same speed together and all slowing down and all increasing speed, all gliding past shops and offices and other buildings and entrances to car parks and maybe entrances to drive through restaurants and other places. You pause to let another car come out from a side turning, so there's you and in front there's another car and a car and a lorry and a bike and a van and a car... and behind there's a bike and a van and a taxi and another bus and a lorry... and a horse! A horse and a rider looking so easy and so casual as they jog easily along.

And the car in front of the car in front of you turns left and the bike turns left and a lorry joins the queue somewhere behind you... and the lights turn orange then red and everybody pauses... then the lights turn orange and red and then go green and everybody moves of easily, steadily, gliding along, just gliding along... and now there's a car and a bus and a lorry and another car and the van seems to have disappeared... and there's a different bike and another car...

and you... and another car and a bike and a large white van and a bus... and that horse.

And after the next set of traffic lights you turn to the right and you join another line of traffic. There's a lorry and a bus and a car and you; and another car just like yours and a van and another car, all moving steadily and easily past shops and offices and other buildings... and there's a crossing where you all stop, pausing for long enough for people to cross the road before you all move off again, the lorry and a bus and a car and you; and another car just like yours and a van and another car, all moving steadily and easily past shops and offices and other buildings and a school and a hall and another restaurant and you realise just how easy all this is as you find yourself in the front of a line of a car and another car and another car and a bike and a van and a bus and a lorry and another car... and you smile to yourself as you see that damned horse, just jogging along on the end of the queue, so easy and so casual.

And you begin to make your way home now and gradually the vehicles in front and the vehicles behind turn where they have to turn and go on their way, the bikes and the vans and the lorries and the busses and the cars... and the horse... until there's just you driving so easily and so effortlessly as you make your way back to your house and then bring your car to a rest at exactly the place where you want to bring it to a rest. And you realise you have a smile on your face, though for a moment or two, you're not exactly sure why. Then you realise that it's simply because you've enjoyed yourself so much... and an idea forms in your mind as you glance at your watch and realise that you actually have time to do it again... so you get back in the car, and feel a real thrill of anticipation as you turn the key in the ignition and the engine purrs into life. And you know that this time, it's going to be even more enjoyable."

At almost any point from the third paragraph of the routine forwards, you may have the opportunity to use the existent ambience of the location within which you are working; if a car drives past and it is audible enough (as it will probably be in most therapist's offices) the following is a useful intervention:

"And you could notice that car that drove past the building just now and, of course, you had no idea of whether the driver was male or female, young or old. And that's just how you'll seem to people that hear you drive past their building; they won't know anything about you and it'll just be a car driving past the building. Just another car with just another driver inside just doing what people who drive cars do... To them, you will seem just like that car that drove past this office just now..."

Ambience and Atmosphere

To get the best out of virtual world work with you clients you need to create an accurate ambience and atmosphere, though <u>without excitation,</u> because you are seeking to normalise the situation as far as possible. 'Normal' situations simply are not exciting.

This is why the work shown in this chapter can often be more successful than going for a 'benefits approach', which relies on enthusing the client for success. Nothing wrong in that, of course – in fact, it is a time-tested and effective way of working. It does have the problem, though, in that you will be coupling excitation with a situation which is already exciting the client, albeit negatively. Consider these two scenarios, this time for an individual who suffers a common form of social phobia – the fear of eating in public. First, we will consider the benefits approach:

"And you can see yourself now looking so calm and so relaxed, just as you are at this very moment, in fact... and you can imagine being truly delighted to notice that people are enjoying your company and you can imagine being delighted, too, at how relaxed you are as you seat yourself at the table... anticipating a wonderful meal and finding a real surge of pleasure and confidence that you are here... noticing how you are actually feeling hungry and being pleased when the first course arrives... and as you begin to eat you are amazed at your confidence and at how much you are actually enjoying..." and so on. As you can see, this should have the effect of creating confidence, but will undoubtedly raise excitement; as long as the excitation stays with achievement, then everything is fine, but if some unfortunate even occurs – a gaffe, maybe – then it could redirect to the original anxiety state.

Now we will consider the virtual world approach:

"And you can just imagine how it would be when you are attending that function feeling as easy and relaxed as you are right now, and of course you haven't got to do it right now so it's easy for you to imagine yourself attending that function while you're easy and relaxed. And there're other diners there chattering before the meal and there's you chattering before the meal with the sound of cutlery on plates, the edges of bottles just touching the edges of glasses, and people having fun, and everybody waiting for the meal and trying to look at their watches without anybody noticing

because it's so long arriving, and you realise that the music in the background has started playing the same song that was playing when you arrived. You realise it's a CD set to play over and over until somebody changes it and you wonder idly how many times you will hear the same tunes during the time you are here. You wonder if anybody else has noticed it when somebody grins and says: 'here goes that damn' song again,' just as the meal is served and you smile in return..."

You will notice that the virtual work is much longer than the benefits approach sample above; remember, you speak very quickly with virtual work, so that you have a constant flow of narrative. In fact, the length of time taken on each passage would be similar, though there is far more information in the second passage. There is also a certain amount of confusing ambiguity but because we want our client to absorb a *concept* rather than a particular *suggestion*, the ambiguity will be useful. The conscious mind will start to seek what is really meant, which means the psyche will be open to the 'hidden' suggestions of normality within our conceptual narrative work.

As mentioned at the beginning of this chapter, practice is needed if you are to get the best from this style of working; it is a good idea to write a few scripts, though not actually with the idea of delivering them. Instead, they will teach you how to use your mind in such a way that you can just 'rattle something off' when you need to – and this is probably the single most important factor of this style of working.

CHAPTER TWENTY
Useful Work materials

In this final chapter, there are some useful work routines and hints, as well as two specific scripts that can help your client to access problems from his earliest years.

Preparation
Many therapeutic endeavours that 'fail' only do so because not enough time was taken during the preparation phase, which commences in the first few seconds of the first meeting with the client.

Perhaps one of the most important things to understand about the initial consultation is that your client's therapy can be wrecked even before you even say a single word. Conversely, those first few seconds of meeting can ensure such a rapport that your job is positively underway before your client even sits down in the consulting chair in front of you.

First Impressions Last...
When we meet somebody for the first time, our first impression is formed within twenty seconds maximum – maybe sooner – and that first impression is incredibly difficult to change at a subconscious level. Twenty seconds is probably about the maximum length of time for a client to get from the first moment of contact to the point where he is

starting to get a conscious 'feel' for the way you are, most of the time.

An explanation might be useful here: the client has never met you before and will have to assess you by reference to the information that he already has stored in the subconscious database about humans. It is a fact that our assessment and identification process works at an incredible speed; we can instantly recognise and classify anything we encounter, provided we have encountered it before. Part of our built-in 'survival pack' insists that we seek to identify every item, every experience, every concept we encounter as rapidly as possible in order to know what action we have to take, if any. So the second we meet somebody new, we *simply cannot stop* that process from starting its work.

Second by second, we start to build up a 'feel' for the individual; when we observe something that we cannot identify, all we can recognise is that this is an unknown quantity. Enough of those sort of indicators, and we may well begin to perceive that this person is 'weird' or even to be feared. If the indicators that we *can* recognise are negative in some way, then we start to form a negative opinion. We might feel that he is unwelcoming, 'shifty', miserable, silly, unknowledgeable or whatever. Most of us have had that sort of experience where we feel uneasy about somebody for no real reason.

A Personal Assessment

All that is happening is that we are comparing everything we are experiencing with all that which we have already experienced. Our assessment of this person is based not on the way he actually is, but how we assess that he *seems* to be, based on what our subconscious has been able to identify as existent in our present knowledge. Always remember that this is exactly the same for our client.

On first meeting, he is unconsciously comparing us with everybody he has ever met and attributing us with the same attitudes and reactions.

Because of this, it is important that we hit as many 'positive buttons' as we can, and as fast as we can. That very first moment that our client sees us is of paramount importance; that is when the initial impression is formed and he will try to relate everything during the next few seconds to that impression. The way you look, move, sound, the way you actually *feel* will be evaluated at the speed of thought. If the overall impression gained is that you are an 'ok person' he will begin to believe that you might possibly be able to assist him with his difficulty.

Follow this up well, and therapy is already under way.

If, on the other hand, you manage to create a negative impression, then, even though the *conscious mind* may very well go through a shift of opinion later on, there will still be doubt present in the psyche. And *doubt* is what we definitely do not want as part of our client's processes. Doubt leads inexorably to expectation of failure.

If we take a dislike to somebody for any reason, it is actually very difficult for another person to convince us that we are wrong. We resist that knowledge, because it conflicts with that which we have already perceived. The conscious critical faculty seeks to maintain the integrity of that already existent belief. The important thing to remember is that it will do exactly the same if we like somebody – we will ignore any advice that suggests that we may be misguided.

So, what you do and how you do it during those first 20 seconds is of paramount importance. What is needed is something like: friendly, welcoming, relaxed, compassionate, concerned... *and 'normal'*. And this is where we hit a sticking point, because 'normal' is very subjective. Friendly and welcoming can seem overwhelming to some; relaxed might be confused with unconcerned, concerned can look like anxiety, compassionate can seem 'over the top', and so on.

Middle of the Road

Clearly we need an approach where we are able to assess our client's 'way of being' at a conscious level as rapidly as possible so that we can get our act right, right from the start. There is nothing wrong with acting in a way that is calculated to set your client on the road to recovery and happiness. So we need an initial 'failsafe' approach that allows us to size up our client quite quickly. 'Middle of the road' is good; 'middle of the road' whilst observing and understanding our client's reaction to middle of the road is better. The ability to *actually use* that reaction, whatever it is, to therapeutic advantage is better still.

You can learn much about this important facet of therapy from **Chapter Three** of this book, on personality and therapy.

Here is something worth remembering: *A good test of whether or not you have conducted a successful initial consultation is how you feel in the few moments after the client leaves your room. If your mind goes with them for just a moment or two, then the chances are you conducted yourself well; and the chances are even higher that your client can feel that your mind has gone with them. In these cases, therapy is off to a flying start.*

Three Wishes

A simple test for the presence of a destructive hidden agenda is to ask the client, during the initial consultation, to tell you what he would ask for if he were to be given three wishes. Ideally, the first wish should reflect the presenting symptom. For instance, if the client has presented with, say, a social phobia of some sort, then the first wish might be for confidence in public. If not the first then the second… and if it does not appear at all then one of two situations exist:

1. A destructive hidden agenda that seeks to maintain the symptom pattern for one reason or another.
2. The client has issues in his life which are more important than the symptom which are possibly invisible even to him.

The situation at (2) is not as rare as you might at first think. Many people suffer from a great difficulty in stating what they actually want and as a result spend their whole lives never quite getting that which they truly seek. Here are some examples:

- The one who would like to play better says he does not mind losing.
- The one who wants money might insist that money does not mean success nor does it bring happiness.
- Somebody who is sexually frustrated but inhibited may state that there are more important things in life.

- The unhappily fat person will say he is far happier fat than he would be if he were skinny.
- The unhappily skinny person states: *'rather skinny than obese.'*
- The woman who thinks herself plain might look at a glamorous woman and say: *'Look at that tart!'*
- The woman who thinks herself 'tarty' might look at a more modestly turned-out female and say: *'Look at that frump!'*

Any one of those might well present with a social phobia but that 'three wishes' question will produce answers revolving usually around personal wealth or world/family peace, dependent upon the image which the client is seeking to convey. He will probably not be aware that he is doing it, most of the time; it is a subconscious process designed to seem plausible and/or 'nice' in order to avoid discussing the unspoken and uncomfortable truth.

Our job is to help the client to attain that which he truly wants and sometimes we need to delve deeply to achieve it. Whether we are working with a hidden agenda or an unadmitted truth – which is much the same thing, most of the time – we need to ask question after question until we lay the real problem bare enough to produce beneficial and lasting change via therapy.

How Others See You

The two questions given here have long been favourites of the author during initial consultation sessions since they give a clear glimpse of how the client might be when therapy is complete. The questions are:

1. *"In a single word or short phrase, how do you see yourself?"*
2. *"In a single word or short phrase, how do others see you?"*

These apparently innocuous questions tell us much. The answer to (1) will often be arrived at only after a good deal of struggling on the part of the client; sometimes we will even hear: *"I don't actually know, really."* At other times, we will hear something derogative. Less commonly, the client will state something positive about self.

It is the answer to (2) which is the most important, in many ways, since, in the unlikely even of having carried out a major consensus of opinion among every acquaintance, friend and family member, the only way that somebody could assess how other people think of him is if *he truly thinks that of himself.*

Now we have the following possibilities:

a) The two answers agree negatively
b) The two answers agree positively
c) The two answers agree benignly, being neither favourable or unfavourable
d) The two answers disagree with (1) being favourable, (2) unfavourable
e) The two answers disagree with (2) being favourable, (1) unfavourable

We will examine each situation.

(a) This may well be evidence of depression; if so and it appears to be of a clinical/endogenous nature (in other words has existed for a very long time and does not waver in intensity) then this client must be referred to conventional medicine. He is 'out of bounds' to the usual therapist, though there may be an exception if you have some conventional medical training.

Where this is not the case, it is likely that the client is suffering from a true inferiority complex and we can expect a lengthy and probably complex therapy if we are to get a full alleviation of symptoms. If there is some sort of reactive depression, alleviating that might well resolve the presenting difficulty, even if that did not appear to be related to a depressive state. (Depression can be enormously difficult to observe).

If there is no evidence of depression, then a complicated therapy will probably ensue, which can embody most of the techniques in this book.

(b) This situation *can* indicate that no therapy is actually needed, so that we would want to know why the client is sitting in front of us. Alternatively, it is a possible indicator of resistance, in which case the client needs to answer the two questions again. Pursue it!

(c) This client is probably 'hiding', seeking to remain invisible to avoid change. It is a kind of passive resistance and it is advisable to delve more to discover the truth.

(d) Evidence of paranoia is showing here. Be sure to ask questions about the abuse of leisure drugs, especially cannabis. This answer can also be indicative of beliefs of inferiority (not a true inferiority complex) which produce a reactive state resembling what some might call a 'superiority complex' in an attempt to maintain personal self-worth.

(e) This is the most common answer and by far the easiest to work with, since we can begin a good therapeutic intervention on the spot by asking the question: *"How did you discover that that's what people think of you?"* This question, followed 'tightly', will not infrequently guide the client to the recognition that is actually his view of self.

Whatever you establish via the questions given here, remember that they are only 'focussing devices' and pointers to what therapy is needed and how it might be conducted. They certainly should not be considered as a therapy within themselves, nor should it be considered that they are *always* 100% accurate – therapy is an art more than a science and relies heavily upon the understanding and rapport between two people who have totally different personal histories. Sometimes, the connection is a little skewed!

Useful Scripts

This first script – a subconscious primer – is ideal for the commencement of analytical styles of hypnotherapy and is based on one that the author has been using successfully as a first session for many years. It can also be used as a 'stand alone' script, used just once, to provide a 'mini analysis'.

It is best used after a personality-related induction to achieve a good state of hypnosis.

"Now just allow your thoughts to drift... all the way back through time, as though there really were no such thing as time... all the way back to those years between when you were born and finally made it to maturity... and for some people, maturity is as early as fifteen or so, while for others it

may be as late as seventeen or even eighteen... just letting your mind drift all the way back to those years, when there was you, and there were the others... things they didn't understand... things you didn't understand... that time of private thoughts and fears and those secrets... when everything was new and for the first time... when you were still finding out and discovering all the things you could do... and the things you couldn't do... and the things you weren't supposed to do, but did anyway... just letting your mind drift all the way back to those years... not searching for anything in particular, not trying to work out why you find what you find there... but just allowing your subconscious mind to go wherever it wants to go...

And I don't know if you'll see pictures in your mind's eye... but if you do, they can be so vivid, so real, that it's just as if you're looking out through your forehead, so that what you saw then you can see again now, and what you felt then, you can feel again now... or maybe you'll just find yourself thinking thoughts, just remembering... or perhaps just feelings will come into your mind and body... feelings or pictures, or just thoughts and memories... or maybe even nothing at all, for some of the time... and whatever happens is right for you, because your subconscious, that powerful and all-knowing subconscious of yours, knows exactly what's right for you... so whatever happens, it's exactly what should happen... for you... exactly the right thing, without you searching for anything in particular, just allowing your mind to drift to wherever it wants to go... and because you have to do absolutely nothing at all, you simply cannot get it wrong... so you can be easy in your mind that whatever you find yourself thinking and feeling, it's the right thing to think and feel...

*And there were so many things that could happen to a child... unpleasant things sometimes, things that the grown-ups maybe knew absolutely nothing about... things that other children did... ... things that other grown-ups did...... some things that were games which went wrong...... or just confusing things that you didn't quite understand...... things that left you feeling uncomfortable or bewildered, or sometimes hopelessly lost or completely alone... and maybe even sometimes leaving you in an unfamiliar place, with unfamiliar people all around you...... and there's sometimes **fear,** too, back there in those childhood years... fear when it seemed there was something that was just too big to deal with all on your own...*

And now I wonder if you can just let your mind drift around those early years, just remembering how things could sometimes feel, back then... remembering so clearly that you can perhaps almost feel that same feeling again now... in your mind... or maybe even in your body... maybe sadness... or anger... or any of those other emotions that you could sometimes feel so sharply when you were just a child... in those years before maturity... jealousy, perhaps, or frustration... or feelings of being left out of things... and I wonder if you can see yourself looking just as you did when you were a small child... just create a really vivid picture in your mind of you as a small child... and now I want you to do a really clever, very special trick... I want you, as an adult, to reach all the way back through time... and just be there with that small child for a few moments... just being there and offering comfort in any way you can... maybe just touching (him/her) *on the shoulder, or stroking* (his/her) *hair... or maybe, in the privacy of your own mind, just sweeping that child up and giving* (him/her) *a huge hug and just making sure that* (he/she) *knows that it's all ok... tell* (him/her) *that you'll always be there always waiting, always helping, always looking after... always loving* (him/her)..."

At this point there will often be a profound emotional response and, not unusually, copious tears as the client accesses childhood hurt. When this happens, urge the client to continue and work through whatever presents (though often there is no actual memory associated). Then continue from the '**' mark later on in the script.

When there is no apparent response, continue with:

"Now, because I'm not a mind reader, I can never know if my client could create the image, how easily he/she could reach back or how that all felt. So tell me (name) *how easily was it for you to make that picture of you when you were small?"*

From here, explore fully whatever the client gives you; how old did the child seem, how did he look, what did it feel like reaching back, and so on. Sometimes, this will trigger emotional response patterns, and occasionally nothing at all will happen, which tells you that this particular client is not good at contacting the emotional self and you <u>might</u> be better of contemplating a different style of therapy – analytical hypnotherapy requires easy accessing of emotions to be successful. It is possible that you and the client would both benefit greatly from using the style of 'conscious' therapy shown at the beginning of the book.

Whatever result you achieve, continue with:
**

"And now I'd like you to let your mind drift to the earliest school memory that you can find... just the earliest memory you have of school days and I want you to tell me what you find there..."

To some, it might seem that this is leading and indeed it is; but it is a 'permissible lead' in that we are asking for a recall of something that must be there, since there are few people, if any, who received no schooling whatsoever. Whatever our client tells you continue with:

"Ok, that's good... now we're going to use a process called... free association... to let your subconscious drift to whatever it wants to drift to... allowing another thought to take the place of that school memory... or maybe just reach down into wherever your memories are stored and grab the first thing you find...without consciously trying to make any connection to anything at all... and again, I want you to tell me what you find yourself thinking of..."

Wait. Urge if necessary but be sure to get a response.

"That's good... and now I want you to that again, just exactly what you did there, just then... and whatever you find yourself thinking is absolutely the right thing for you to think... whatever it is, however silly it seems to you, or however embarrassing it seems...just letting your mind drift

again now... and once again just grab the first memory that you find there, something that happened one time, and just tell me what you find... "

Wait, urge if necessary, and be sure to get a response.

"Good... and now I want you to find two memories one after the other without waiting for me to prompt you... just find the first one and tell me about it... then let it go, just drift away... then grab another one and tell me about that... "

Wait, urge <u>only if necessary</u> and be sure to get two memories.

"That's good... and that's all you have to do each time you come to see me is exactly what you've just done there today... just grabbing one memory after another and telling me the thoughts as they come to you.

And now you can let your mind drift away from the past... coming back to the here and now, coming back up to date, back to this room, to the here and now, with the speed of an express train so that all those memories and feelings are not only years behind, but thousands upon thousands of miles behind, too... so that you can leave behind any unpleasant feelings we disturbed today... just leaving them here with me, when you go... and next time you come to see me, it's going to be twice as easy to be twice as relaxed... easy to remember things... easy to tell me the things you remember... but in the meantime, you'll find yourself with all sorts of flashbacks to those childhood years... all sorts of little memories occurring to you, just when you least expect it... and sometimes in dreams, too... and you'll find that you remember your dreams and you can write those dreams down and bring them to me the next time you come to see me...

Next time you come to see me, it's going to be twice as easy to be twice as relaxed, easy to remember things, easy to tell me things... but in the meantime, you're going to find yourself with a good feeling of being at ease within yourself... when you close my door behind you as you leave, you're going to find yourself with a good feeling, a feeling that it's all going to be all right... in fact, you're going to find that things that used to upset you are going to now just calm and relax you, and the more they could previously upset you, the more they're going to now just simply calm and simply relax you... so that all the things you used to have trouble in dealing with are going to seem so easy to you from now on, you'll find yourself wondering if they were ever truly a problem in the first place... so easy to you from now on, you'll find yourself being an inspiration to other people... and that feels good...

And next time you come to see me, it's going to be easier to relax, easy to remember things, easy to tell me things... just knowing within yourself that you're going to tell me everything you remember, and everything you tell me will lead you one step closer to the time when you can be... exactly as you wish to be... one step closer to you being... the best person you can be.

And now it's time for me to bring the session to an end.... Etc.

Very often the next time you see the client, they will have a success story to tell you of something they achieved which has delighted them, or of a dream which has seemed particularly profound. Sometimes, you will hear about a memory that has lain unremembered for maybe scores or years and the recall of which has changed your client's life dramatically. Sometimes, of course, you will hear none of this but the subconscious has still been accessed and will still be searching for that which is the cause of your client's symptoms.

The Time Capsule
This script can be used as an indirect approach to discovery and it particularly suits the scientifically minded individual. It also has a built in advantage of dissociation, making it suitable for use where there is a need to view past events clearly but from a place of relative safety.

It has many places where your client can investigate, in his mind, the future effects of changing or not changing. This allows him to produce the desire for a course of action *from the inside,* which will always be more powerful than anything that you can give him from your own mind. At those points, you would need to pause long enough for your client to access the relevant part of his thought processes. Where you see an emotional response, which is not at all unusual with this script, you can begin to work at exploring the memory or sensation; when it is complete, simply return to the capsule to continue working.

Although written for analytical therapy you will see that it also lends itself admirably to PLR (Past Life Regression) experiments.

"And now I want you to imagine a shimmering, transparent capsule... a shimmering, transparent capsule suspended by a silvery thread somewhere in a timeless place... it's been suspended there since before time began...

in this secret place where nobody ever goes... where nobody has ever yet been... and it's a strange thing that nobody knows who put it there... and even stranger that nobody knows from where or whence it came... and as you gaze upon this mystery, it begins to seem somehow familiar to you for some reason you don't quite understand... as if you've seen it before somewhere... sometime... and then it gradually dawns on you that you know what it's for... even though you don't know how you know... you just somehow realise that you can use the power of your mind to move inside it... simply by using the power of your thoughts... to glide effortlessly into this place of total safety... where nothing can harm you... where you are protected from everything... even protected from time itself...

Outside of this magical capsule, nothing ever changes... because time simply stands still... so you can actually move through time... moving back, back through the years as though there were no such thing as time... moving back to times past... maybe even back to times before your own lifetime even began... or perhaps moving forward through time... to a time yet to come, yet to be... simply by using the power of your mind... simply thinking where you want to be... and you can see without being seen, hear without being heard... and you can feel what you choose to feel when you observe these things... and all the time you are absolutely safe in this magical capsule... a silvery capsule where you are protected from the world...

And I can only wonder if you're going to find yourself moving back to a time past, perhaps to make sense of something that that you didn't quite understand the first time around... or if you're going to move forward to sense how your life might be in a little while... if you don't make a change... or perhaps if you do make a change of some sort... maybe a specific change that you have perhaps already been thinking about... just allowing your subconscious, that powerful subconscious of yours, to sense the outcome... and of course, it's nobody's business but yours what you decide to do... where you decide to go... and maybe you'll decide to stay just where you are and enjoy the feeling of relaxation and calmness... or perhaps allow yourself to journey to some imaginary place... a place created by the creativity of your imagination... where there might be castles and kings... or ancient walled cities high on a mountain, that nobody has seen for centuries... perhaps mythical gilded palaces in some Oriental land... gently sloping hillsides which lead to tranquil lakes or gently flowing rivers... where there is just the merest whisper of a breeze... or deep and mysterious canyons, with waterfalls thundering and roaring between glittering, multi-coloured walls of quartz and crystal... waterfalls that create miniature rainbows that arch through the mist and spray, in the warm rays of a setting sun... waterfalls that you can perhaps move behind to discover mystery worlds in the caves beyond...

Maybe you will find a world where everything is exactly as you want it to be to make it absolutely perfect... or perhaps one which is so different from the one we live that it's almost too difficult to understand... and perhaps, too, there will be people there... kind people who will help you to easily achieve your every goal, your every wish... or perhaps instead this world is a benign place, where you can discover how to realise your own goals... a place that actually works with you to allow your confidence to grow, day by day... a

365

place where you feel you might almost move mountains if you needed to do so... a place where you can easily learn skills, discover strengths and resources you were not previously aware of... strengths and resources that can persist and remain and stay with you wherever you might find yourself...

But of course you might decide that you don't wish to travel anywhere in this magical capsule... deciding instead to search for a truth... or an answer to a problem, perhaps... maybe searching deep, deep, inside yourself in this wonderful relaxed state that we call hypnosis... searching inside yourself and becoming aware of resources that you already have... strengths you already possess... and this could be an even more magical journey as you go deeper and deeper now... allowing yourself to become aware of problems that you have solved successfully in the past... or maybe problems for which there was no solution then... and you could realise that your subconscious mind, which simply does not understand time... could still be trying to solve some of these problems from the past... realising in almost the very same instant that it can simply cease to do so... because these things are from the past and can stay in the past... because they are out of date now... and it's safe to simply leave them back there where they belong... and it may be that you become aware that you need to forgive yourself... or somebody else perhaps... for things that happened back there, back then... and you'll find that so easy to do, now... so that you can just consciously let go of those things... so that they no longer absorb energies... now that your subconscious can accept that there is no longer any need to solve these problems... no longer any need to be concerned with these difficulties... so that those energies are now going to be available to you in your everyday life... and it could be that... while you're cocooned in the safety of this magical capsule... that you'll find your mind drifting to a conflict with some other person at some time in your life... maybe when you were just small.. or perhaps when you were not so small... but a conflict that looks so different now... so much less important... now that you can observe it in safety and from a distance of time... and I can only wonder where your mind has been drifting while I've been talking... or even if it has not drifted anywhere at all, but simply considered the possibilities presented to you... and whatever has happened, or is happening now... is absolutely the right thing for you... absolutely the right thing for your mind to do... and now I'd like you to become aware of your presence inside that magical capsule... suspended in total safety in some secret place by a silvery thread... become aware of new resources within you... and realise that at this very moment... you are in more in touch with that all-knowing subconscious mind of yours than you have ever been before..."

It is to be hoped that with the material in this final chapter, you have acquired proficiency with some new tools, or perhaps hone some old ones. It is also to be hoped that what you have found here will give you steadily increasing confidence in your therapeutic endeavours, steadily more success with and for your clients and steadily increasing prosperity!

Until the next time…

Terence Watts

BIBLIOGRAPHY

Anastasi, Anne. *Psychological Testing*, London, UK: Collier Macmillan 1988

Bandler, R & Grinder, J. *Frogs Into Princes.* Moab, Utah, USA: Real People Press 1975

Bandler, R. & Grinder, J. *The Structure of Magic Vol. I.* Palo Alto, USA: Science & Behaviour Books, inc.: 1975

Bandler, Richard. *Using your brain for a change.* Moab, Utah, USA: Real People Press 1985

Barnett, E.A. *Analytical Hypnotherapy Principles & Practice.* Glendale, California, USA: Westwood Publishing 1989

Barret, Paul. *Charles Darwin's Notebooks: 1836-1844: Geology, Transmutation of Species, Metaphysical Enquiries.* Ithaca, New York, USA: Cornell University Press.

Bergin, Allen E. & Garfield, Sol L. (editors). *Handbook of Psychotherapy and Behaviour Change.* New York, USA: 1994

Elman, Dave. *Hypnotherapy.* Glendale, California, USA. Westwood Publishing 1964

Freud Sigmund. *The Psychopathology of Everyday Life.* London, UK: Penquin Books 1991 (orig. pub. 1901)

Hogan, Kevin. *The New Hypnotherapy Handbook.* Eagan, MN, USA: Network 3000 Publishing 2001

Hunter C. Roy. *The Art of Hypnosis.* Dubuque, USA: Kendall Hunt 1994

Johansen, Donald & Edey, Maitland. *Lucy: The Beginnings of Human Kind.* London, UK. Paladin 1981

Jung, C.G. *Memories, Dream and Reflections.* London, UK: Fontana 1962

Markham, Ursula. *The Elements of Visualisation.* Shaftesbury, Dorset, UK: Element Books 1989

Myers, David G. *Psychology.* New York, USA: Worth Publishers Inc. 1995

Sasz, Thomas. *The Ethics of Psychoanalysis.* Syracuse: Syracuse University Press 1988

Spelling, Abraham P. *Psychology Made Simple.* Oxford, UK: Butterworth-Heinemann 1982

Watts, Terence. *Warriors, Settlers & Nomads.* Carmarthen, Wales, UK: Crown House Publishing 2000

Watts, Terence & Philips Georges. *Rapid Cognitive Therapy.* Carmarthen, Wales, UK: Crown House Publishing 1999

Yapko, Michael D. *Trancework.* Philadelphia, USA: Brunner/Mazel Publishers 1990

Printed in the United Kingdom
by Lightning Source UK Ltd.
111535UKS00001B/25-42

9 780970 932136